# The Women's Annual
## Number 5
### 1984-1985

G. K. Hall

# WOMEN'S STUDIES

Publications

**Barbara Haber**
**Editor**

# The Women's Annual

Number 5

1984-1985

Edited by
Mary Drake McFeely

© 1985 G.K. Hall
"Women, Health, and Aging" © 1985 Partnership for Health

Library of Congress has cataloged this serial publication as follows:

**The Women's annual, . . . the year in review.**—1980-
  Boston: G.K. Hall & Co.,

  (Reference publication in women's studies)

  Annual
  Editor: Barbara Haber.
  ISSN 0276-7988 = The Women's annual, the year in review.

  ISBN 0-8161-8717-7
  ISBN 0-8161-8741-X (pbk.)

  1.  Feminism—United States—Yearbooks.  I.  Haber,
Barbara.  II.  G.K. Hall & Company.  III.  Series.
HQ1402.W65          305.4'2'0973                    82-641994
AACR  2  MARC-S

*This publication is printed on permanent/durable acid-free paper*
MANUFACTURED IN THE UNITED STATES OF AMERICA

# Contents

# Introduction

The word for the women's movement now is perseverance. Times are wrong for revolution and scarcely right for reform; just holding on to the gains of the past requires constant effort and vigilance. Still, the writers of this fifth *Women's Annual* have more to report than mere losses or retrenchment. Women are continuing to build upon the solid foundation of their earlier work.

One message that emerges from a review of issues concerning American women is that important changes did take place during this year. That the changes involved both brief moments of exalted triumph and major disappointments was perhaps epitomized in the candidacy of Geraldine Ferraro for vice president of the United States. It is not surprising that she is mentioned several times in this year's *Women's Annual*.

As in previous editions, these essays survey major events, issues, and accomplishments in the humanities, in feminist theory, and in popular culture. Because the year's political events were extraordinary, politics and law are discussed in separate chapters. This year for the first time, we include a chapter on women in science. There are also essays concentrating on specific topics: health issues of aging, an important topic as the number of older women increases; an exciting new approach to curriculum in higher education; women pioneering in "nontraditional" occupations; and new findings on the psychological well-being of women who combine family responsibilities with work outside the home. No single volume can encompass all the issues or report all the research of importance to women; some topics have been covered in earlier volumes, and others must wait for another year.

Although the range of subjects is broad, there is a sense of connectedness among these ten essays on different topics by different authors. Strong links bind women scholars, who are questioning old assumptions in a variety of disciplines—women in politics, women pioneers working in nontraditional occupations, women pressing for better health care. There is an immediacy about feminist research: whether their work involves the study of philosophy or the everyday life of working women, feminist scholars are aware of the potential of new points of view and new questions for reshaping society.

Feminist research has richly invigorated our thinking about women. Josephine Donovan and Elissa Gelfand survey the work of scholars in the humanities and feminist theorists who are bringing entirely new perspectives to the study of literature, philosophy, and history. Theirs is no ivory tower; the study of gender issues in the humanities has strong political potential. Gelfand compares the thought of French and American theorists and thereby provides a useful view of feminists in this country, showing the influence on them of French and Canadian work. Donovan reminds us that the body of feminist scholarship is now large and well established. The books multiply. Ten volumes of *Signs* and an equal stack of *Feminist Studies* are constantly in use, the findings reported in their pages stimulating further research. *The Women's Review of Books*, which began publication late in 1983, keeps abreast of feminist scholarship with substantial and thoughtful reviews.

Women researchers make a difference. Women scientists, Betty Vetter suggests, may ask different questions than men ask—or may deliberately choose not to pursue some forms of scientific research. Rosalind Barnett shows what happens in social science research when a study is set up with women as the norm, not the aberration. The sample group is different and so are the questions asked. The results alter long-standing views of how women cope with family life and work.

Research lays groundwork and stimulates more research, but it also changes basic assumptions. As we educate tomorrow's scholars, professionals, citizens and workers, their perceptions of the world are formed. Susan Van Dyne and Marilyn Schuster describe a radical development in education, a change that would not have been possible without the solid foundation of feminist scholarship we now have. In "reimagining the core of the liberal arts curriculum," curriculum transformation moves beyond separate women's studies and minority group studies programs to integrate the perspectives of and material on women and minorities into courses in all fields. The potential for changing the viewpoint of young Americans is enormous. Already in motion in colleges, curriculum transformation is beginning to appear in secondary schools. Its proponents are patient, building change with great care in one institution at a time, but their carefully recorded experience will enable others to follow. The change represented by this exciting approach would help to alter the attitudes of guidance counselors and teachers, who, Carroll Wilkinson tells us, consciously or unconsciously often close the door to young girls' explorations of occupations not traditionally held by women.

Wilkinson looks at women pioneering in a great variety of occupations formerly closed to them, from coal mining to space flight. "First women" often must lead a lonely life, but they are finding one another and forming networks, as evidenced by Wilkinson's list of organizations. Betty Vetter shows us, in statistics and narrative, what women in the sciences are achieving. Women lawyers are making progress, Lynn Holmes reports, but they are not making as much money as their colleagues. Advances may be slow and hard to achieve, and for many women, the primary goal is not a triumph for feminism but a job and a paycheck.

Women workers took some steps toward equality as legislative activity concentrated on economic equity. Stalled in a political climate unfriendly toward such civil rights issues as reproductive rights or the Equal Rights Amendment, feminist activists turned their attention to one-step-at-a-time economic issues: equity for women in pensions, insurance, and pay. Lynn Holmes describes these efforts, what they achieved or failed to achieve, and why.

It is hard to reconcile these images of hard-working, serious women with Andrew Hacker's picture of woman as the thief of man's work and self-esteem, presented in an article, "Women Vs. Men in the Work Force," in the *New York Times Magazine*, 9 December, 1984. He—and other writers—pose the threat that women who dare to compete will have to live with the emasculated man they have created in the process. It is equally hard to imagine the women discussed in these essays having time for the preoccupation suggested in Bergdorf Goodman's advertisement in the *New York Times* of 17 February, 1985; "Freud said a woman's basic fear is that she will lose love. B. G. says her real fear is not finding the right shoe." For the six out of ten working mothers of children under eighteen, the right shoe probably belongs to one of the kids and it might be under a bed somewhere.

Many of the women characters in film, television, and popular fiction have born too little resemblance to contemporary women in real life. There are still plenty of old-fashioned stereotypes, especially in the romance fiction that fills the supermarket book racks. But Katherine St. Clair finds progress even in the world of popular culture. She demonstrates that, despite the glacial pace of change in television and film, new and more realistic female characters are appearing, women who cope with careers and family, decide to marry or not, work out friendships, in situations that we can sometimes recognize from our own lives.

Women, whatever their marital or parental condition, are already juggling multiple responsibilities. Ever since women went out to work in factories in the nineteenth century, they have been managing two or three roles simultaneously. The news lies in the findings of research on women, work, and stress by Rosalind Barnett and her colleagues. They challenge the long-established view that women are naturally homebodies, whose health cannot endure being buffeted by the hard circumstances of the world of work. These conclusions contradict the concept that venturing away from the hearth is inevitably risky for women, a concept that has haunted women workers and women scholars for decades.

Barnett's evidence indicates that domestic life and child rearing may contribute more to stress among women than work life. Josephine Donovan describes some recent historical research on alternative communities; chapters on aging and on work point to the continuing need for such communities. The self-contained family unit endures as a model despite its obvious failings and the declining number of traditional families. Impractical and inefficient for working mothers, lonely and unmanageable for aging women, the single-family housing unit, whether it is a suburban house or a city apartment, remains nearly always the only choice. Alternatives that

offer greater community support—child care, shared cooking arrangements, companionship for the elderly—have been proposed but seldom
adopted.

The high point in politics was the Democratic National Convention.
Later in the year, the political scene was discouraging, but if there were
few triumphs for women in the results of the 1984 elections, Peggy Simpson's analysis shows clear indications that both major parties acknowledged
women as a political force to reckon with. At the same time, both Simpson
and Holmes present evidence that even in a time of retrenchment, women
are pressing ahead where they can, turning to state and local action when
the federal government is intractable.

Not only government but the medical profession and scientific research seem to be failing in their attention to the problems of aging women.
Perhaps our least satisfactory news this year is in the area of older women's
health and physical well-being. Aging is the focal point of our chapter on
health, for women over sixty-five represent a large and growing proportion
of the population. Yet, our report shows, their health problems have not
received a proportionate share of attention. Some of these problems stem
from exposure to health hazards throughout their lives—smoking, hazardous working conditions, environmental pollution—which indicate the need
to eliminate or reduce these risks. Also, doctors need a change of attitude;
preventive care and chronic diseases have not been of compelling interest to
the medical profession. And correcting a central cause of poor health, the
poverty in which elderly women live, ranks low on the list of government
priorities.

If older women receive a message that they got themselves in this fix
by having the temerity to live so long, younger women are victims of a similar vindictive illogic. The United States has the highest rate of teenage
pregnancy of any industrialized country. Education and counseling on sexuality and family planning continue only under constant protest. Statistics
gathered by the Alan Guttmacher institute show that over 3 million American women who do not wish to become pregnant still use no form of birth
control. Legal abortion languishes in limbo, the New Right standing ever
ready to stop it through the legislative process or through the courts. The
federal government turns a deaf ear and a blind eye to terrorist attacks on
abortion clinics, and the president takes time to give warm greetings to an-
tiabortionists massing in Washington on the anniversary of *Roe* v. *Wade*. An
insistence on the humanity of the fetus contrasts starkly with cuts in federal
aid to pregnant women and to children, so starkly that the motivation and
rationale are hard to discern.

Although no chapter of this volume specifically addresses the issues of
war and nuclear weapons, women continue to play a central role in the
struggle to ensure a future for the world. As "star wars" move from fiction
toward reality, like a Woody Allen character stepping from the screen into
our lives, the publications and speeches of women like Helen Caldicott and
the regional efforts of women like Frances Crowe of Massachusetts to
awaken people to the destruction of our future continue unabated. As defense spending consumes the national budget, less and less is available for
items crucial to women—aid to children, education, medical care for the
aged, alleviation of poverty. In a nation hypnotized by weapons, women

who are campaigning to break that fascination deserve our respect and applause.

While showing us where we are, the contributors to this volume also provide signposts to the next destination. If we must settle now for modest gains, we can continue to move toward our goals.

Thanks to the enthusiasm and diligence of the contributors, editing this volume has been a satisfying task. I am grateful to Janice Meagher and Barbara Haber for their ideas and assistance, and especially to Jill Conway, Billie Bozone, and my other colleagues at Smith College, whose support and encouragement made my work on the book possible.

Mary Drake McFeely

# Education
## Transforming the Liberal Arts

*Susan Van Dyne and Marilyn Schuster*

## Setting the Context

The eighties are a crucial decade for women and minorities in higher education. For the first time in history, women now represent the majority of the college population, and by the end of the century, over 30 percent of college-age students will be members of so-called minority groups. More, a growing percentage of women undergraduates (over 20 percent in some institutions) are older returning students. These students challenge institutions of higher education to create a curriculum that meaningfully answers their needs. At the same time, scholarship on women and women's studies programs have come of age after nearly twenty years of work focused on women's experience. There are now over 30,000 women's studies courses, 452 official women's studies programs, and 40 centers for research on women across the country (Howe 1985).

Even as women become the majority in the undergraduate population and scholarship on women and minorities brings new data and new perspectives to the academic disciplines, higher education in the United States is in a state of conflict and crisis. The year 1984 may prove to have been a decisive year for identifying goals and defining the content of the liberal arts curriculum for the rest of the century, and for determining the place of women in the academy. Two reports that were published or prepared in 1984 represent opposite approaches to the same problem. "To Reclaim a Legacy," written by William Bennett (1984), was based on the National Endowment for the Humanities "Study Group on the State of Learning in the Humanities in Higher Education." The Association of American Colleges report "Integrity in the College Curriculum: A Report to the Academic Community" (Integrity. . . 1985) is based on the "Project on Redefining the Meaning and Purpose of Baccalaureate Degrees" of the Association of American Colleges. Both reports begin with an indictment of the present state of the undergraduate curriculum. They reinforce the sense of crisis in

American higher education, citing lack of coherence in the curriculum, the need for a renewed sense of shared purpose and values, the increasingly narrow research interests of faculty members who are not necessarily trained or rewarded for good teaching, and the tendency of students to define their education in terms of specific vocational goals.

Although both reports recognize pervasive problems of meaning in the undergraduate curriculum and of morale among educators, they point to opposite solutions. The Bennett report prescribes a return to the curriculum of the fifties and early sixties, based "on monuments of Western civilization," that would define what the educated person needs to know by establishing a common reading list. Seeing the changes in knowledge of the last two decades as a threat to education as he knew it, Bennett would discard the insights of ethnic and women's studies and of student-centered learning. The AAC report, on the other hand, looks for coherence based on common learning experiences and necessary skills rather than on a fixed reading list. The stress is on "integrity" rather than a "legacy" and allows for the incorporation of two decades of scholarship that has redefined the disciplines and produced many new types of courses. The AAC report identifies as one of nine experiences essential to men and women engaged in baccalaureate education international and multicultural experiences that pay attention to "the insights and understandings, the lives and aspirations of the distant and foreign, the different and neglected."

## What Curriculum Transformation Is (and Isn't)

By 1984, over fifty colleges and universities had developed curricular plans to restore quality and responsibility at the core of the liberal arts by integrating recent scholarship on women and nonwhite cultural groups rather than by ignoring it. A directory of projects is compiled annually by Barbara Kneubuhl and Peggy McIntosh at the Wellesley College Center for Research on Women (1984). A special issue of the *Forum for Liberal Education* gave progress reports on exemplary projects nationwide (1984). These issues are also increasingly important in private secondary schools. The national conference of the National Association of Independent Schools in March 1985 identified gender, race, ethnicity, and socioeconomic status as central themes.

Curriculum transformation is the effort to bring the material and perspectives of scholarship on women and minorities into the full range of the undergraduate curriculum. The term *curriculum* is used here in the broadest sense to include not only individual courses but patterns of course selection, advising, pedagogical practice in the classroom, and the relationship between the curriculum and extracurricular activities in a student's overall education. Curriculum transformation does not necessarily mean the creation of new courses but the reformulation of standard courses in all departments to bring them up to date with new scholarship and to make them responsive to the needs and experience of the entire student population— women and men, blacks and whites. Some early efforts used the term *mainstreaming* to indicate that the goal was to bring the study of women into the educational mainstream or the regular departmental offerings as these have been traditionally defined. *Transformation* more aptly indicates that scholarship on women and minorities has so redefined the disciplines that the core of undergraduate study is profoundly changed with the integration of the new research (Howe 1982).

Successful efforts at curriculum transformation have also demonstrated that transformation of the academic disciplines and institutional power structures is far from a dilution of women's studies. Transformation does not mean assimilation of the scholarship most compatible with the traditional liberal arts at the expense of difficult issues, such as institutional misogyny, racism, and homophobia. The experience of emerging curriculum transformation projects has shown that effective transformation is impossible without a base of researchers and teachers whose primary concern is women; similarly, women's studies departments and programs become marginalized and risk having little effect on the experience of most faculty members and students if they are not linked to curriculum transformation projects.

## Strategies for Curricular Change

Three strategies have been used to make higher education more responsive to students who are female and to those who belong to cultures designated as minorities in the American educational system. The focus of curricular reform and the means for achieving change shift with each strategy: (1) nonsexist, nonracist, nonelitist; (2) sex-equity or affirmative action; and (3) gender, race, and class as categories of analysis.

The first strategy to evolve was an effort to correct for existing bias. Reviews of the language and images of textbooks and of teachers' presentation of material revealed that our educational materials and our teaching habits persistently excluded or trivialized women, as well as men and women outside the dominant race, class, or culture. This strategy is critical for raising consciousness; as a first step, the concern to become nonsexist, nonracist, nonelitist devotes primary attention to monitoring and deleting material that explicitly or implicitly demeans any group and to alerting faculty to possible bias in interactions with students. Bernice Sandler directed a project for the Association of American Colleges that identified teaching behaviors that disadvantage female students (1982). But to rest satisfied with this strategy alone ignores the possibility that a superficial improvement in unacceptable language or attitudes may camouflage a deeper, unspoken misogyny or racism that may operate in the classroom.

The next strategy attempts to produce sex-equity or affirmative action in course materials by adding a representative number of women figures or a sampling of racial and cultural diversity to the syllabus. This strategy may, unfortunately, be shortsighted if a "representative number" from these groups is defined as an approximate ratio to their presence in the current student population. Teachers might more fruitfully ask themselves, does my syllabus recognize that half of human experience has been women's and that the majority of the world's population is not white?

The most transformative strategy employs gender, race, and class as categories of analysis. Along with a change in the actual figures on the syllabus, this strategy introduces a shift in the perspective or lens through which we see them. We ask new questions about the course materials and about ourselves as interpreters: how might the variables of gender, race, and class influence the experience, perception, or analysis of each of the items on the syllabus? None of these strategies may be overlooked and each is essential to achieve long-term personal and institutional change.

## The Impact of Scholarship on Women and Minorities on the Disciplines

Transformation of the traditional curriculum began by a negative definition of the curriculum that excluded women; we identified what was needed by cataloging what was missing or marginalized. Reimagining the core of the liberal arts curriculum means exposing the conflict between opposing world-views: an exclusive, white, male, Western European view of human experience that calls itself humanist, in contrast to a much more inclusive vision of critical differences in gender, ethnicity, and socioeconomic background. The vision of a curriculum responsive to women and minorities is no longer merely a negative definition of what we must overcome—sexist, racist, or class bias, exclusively patriarchal values, and female students who are invisible in the classroom. The evolution of curriculum change efforts parallels the directions of the last twenty years of scholarship on women; the insights from that research have altered the content of many academic disciplines. Accumulation of this new data, in turn, generates new questions about the nature of women's experience and that of other groups not currently represented in the traditional syllabus. The experience of the women's studies classroom has provided insights into the interrelationship of course content and classroom practice. Because of the important landmarks in the scholarship on women, the experience of the women's studies classroom, and the example of curriculum change projects across the country, we can begin to identify the interactions among research questions, course design, and classroom practice that stimulate the transformation of the curriculum.

The accumulation of data gathered about the experience of women and minorities and analyzed in their own terms causes us to question in profound ways the frameworks that organize our traditional courses. In history, we are led to question the validity of current definitions of significant historical periods. In political science, the examination of women's experience tests conventional definitions of power. Analysis of the cultural production of women and of noncanonical forms of art and of writing (quilts, diaries, letters, journals) tests the exclusive nature of conventional standards of excellence and broadens our sense of what meaningful art and literature are. When the experience of women and minority ethnic groups is looked at in its own terms and is included in the data from which theories of behavior are derived, definitions of normative behavior or stages of development change significantly.

Teachers who have taught women's studies courses or who have read extensively in the scholarship on women and ethnic minorities are the most likely to undertake the most thorough form of curriculum transformation.

They are willing and able to test the paradigms that have conventionally organized knowledge on the syllabus to exclude or marginalize women and other subordinate groups and to formulate new structures. In institutional terms, the movement from women's studies to integrating or transforming the core curriculum is rarely seen as a natural or necessarily welcome outgrowth by faculty members unfamiliar with the scholarship. When faculty members face the difficult questions posed by the new scholarship, they often feel that not only their own credentials as well-educated, impartial teachers are in doubt but the worth and integrity of their academic disciplines. Perhaps because questioning the paradigms we use to perceive, analyze, and organize experience pointedly asks not only what we know but how we came to know it, the intellectual and emotional investment on both sides of the debate may be higher than at earlier points in the process of change. Even those who are willing to admit the validity of the feminist critique of the disciplines—that periodization in history does not mark the significant changes in women's estate, that canons of great art and literature are derived from and reinforce male practice as most valuable, that the scientific method defines objectivity in androcentric rather than gender-neutral terms—may resist the deconstruction of their own discipline.

## Reconstructing the Syllabus

Given the revolutionary nature of the questions raised by scholarship on women and minorities, it requires significant new learning and rethinking to incorporate these insights into conventional courses. Initial efforts at curriculum transformation assumed that one could add a unit on women in a traditional course and thus understand women's particular "contribution" to established fields of knowledge. Another early assumption was that if one wanted to reach most students one should target introductory or survey courses first and redesign intermediate- or advanced-level courses later. The first lesson from these efforts was that, although adding a unit on women is better than not representing women's experience at all, it tends still to create the impression that women's experience or cultural production is peripheral to human experience or that it is anomalous within the greater sweep of history or art or literature. Simple inclusion of the new knowledge within the inherited framework was problematic because disciplinary paradigms continued to control our interpretation of the fresh data. As long as we agreed to view women through the lens of the dominant group or gender, the most noticeable characteristic of their experience was oppression. Fortunately, the examples of black studies and women's studies offer alternatives to this analysis. If we adopt an insider's view, rather than the exclusionary perspective of the conventionally designed syllabus, we realize that the identities of women are richly diverse and can be defined independently of the dominant group.

During the last three to five years, the experience of mature transformation projects has proven that the introductory and survey courses are the hardest to change because they are the courses that are designed to introduce students to the criteria and essential questions of the discipline and so require the most thorough overhauling in order to be responsive to the new research. Further, faculty members need the confidence and competence gained in transforming upper-level courses to imagine workable alternatives for the introductory courses.

Because effective curriculum transformation is a long-term effort, change needs to be incremental, undertaken at a pace that is not discouraging to the faculty members involved and in a direction that builds on individual and local strengths. The syllabi in a specific field will be easier to redesign if teachers have had a chance to examine critically together landmark essays and books from the new scholarship and to identify the conventions that shape our presentation of knowledge in the classroom. In interdisciplinary groups faculty members may discover new methods of organizing essential data and strategies for making methodology and tools of analysis more apparent or for realizing transcendent goals such as "enabling students to think critically" rather than merely converting a body of material. For example, social scientists or scientists who have organized courses around "problems" or "topics" may help humanists out of the often limiting structure of "chronology." Humanists, on the other hand, may help colleagues in other fields recognize the importance of social and historical context in the shaping of problems and topics, and the desirability of including the philosophy or history of science, for example, in a basic science course.

Teachers may be freer to redesign courses at the intermediate or advanced level, introducing new units on women and minorities gradually, testing new methods of organization or new pedagogical tools before tackling courses that are the most central to the departmental agenda. One of the most difficult hurdles for faculty members, particularly established, tenured scholars, is to become students again, to recognize the changing shape of knowledge and their changed responsibility to their discipline (McIntosh 1982). The experience of many curriculum transformation programs has been, though, that the excitement of genuine intellectual exchange with colleagues that faculty development seminars encourage immediately compensates for an initial sense of loss of old certainties and conventional authority.

## Reorganizing Power in the Classroom

Just as established mastery of old material is superseded by the excitement of new learning, new perspectives generate a reexamination of pedagogy. Unspoken power relations surface when women appear at the head of the classroom or when a woman teacher occupies one of the chairs in a circle of students. How does this relation change when the teacher is a man or a woman team-teaching with a man? The experience of women teachers, particularly in women-focused courses, shows that we need to move beyond an analysis that identifies women teachers as unambiguous role models and mentors to be emulated. As Jean Baker Miller suggests, the teacher/student relationship is founded on an assumption of temporary inequality in which the goal of the participant with more power or knowledge is to end or reduce that inequality by sharing these resources (1976). Yet the temporary inequality of the teacher/student relationship is enmeshed in a cultural context of more permanent inequalities, in which dominant groups, such as men and whites, inhibit access to their power by subordinate groups, such as women and nonwhites.

Power relationships are at the root of the paradigms that inform classroom interaction (Schuster and Van Dyne 1985; Culley and Portuges 1985). How is power felt in the woman-focused classroom? Frequently our pedagogy departs intentionally from conventional models. The same critique that transforms the traditional syllabus in order to take women seriously as a legitimate subject of study and that strives to examine women's experience in its own terms reminds the teacher to respect an individual student's right to report her own experience. Aware that power may have been hoarded by dominant groups to the disadvantage of women in the past, the women-focused teacher is self-conscious about broadening the authority group in the classroom, including students as significant sources of approval and intellectual validation for their peers. Wary of the pitfalls of competitive hierarchical modes of evaluation and judgment, she or he is likely to foster collaborative learning and shared responsibility for measuring achievement. Intellectually rigorous about uncovering the cultural biases that may mar our generalizations, the women-focused teacher will try to illuminate differences among students as much as promote a sense of community in the classroom. Ideally, students learn to value the authority of their own experience as they become critical of the forces that have defined it.

## Characteristics of a Transformed Course

Taking into account the changes in content, organization, perspective, and pedagogy brought about by research on women and minorities, we would propose the following as characteristics of a transformed course (Schuster and Van Dyne 1984). A transformed course would:

- Be self-conscious about *methodology* and use gender as a category of analysis, no matter what is on the syllabus (even if all males)

- Present changed content in a *changed context* and be aware that all knowledge is historical and socially constructed, not immutable

- Develop an *interdisciplinary perspective*, to make visible the language of discourse, assumptions of a field, and analytical methods by contrast with other fields

- Pay meaningful attention to intersections of *race, class, and cultural differences within gender* and avoid universalizing beyond data

- Study new subjects in their *own terms*, not merely as other, alien, nonnormative, and non-Western, and encourage a true *pluralism*

- *Test paradigms*, rather than merely "add on" women figures or issues, and incorporate analysis of gender, race, and class by a thorough reorganization of available knowledge

- Make student's experience and *learning process* part of the explicit content of the course, thereby reaffirming the transcendent goals of the course

- Recognize that, because *cultural patterns of authority shape classroom behavior*, the more conscious we are of this phenomenon, the more likely we are to turn it to our advantage in teaching the transformed course

## Curriculum Transformation Comes of Age: Three Models

Transforming institutional structures in order to translate the insights of feminist scholarship and pedagogy effectively is a particularly difficult task at this historical moment. The crisis of confidence outlined in the reports on higher education is matched by a material, budgetary crisis that has put many faculty members on the defensive, making them more protective of their own special interests at the very moment that interdepartmental co-operation and a broader institutional vision are called for. The most successful curriculum and faculty development plans demonstrate that pooling available funds and organizing interdepartmental groups of teachers together around a common intellectual task lead to a better return on investment in faculty development and often increase the rate of curriculum change.

A review of curriculum transformation projects suggests three primary models that have been tried in a variety of contexts:

1. A top-down model that begins with an administrative directive to make sweeping changes in the curriculum by integrating introductory courses in all departments or otherwise affecting a significant number of basic courses.

2. A piggy-back model in which interdisciplinary courses or programs already sanctioned within the institutional agenda are targeted by women's studies groups or by administrators as the best way to begin curriculum transformation and to reach a broad range of faculty.

3. A bottom-up coordination or consortial model that originates with faculty expertise and student interest and seeks to highlight, connect, and maximize internal or regional resources. Retraining is accomplished through collaboration among peers.

In thinking about these models, we asked how each would answer these questions: Who can change? Where is the locus for change? What are the incentives for change? And how do we evaluate change? In seeking answers to these questions, we've tried to bring into view the assumptions and priorities that may govern the outcomes of these important experiments.

### The Top-Down Model

A distinguishing characteristic of the top-down model is a comprehensive administrative mandate. The initial charge at Wheaton College, for example, was "to integrate scholarship about women into the whole curriculum." Established departments or divisions are most frequently the locus for change in this model, with a special focus on the introductory courses within the departments. Yet the conventional introductory courses in traditional departments are, as we've pointed out, the hardest to transform.

A second discovery is that using the departmental structure as a locus for change is not enough. Because this model is often adopted by institutions without a core of women's studies faculty, they discover they've tried to skip a step that is essential to effective transformation: the creation of women-focused courses that don't fit departmental categories. Although projects designed according to the top-down model, particularly those that require tangible products of faculty participants, do succeed in transforming some basic courses, the most positive outcome is likely to be the creation of a network of faculty members who might begin to provide the missing step: women-focused and feminist theory courses (Spanier et al. 1984).

## The Piggy-back Model

Projects structured along the lines of the piggy-back model hope ultimately to transform the whole curriculum, but take as the locus for change a course or department that already stands outside the conventional disciplines and yet enjoys a privileged place in the institution's established agenda. Whereas the first model begins with a departmental base, this model is interdepartmental or interdisciplinary at the start. A project at Lewis and Clark College in Portland, Oregon, started as a piggy-back plan targeting the general studies program, because it is interdisciplinary and multicultural and involves a large number of faculty who teach in teams. The objective was to train faculty participants who would bring their new knowledge back to the general studies program and who, while team-teaching, would in turn teach the others what they'd gained in the seminar. The program organizers hoped that faculty participants would also spontaneously transform their upper-division courses (Arch and Kirschner 1984). Colby-Sawyer College in New Hampshire and Skidmore College in New York have recently emphasized the inclusion of materials on gender and race in the design of new interdepartmental courses that will serve as core courses required of all students.

The clearest advantage of the piggy-back model is the legitimacy and visibility afforded by association with a strong requirement or program that is already central to the institution's curriculum. A risk of this model is that the program or core courses it targets will swallow up the entire integration effort.

## The Bottom-up Model

The bottom-up model presupposes a network, however loosely defined, of feminist scholars, women-focused courses, and other resources. All the questions—who can change, what the locus for change is, what stimulates change, and how we measure it—are answered differently than for the other two models. The immediate objective of this model is to make visible and accessible all the resources within a region or institution that facilitate curriculum transformation in order to create a community for previously dispersed feminist scholars and teachers, and then to include others who are new to women's research and teaching in the community.

Smith College has adopted this model on an individual campus, and the Great Lakes Colleges Association Summer Institute exemplifies this model on a regional scale. In a sense these projects attempt to create a new locus in which to operate and effect change. Just as the top-down model is departmental and targets introductory courses and the piggy-back model is interdepartmental, the bottom-up model is counter- or extradepartmental.

Because true transformation is a long-range undertaking and must be on-going to be effective and because external sources of funding are drying up, we need to look to the experience of successful programs for models that can be undertaken economically within our current institutional resources. The commitment to research and teaching about women, which is easy to articulate when an outside funding agency is paying for it, must become an integral part of fund-raising objectives, of appeals to alumni donors, and of the operating budget when no more grants are forthcoming.

Betty Schmitz summarizes the conditions necessary to initiate a successful project to integrate scholarship on women into the curriculum. Her analysis is based on directing and designing three mature projects at Montana State University, the Northern Rockies Program on Women in the Curriculum, and, with Myra Dinnerstein, director of the Southwest Institute for Research on Women, the Western States Project on Women in the Curriculum (Schmitz et al. 1985). The conditions are:

- A key group of committed individuals who will act as change agents
- Administrative support for the project
- Women's studies expertise and resources on campus
- Resources to support faculty development activities
- An impetus for reform or specific opportunity for faculty development
- A reward mechanism for participating faculty
- A legitimate home base for the project within the institutional power structure
- Salary or released time for a project director to oversee the effort for a specific period of time

In gaining commitment to these goals from administrators and teachers, we need to counter their impatience for the finished product, their understandably urgent demand for the transformed syllabus, the fully integrated textbook, the inclusive general education requirements, the truly liberal core curriculum. The shape and substance of these products become clearer the more we understand about the change process itself. The curriculum, like education, is not static, and our eagerness to have closure, to touch actual products, should not make us forget that because knowledge is historical we will need to revise the curriculum continually.

## References

Arch, Elizabeth, and Susan Kirschner. 1984. 'Transformation' of the curriculum: Problems of conception and deception. *Women's Studies International Forum* 7, no. 3:149–51.

Bennett, William J. 1984. To reclaim a legacy. Reprinted in *Chronicle of Higher Education*, 28 November, 1984.

Culley, Margo, and Catherine Portuges, eds. 1985. *Gendered subjects: The dynamics of difference in the classroom*. Boston and London: Routledge & Kegan Paul.

*Forum for Liberal Education.* 1984. 6, no. 5.

Howe, Florence. 1982. Feminist scholarship: The extent of the revolution. *Change,* April, 17–18.

———.1985. *Myths of coeducation.* Bloomington: Indiana University Press.

Integrity in the college curriculum: A report to the academic community. 1985. Reprinted in *Chronicle of Higher Education,* 13 February, 1985.

Kneubuhl, Barbara, and Peggy McIntosh, comps. 1984. *Directory of projects: Transforming the liberal arts curriculum through incorportion of the new scholarship on women.* Wellesley, Mass.: Wellesley College Center for Research on Women.

McIntosh, Peggy. 1982. Warning: The new scholarship on women may be hazardous to your ego. *Women's Studies Quarterly* 10, no. 1:29–31.

Miller, Jean Baker. 1976. *Toward a new psychology of women.* Boston: Beacon Press, 3–12.

Sandler, Bernice. 1982. The classroom climate: A chilly one for women? Project on the Status and Education of Women for the Association of American Colleges, Washington, D.C.

Schmitz, Betty, Myra Dinnerstein, and Nancy Mairs. 1985. Initiating a curriculum integration project: Lessons from the campus and the region. In *Women's place in the academy,* edited by Marilyn R. Schuster and Susan R. Van Dyne. Totowa, N.J.: Rowman & Allanheld.

Schuster, Marilyn R., and Susan R. Van Dyne. 1984. Placing women in the liberal arts: Stages of curriculum transformation. *Harvard Educational Review,* 54, no. 4:413–28.

Schuster, Marilyn R., and Susan R. Van Dyne, eds. 1985. The changing classroom. In *Women's place in the academy.* Totowa, N.J.: Rowman & Allanheld.

Spanier, Bonnie, Alexander Bloom, and Darlene Boroviak, eds. 1984. *Toward a balanced curriculum: A sourcebook for initiating gender integration projects.* Cambridge, Mass.: Schenkman Publishing Co.

## Bibliography of Essential Resources for Curriculum Transformation

Chapman, Anne. *Feminist Resources for Schools and Colleges.* 3d ed. Old Westbury, N.Y.: Feminist Press, 1985. Annotates classroom resources for secondary school and college teachers in American and European history, literature, social sciences, mathematics, and art.

Culley, Margo, and Catherine Portuges, eds. *Gendered Subjects: The Dynamics of Difference in the Classroom.* Boston: Routledge & Kegan Paul, 1985. An anthology focusing on feminist pedagogies, the collection examines empowering strategies learned inside and outside of traditional classroom settings.

Dinnerstein, Myra, Sheryl R. O'Donnell, and Patricia MacCorquodale. *How to Integrate Women's Studies into the Curriculum.* Working Paper, no. 9. Tucson: Southwest Institute for Research on Women, 1982. An introductory essay with helpful practical strategies plus seventeen initial reports of integration projects begun in 1981.

Fowlkes, Diane L., and Charlotte S. McClure, eds. *Feminist Visions: Toward a Transformation of the Liberal Arts Curriculum.* University: University of Alabama

Press, 1984. Selected papers from a 1981 conference, "A Fabric of Our Own Making: Southern Scholars on Women," at Georgia State University. Contains essays on feminist scholarship in various fields, some with a southern focus.

Fritsche, JoAnn M. *Toward Excellence and Equity: The Scholarship on Women as a Catalyst for Change in the University.* Orono: University of Maine at Orono, 1984. A practical step-by-step guide for planning, implementing, and evaluating curricular change derived from the experience of a state university system. Available from the author, Director of Equal Opportunity and Women's Development Programs, 324 Shibles Hall, University of Maine at Orono, Orono, ME 04469.

Howe, Florence. *Myths of Coeducation, Selected Essays, 1964–1983.* Bloomington: Indiana University Press, 1984. Excellent essays on the history of women's education, the special mission of women's colleges, the evolution of women's studies, and the philosophy of curriculum transformation.

Langland, Elizabeth, and Walter Gove, eds. *A Feminist Perspective in the Academy: The Difference It Makes.* Chicago: University of Chicago Press, 1983. An anthology examining the impact of the scholarship on women in the fields of American history, anthropology, economics, literature, political science, psychology, religion, and sociology.

Reed, Beth, ed. *Toward a Feminist Transformation of the Academy.* 6 vols. Ann Arbor, Mich.: Great Lakes Colleges Association Women's Studies Program, 1979–. Proceedings of the annual Great Lakes Colleges Association Women's Studies Conference. Available from GLCA, Women's Studies Program, 220 Collingwood, Suite 240, Ann Arbor, MI 48103.

Schmitz, Betty. *Integrating Women's Studies into the Curriculum: A Guide and Bibliography.* Old Westbury, N.Y.: Feminist Press, 1985. A handbook of practical strategies for those beginning integration projects; includes descriptions of effective faculty recruitment, seminar and conference programs, evaluation instruments, a current list of integration projects, and an extensive annotated bibliography.

Schuster, Marilyn, and Susan Van Dyne, eds. *Women's Place in the Academy: Transforming the Liberal Arts Curriculum.* Totowa, N.J.: Rowman & Allanheld, 1985. Eighteen original essays. Part I proposes an analysis of the curriculum change process emphasizing the connections between women's studies and black studies and between women's studies and integration projects. Part II evaluates the resources, design, context, and outcomes of faculty development projects. Exemplary transformed courses are analyzed in Part III, and there is a resource section with an extensive bibliography and guidelines for syllabus redesign.

Spanier, Bonnie, Alexander Bloom, and Darlene Boroviak, eds. *Toward a Balanced Curriculum: A Sourcebook for Initiating Gender Integration Projects.* Cambridge, Mass: Schenkman Publishing Co., 1984. The proceedings of the dissemination conference in June 1983 that concluded a three-year grant to balance the Wheaton curriculum. Contains some essays by leading scholars and directors of other successful projects.

Tinsley, Adrian, Cynthia Secor, and Sheila Kaplan, eds. *Women in Higher Education Administration.* San Francisco: Jossey-Bass, 1984. A sourcebook that examines the careers of women administrators and identifies institutional strategies to recruit and support women, foundation programs to increase professional skills, and the special barriers faced by minority women. Also provides structured exercises to analyze career paths and goals.

Working papers on curriculum change in humanities and social sciences, the Wellesley College Center for Research on Women Working Paper Series, 1983–84. The working papers are contributed by participants in a regional seminar that examined the impact of feminist scholarship on specific academic fields; 1982–83, humanities; 1983–84, social sciences; 1984–85, sciences. For brochure and ordering, contact Peggy McIntosh, Wellesley College Center for Research on Women, Wellesley, MA 02181.

## Materials for Transforming Courses by Field

Each of the following resources contains extensive bibliographies.

### BIOLOGY

Bleier, Ruth. *Science and Gender: A Critique of Biology and Its Theories on Women*. New York: Pergamon Press, 1984. An interdisciplinary perspective on biology that investigates the cultural construction of women's biology and of biological theories.

Hubbard, Ruth, and Barbara Henifin, eds., *Biological Woman: The Convenient Myth*. Cambridge, Mass.: Schenkman, 1982. An anthology of feminist essays on women's health issues, such as menstruation, sterilization, and hazardous work conditions. Includes feminist critiques of theories about women's sexuality and socialization.

### BLACK WOMEN'S STUDIES

Hull, Gloria T., Patricia Bell Scott, and Barbara Smith, eds. *But Some of Us Are Brave: Black Women's Studies*. Old Westbury, N.Y.: Feminist Press, 1982. An anthology including analytical essays on black feminism, slavery and racism, black women's education, health, and literature. Contains extensive annotated bibliographies and is an essential resource for nonprint materials (films, cassettes, music, slides ) and for model syllabi.

### ECONOMICS

Gappa, Judith M., and Janice Pearce. *Sex and Gender in the Social Sciences: Reassessing the Introductory Course. Principles of Microeconomics*. San Francisco: San Francisco State University, 1982. The series, which also includes psychology and sociology, provides instruments to evaluate core courses and identifies supplementary classroom materials and strategies for reorganizing the syllabus. Available from Judith M. Gappa, Associate Provost, San Francisco State University, 1600 Holloway Ave. N-AD 455, San Francisco, CA 94132.

### GEOGRAPHY

Rengert, Arlene C., and Janice J. Monk, eds. *Women and Spatial Change: Learning Resources for Social Science Courses*. A Publication of the Association of American Geographers. Dubuque, Iowa: Kendall/Hunt Publishing Co., 1982. Develops modules about women to be included in new definitions of human and cultural geography. Topics include home and agricultural landscapes, migration, industrialization, and day care.

### HISTORY

Fox-Genovese, Elizabeth, and Susan Mosher Stuard. *Restoring Women to History: Materials for Western Civilization I and II*. 2 Vols. Bloomington, Ind.: Organization of American Historians, 1983. Available from OAH, 112 N. Bryan, Bloomington, IN 47401.

*Her Story: 1620–1980: A Curriculum Guide for American History Teachers.* Princeton, N.J.: Woodrow Wilson National Fellowship Foundation, 1981. Includes historiographical essays on each period plus primary documents for classroom use and annotated bibliographies.

Lerner, Gerda. *Teaching Women's History.* Washington, D.C.: American Historical Association, 1981. Separate essays present an overview of information about women to be included in topics such as community, education, family, religion. Special attention is given to the history of women in a variety of ethnic groups. Available from AHA, 400 A Street SE, Washington, DC 20003.

Organization of American Historians. *Restoring Women to History: Materials for U.S. I and II.* 2 vols. Bloomington, Ind.: Organization of American Historians, 1983. Available from OAH, 112 N. Bryan, Bloomington, IN 47401.

## LITERATURE
Lauter, Paul, ed. *Reconstructing American Literature: Syllabi, Critiques, and Issues.* Old Westbury, N.Y.: Feminist Press, 1984. A valuable introductory essay on the process and goals of transforming American literature courses plus sample syllabi developed by teachers at a wide variety of institutions. Especially helpful for inclusion of noncanonical materials from different class and ethnic backgrounds.

## POLITICAL SCIENCE
American Political Science Association. *Citizenship and Change: Women and American Politics.* Washington, D.C.: American Political Science Association, 1983–84.

These units are currently available within the series:

Diamond, Irene. *Family and Public Policy.*

Gelb, Joyce, and Ethel Klein. *Women's Movements: Organizing for Change in the 1980's.*

Hedblom, Milda K. *Women and American Political Organizations and Institutions.*

Pinderhughes, Dianne. *Images and Films: Race and Gender.*

Sapiro, Virginia. *Women, Political Action, and Political Participation.*

Shanley, Mary. *Feminism: Ideology and Theory.*

Slavin, Sarah. *Constitutional Principles.*

Steihm, Judith H., with Michelle Saint-Germain. *Men, Women and State Violence: Government and the Military.*

Talarico, Susette, Beverly B. Cook, and Karen O'Connor. *Judicial Process and Behavior.*

## PSYCHOLOGY
Gappa, Judith M., and Janice Pearce, gen. eds. *Sex and Gender in the Social Sciences: Reassessing the Introductory Course.* See under Economics.

Russo, Nancy Felipe, and Natalie J. Malovich. *Assessing the Introductory Psychology Course.* Washington, D.C.: American Psychological Association, 1982. Available from APA, 1200 17th St., NW, Washington, DC 20036.

## SOCIOLOGY
Gappa, Judith M., and Janice Pearce, gen. eds. *Sex and Gender in the Social Sciences: Reassessing the Introductory Course.* See under Economics.

Thorne, Barrie. *Guidelines for Introductory Sociology*. Washington, D.C.: American Sociological Association, 1982.

Jenkins, Mercilee M. *Guidelines for Student-Faculty Communication*. Washington, D.C.: American Sociological Association, 1982. A helpful guidebook for teachers in any field to identify bias and to develop strategies for overcoming it. Includes a self-evaluation questionnaire for teachers and a student perception questionnaire.

The latter two resources are available as one document from the American Sociological Association Teaching Resources Center, 1722 N St., NW, Washington, DC 20036.

Goldsmid, Paula L., ed. *Teaching the Sociology of Sex and Gender: Syllabi and Related Materials*. Washington, D.C.: American Sociological Association, 1980. Available from the American Sociological Association Teaching Resources Center, 1722 N St. NW, Washington, DC 20036.

# Health
## Women and Aging

*Norma Meras Swenson, Diana Laskin Siegal,*
*and Paula Brown Doress*

Women's life expectancy is now almost eight years longer than men's and is expected to extend still further. While the proportion of all the elderly (sixty-five and over) to the whole population is growing—12 percent today, 20 percent projected by 2020—women outlive and thus outnumber men; frequently they outlive their children as well.

Greater longevity raises a host of concerns for women—concerns about chronic illness, insufficient economic resources, giving or needing care, surviving family members and closest friends. Yet until recently, women's issues and concerns have been overlooked because so much of the policy-making on aging is still based on research by and about men, much of it done many years ago (Boston Women . . . 1984).

Whatever their earlier life-styles and circumstances, almost all older women will be forced to adapt in response to medical and social policies in setting which they had virtually no voice. In 1984, much attention was given to expensive medical heroics like the artificial heart. Meanwhile, millions of elderly women, living alone and at or near poverty, witnessed during this year the Reagan administration's massive new attacks on federal health and human service budgets, targeting programs whose beneficiaries are almost all women (Piven 1984). Unless changed, these policies may facilitate the recommendation voiced by the governor of Colorado in 1984 that the elderly who are ill have "a duty to die and get out of the way" (Governor Lamm . . . 1984).

This article is part of a larger untitled work on the subject of the health of older women to be published in 1986.

## Poverty and Isolation

The major health issues for older women are poverty and isolation. Women are the majority of the older poor, and close to half live alone or in institutions. These facts have major implications for older women's health, since poverty, isolation, and institutionalization have lethal consequences for any population group (Conrad and Kern 1981).

Poverty, of course, means malnutrition, poor housing, inadequate protection from cold, high heat and repair bills, inadequate clothing. Older persons are more sensitive to cold and more vulnerable to respiratory conditions, pneumonia, and hypothermia. Poverty means delaying preventive care and care at early stages of disease. It means going without hearing aids, glasses, dental care or dentures, special diets, vitamin and mineral supplements, exercise facilities, routine foot care. None of these is covered by Medicare and in some states not by Medicaid either. Poverty also often means giving up a sense of control over one's life, which in itself can adversely affect health (Langer 1983). Even those just above the poverty level are subject to the constant stress of economic worry and may have to choose among necessities that affect health.

Because age discrimination begins earlier for women, many are prevented from advancing in or even entering the paid work force in mid-life, when men typically reach the peak of their job status and earning power. Women are also denied any financial recognition for their years of unpaid labor doing housework, caring for children and for the ill or disabled at home, and for maintaining the official family breadwinner.

Women incur devastating economic losses through widowhood, divorce, or ending a relationship, or through their own or their partner's illness or disability. Usually women lose their health insurance when they lose a relationship or a job that is their source of economic support. For example, at least 4 million mid-life women lack health insurance. Eighty-five percent of surviving spouses are widows and they are among the poorest older women (Older Women's League 1984). Only 2 percent of widows ever collect on their husbands' pensions; one quarter are destitute after two months; and over half in eighteen months, though on average a widow survives her husband by eighteen and a half years (Chauncey 1984).

A working woman who begins her career earning $.76 to a man's dollar actually experiences a decline in relative earnings to $.53 by the end of her working life (National 9 to 5, 1980). By mid-life, one out of four women is single (ever-single, widowed, divorced) and more than half work outside the home to support their families (Lewis 1985).

By the time they are classified as old (sixty-five and over), women have a median annual income of only $800 above the official poverty level—$5,599 per year, compared with $9,766 for older men. Fully one-third of women age sixty-five and over are now officially below the poverty line, and each year the numbers grow, as formerly comfortable or even affluent women exhaust their financial resources, are unable to work, and have no family to care for them. Over 80 percent live alone. Although only about 5 percent of those over sixty-five are institutionalized, about 75 percent of these are women over eighty in nursing homes (Lewis 1985).

Half of all black and one quarter of all Hispanic older women live below the poverty line, compared with 15 perent of white women. However, white women's greater longevity and numbers make them the overwhelming majority of the elder poor (Lewis 1985).

## Double Jeopardy: Ageism and Sexism

Most women want to live as long as possible, yet few look forward to growing older. Ageism—the widespread bias and institutionalized discrimination against persons because of their chronological age—is so deeply ingrained in our culture, it exists even among the persons and institutions women turn to for help and support.

Ageism in regard to health manifests itself first and foremost in the attitude that aging is a disease. There is a school of thought within the new science of gerontology which hopes "to cure and prevent the disease we now call old age or senescence" (Gelein 1982). Thus many people equate getting old with getting sick or frail. By age sixty-five most elders do have one chronic condition, but not necessarily one that limits mobility or functioning. In Western medicine, however, the emphasis in training, research, and care is on trauma and acute care conditions, not on chronic care. Many health practitioners dismiss complaints of older persons with the classic put-down, "What do you expect at your age?" an attitude that medicalizes the normal aging process and causes physicians and patients to overlook manageable complaints and problems.

For example, menopause is a normal life transition that most mid-life women go through with relatively few discomforts (McKinlay 1984). Yet medical practitioners conventionally view it as a disease to be treated with hormones or tranquilizers. Often physicians take illnesses more seriously in men than in women; dismissing the variety of complaints reported by mid-life women as menopausal, they may overlook symptoms of what might actually be heart disease, hypertension, or gall bladder disease (DeLorey 1984).

In spite of research criticizing medical education for systematically teaching mistrust of women's complaints (Scully and Bart 1973; Howell 1974) and for training gynecologists to manipulate women to accept surgery (Scully 1980), review of recent medical tests shows that these attitudes persist (Boston Women . . . 1984). The result for older women is best summarized by a remark of Dr. Robert Butler, past director, National Institute on Aging:

> Older women cannot count on the medical profession. Few
> doctors are interested in them. Their physical and emotional
> discomforts are often characterized as post-menopausal
> syndrome, until they have lived too long for this to be an even
> faintly reasonable diagnosis. After that they are assigned the
> category of senility. (Butler 1975)

Medicalizing can also lead to overtreatment. Women are often defined in terms of their reproductive capacity and their bodies are considered obsolete when they can no longer reproduce. This bias partly underlies the high rate of unnecessary hysterectomies (removal of the uterus). In recent years, 50 percent of women have had a hysterectomy by age sixty-five, often accompanied by an oophorectomy (removal of the ovaries). Studies show between 30 and 50 percent of such surgery is unnecessary (Boston Women . . . 1984).

Other examples of overtreatment include high rates of multiple prescription drugs given to elderly women, especially tranquilizers. Over two-thirds of all psychotropic drug prescriptions are for women (Lewis 1985).

How can women best deal with these issues? Women in self-help groups learn from and support each other. For example, sharing information about changes in menstrual flow in the decade prior to menopause has helped many women resist pressures to undergo unnecessary hysterectomies. They learn about exercise, herbs, vitamins, dietary changes, fans for hot flashes, unhurried love-making, and lotions for vaginal dryness. Women reduce social discomfort by breaking the taboos on acknowledging menopause and even celebrating it as a significant rite of passage into a new stage of life.

An example of a problem that is overlooked but has serious consequences for older women is urinary incontinence: stress incontinence (the leakage of urine with a sneeze, cough, laughter, or physical exertion), or urge incontinence, the feeling, often uncontrollable, of frequent need to urinate. Some problems may develop after childbirth, but around menopause and thereafter, the frequency of these complaints rises considerably; by old age it becomes a major problem. Half the elderly in institutions are labeled incontinent (E. Brody 1985), but many are "situationally" so, that is, they would not have this problem if their needs were responded to in a timely manner. Even among those with organic problems, much could be done both medically and with retraining (Butler and Lewis 1983).

The extent of the problem is indicated by the appearance of ads in newspapers and magazines for "adult diapers" and the publication in 1984 of a *Resource Guide of Incontinence Aids and Services* (HIP 1984). Women are beginning to overcome their shame and embarrassment in order to study urinary control questions, share experiences, and learn prevention and self-help techniques like the Kegel exercises, leg lifts, and exercises to strengthen abdominal muscles.

Shockingly little is really known and understood about urinary control and function in women, and few doctors (mostly Europeans) are interested in developing more precise methods of distinguishing between the types of incontinence and improving techniques for correcting them. These same issues are involved in recurring bladder and kidney infections, also common among older women.

## The Effects of Smoking on Health

Reports in 1984 continue to show the many ways in which smoking is a major health hazard and a major factor in premature death for older women. Smoking is linked to 30 percent of all cancer deaths and to cardiovascular diseases, emphysema, colds, gastric ulcers, chronic bronchitis, and stroke. Smoking also increases the susceptibility of workers to lung diseases arising from exposure to toxic substances (Cancer Facts . . . 1985). Heart disease is ten times more common in women who use birth control pills and also smoke.

Evidence is mounting that smoke inhaled by a nonsmoker (sidestream, ambient, or passive smoking) also causes disease. A nonsmoker in a family that consumes more than two packs a day inhales the equivalent of one or two cigarettes. The air quality in some lounges and restaurants exceeds outdoor air pollution emergency levels (Kenney 1984).

## Prevention

Older women *are* remarkably healthy. To speak of poverty and isolation as health issues of older women is to understand that health goes beyond the mere absence of disease, far beyond the medical model that recognizes only those biological processes going on within the body (Mishler et al. 1984). For example, social class, work, food, housing, substance habits, water, and air actually have more influence on health status than medical care (Brody 1984; Conrad and Kern 1981). Wellness approaches to health recognize that daily habits and environmental factors are more influential in maintaining health and preventing disease than are visits to a health practitioner.

A series of recommendations issued in 1984—by the National Academy of Sciences, the American Heart Association, and the American Cancer Society—involved exercise and dietary changes for the prevention of diseases that affect older women (Gorbach 1984). Heart and circulatory disease, the leading cause of death of women after age fifty-five; cancer, especially breast cancer, the leading cause of death of women between forty-five and fifty-five; adult-onset diabetes, which afflicts more women than men and is the most common cause of blindness; osteoporosis and osteoarthritis, which affect mostly women: all these would doubtless show marked reduction in incidence if the officially recommended prevention regimes were combined and applied well before mid-life. Such a regime would involve:

- Regular exercise to help keep joints limber, help prevent osteoporosis, heart disease, and arthritis, and maintain optimum weight so as to prevent diabetes

- Reduction of fats to 30 percent or below (no less than 10 percent) of total dietary calories to help prevent circulatory disorders, reduce gall bladder disease and breast cancer, and maintain optimum weight

- Increasing complex carbohydrates (grains), legumes (dried peas, beans, lentils, etc.), fiber, fresh fruits and vegetables, and calcium (dairy and some other sources) to help prevent diabetes, osteoporosis, and heart disease (including hypertension and strokes)

- Elimination or reduction of alcohol, sugar, caffeine, salt, red meat, white flour products, and high phosphorous snacks to help in every one of the above processes.

These changes are also useful as therapy or prevention of more serious illness after a diagnosis has already been made. Much Type II diabetes and hypertension, for example, can be controlled by diet and exercise. Control by these methods if possible is preferable to use of insulin and antihypertensive drugs. Fatality rates from strokes, slightly more common in women than in men, are already lessening, possibly as a result of more active preventive programs and management for hypertension (Lewis 1985).

The danger, of course, is that of blaming the victim, of penalizing people who fail to alter life habits like smoking or exercise in the desired direction and according to the most recent research. Many key health promotion or prevention activities require collaborative efforts like improving the water supply, restricting tobacco and alcohol advertising, or deciding as a community to provide blood pressure screening to all people over forty-five.

## Occupational Health

One major area that remains virtually unexplored is the impact of work on mid-life and aging women's health. Occupational health is a relatively new field in the United States, and what research has been done has looked mainly at the impact on male workers. Recent work on women has tended to focus on the impact of work environments on women's reproductive health (Women's Committee . . . 1984). Since half of mid-life women are in the work force, the effect of the workplace on the health of older women workers—specifically, women in electronics, asbestos manufacture, clerical work, medical care and related clinical work—needs study. Women may feel justifiably that speaking out against occupational hazards will put them at higher risk of losing their jobs. Since no progress is made without pressure for change, however, we need to support those willing to be advocates on these issues.

Women constitute the vast majority of the 10 million workers using Video Display Terminals. Since VDTs were put into the workplace fifteen years ago, without testing, evidence and claims against hazards and improper use have mounted. The organization 9 to 5 reported thirteen successful requests for worker's compensation for VDT-related injuries in 1984—eight for carpal tunnel syndrome[1] and most of the remaining for eye problems. Legislation to regulate use of VDTs was introduced in fourteen states in 1984 but none passed. The governor of Massachusetts and the city of Berkeley, California, issued guidelines for the safer selection and use of VDTs to protect their governmental employees (Meyer 1985).

Health and work are related in other ways. Widespread discrimination against cancer patients by their employers continued in 1984 despite legislation in thirty-seven states specifically prohibiting such discrimination. Reports of dismissal, denial of employment or promotion, and termination of workers with cancer are documented in growing numbers. The American Cancer Society issued a major report (Lazarus 1984; Canellos 1985).

During 1984 women brought suits in several jurisdictions for protection from smoking in work situations. Increasingly workers are winning the right to smoke-free environments or to separate ventilation systems (Moore 1985).

## Hormones and Osteoporosis

Many articles on osteoporosis were published in 1984 in popular magazines and newspapers. One major event stimulating these articles was the April National Institutes of Health (NIH) Consensus Development Conference (CDC) on Osteoporosis.[2] The issue of osteoporosis had been addressed briefly at a previous NIH CDC in 1979 on the use of menopausal estrogens. At that time no data clearly demonstrated benefits in treating or preventing osteoporosis through the use of estrogen, and in fact, the final recommendation specifically so stated, leaving alleviation of hot flashes and vaginal dryness as the only "proven" benefits of menopausal estrogens. Clear warnings as to its demonstrated carcinogenicity in long-term use, based on at least five excellent studies, were also included as support for this restricted recommendation. Subsequently, consumer advocates fought successfully to include this information in a "patient package insert" so that women could learn risks and benefits directly.

The 1984 group, which convened to look at the disease osteoporosis rather than the drug estrogen, concluded that the sequelae of spontaneous bone fractures from osteoporosis in elderly women were so serious, including high rates of postfracture death from associated complications, that routine long-term administration of estrogens to healthy mid-life women was justified as prevention. The report concluded that the mainstays of prevention and management of osteoporosis are estrogen and calcium and that exercise and nutrition (including vitamin D) may be important adjuncts. (NIH 1984).

On analyzing this unprecedented conclusion, several factors stand out. On ethical grounds, *clinicians and researchers require greater justification whenever a potent, possibly disease-causing drug is used on healthy persons for prevention.* Also, the rationale that this practice will give future benefit is flawed in several ways. First, only about 20 to 25 percent of postmenopausal women develop osteoporosis, so that it is questionable that *all* women should receive the drug in the expectation of benefiting *some.* Examining risk factors might more carefully pinpoint benefit of the drug to specific women. For example, it is known that women who are white, thin, sedentary, smokers, alcohol users, meat eaters, and who eat few calcium-rich foods and have had their ovaries removed are at highest risk. Second, at least some of the target group could have their potential osteoporosis prevented by timely intervention in their habits. This would leave a considerably smaller group for whom the hormonal treatment might be appropriate.

Next, whereas estrogen therapy may be balanced by progestin in order to attempt to eliminate the carcinogenic potential of the unopposed estrogen, *no specific evidence is available guaranteeing the benefits of estrogen, when combined with progestin, in retarding osteoporosis.* Furthermore, progestin itself has risks, known and unknown, that should be considered by both practitioner and client: potentially elevated low density lipoprotein (LDL) levels, which might predispose women to heart attack and stroke (LDL is a type of dangerous blood cholesterol, predictive of heart attack, as opposed to high density lipoproteins, HDL, which are protective against heart disease); risk of gall bladder disease; weight gain; hair loss; depression; and loss of libido. Furthermore, the twofold increased risk of breast cancer from taking estrogens over a long term (verified between the first and second NIH conferences [DeLorey 1984; Boston Women . . . 1984, 448 n.]) was not identified by the expert panel as a risk worthy of mention in the 1984 deliberations. Whether estrogen combined with progestin would have the same or a different effect on breast cancer is unknown.

These proceedings illustrate clearly the triumph of commercial interests in persuading the medical community to find acceptable use for a product that was declining in popularity because of serious, publicized cancer risks (Boston Women . . . 1984). It also illustrates the triumph of a medical regimen (estrogen) over social measures (exercise programs for mid-life and aging women) and nonmedical support and self-help (calcium and sunshine). Another question deserving further research is this: what proportion of women with osteoporosis have had ovaries removed, and what role, along with other preventive measures, might prevention of oophorectomy play in curbing the disease?

## Cancer

News of treatments of several cancers that affect older women generated concern and hope during 1984. *Breast cancer* is still one of the leading causes of death in mid-life women ages forty-five to fifty-four and a continuing cause in postmenopausal women. New five-year treatment trial results, showing that since the 1979 NIH Consensus Development Conference which discredited the Halsted radical mastectomy, three treatments of women with Stage I and II breast cancer (no cancer found in a sampling of underarm nodes) have similar outcomes: (1) modified radical mastectomy, (2) lumpectomy (original lump and small amount of surrounding tissue removed) followed by radiation, and (3) lumpectomy alone (McCann 1984). (However, the full research report showed that lumpectomy plus radiation is superior to lumpectomy alone [Fisher et al. 1985b].) These results are virtually identical to Canadian and European trials for which similar ten- or twenty-year survival results exist. These results mean, in effect, that (1) a woman does not need to have a modified radical (or total) mastectomy, although she may if she chooses to, with the option of reconstruction (an implant, done either at the time of surgery or some weeks or months later); (2) a woman need not lose her breast, but may choose radiation; and (3) she may choose lumpectomy alone.

Consumer advocate and breast cancer patient Rose Kushner criticized a growing trend to offer chemotherapy to women for whom no benefit can be demonstrated (Kushner 1984). Calling it the "Halsted of the eighties," Kushner described how an innovation useful for some patients diffuses rapidly. This moves it to a place in medical practice where it becomes part of the "accepted community standard of care," *simply because other doctors are offering it, not because it is appropriate for a particular patient* (Oakley 1984). At this point, a doctor or hospital may be afraid *not* to offer the technology in question.

The best answer on choice of treatment comes from actual clinical practice, and since one particular endocrine treatment, tamoxifen, has been shown to *shorten* the lives of breast cancer patients when it was given inappropriately (Boston Women . . . 1984), a woman needs to be well-informed and to ask questions about any recommended breast cancer treatment—especially questions about its usefulness in her particular case. Seven states (California, Georgia, Hawaii, Massachusetts, Minnesota, Virginia, Wisconsin) now have laws requiring that information be given to women about options in the treatment of breast cancer. As part of informed consent, such laws can help make it easier for women to ask "What about *my* case?" when any treatment is offered.

Recent work has reevaluated the original so-called breast cancer risk factors. The few women at "high" risk are: (1) women with a previous breast cancer; (2) women whose mothers or sisters had breast cancer but only if this cancer appeared premenopausally (more so if the cancer was in both breasts); and (3) women exposed to considerable radiation or who have taken estrogens for extended periods for menopause and via DES (diethylstilbestrol). Compared to the long list of a few years ago, this is reassuring (Boston Women . . . 1984).

The practice of "prophylactic" mastectomy followed by reconstruction for women "at risk" of breast cancer is still growing, despite new studies that show that removing the breast does *not* necessarily prevent breast cancer (which is then more difficult to detect) and despite reports of complications and dissatisfactions with the old procedure almost 50 percent of the time.

Women who have painful, lumpy breasts, so-called fibrocystic disease, are not at higher risk than other women of developing breast cancer—a further reason why "prophylactic" mastectomies on such women are inappropriate. Many doctors now call this a condition, not a disease, since it is so common and causes no other known disease or complication (Love 1982). Women and doctors are reporting some positive results in relief from lumpy breasts by eliminating caffeine and reducing fats in the diet. Meanwhile, women can speak up and ask for needle aspirations. This procedure can be performed in a doctor's office. A needle is inserted into the lump and any fluid present is drawn out for examination. Only if it is not a cyst (fluid-filled sac) might it be important to go ahead with a surgical biopsy. Other studies show that while the capability for performing surgical biopsies under a local anesthetic on an outpatient basis varies from one part of the country to another and from one surgeon to another, the practice is growing rapidly, largely because of cost savings (Homer 1984).

The *lung cancer* death rate for women is increasing rapidly; it has surpassed that of colorectal cancer nationally and that of breast cancer in some states. By 1986 lung cancer will become the number one cancer killer of women. Since lung cancer in women grows more slowly than in men, women with the disease generally live longer than men. However, overall survival rates are low and only 9 percent of all lung cancer patients live five or more years after diagnosis. The American Cancer Society estimates that smoking is responsible for 75 percent of lung cancer in women and that the death rate for women smokers is 67 percent higher than for nonsmokers (Cancer Facts . . . 1985).

In 1984 the National Cancer Institute's total research budget was $907.6 million. Of this 5.9 percent was spent on breast cancer research and 4.4 percent on lung cancer research (Carlsbert 1985). Women will need to watch future funding and actively support public and private research on prevention and treatment.

## Hysterectomy and Oophorectomy

Among important organs, only the uterus and ovary are so readily removed without first assessing their degree of malfunction (Greenberg 1981).

Because so many doctors believe in prophylactic removal of healthy organs to prevent possible later cancers, most women are not told of the possible long-term effects and risks of these procedures nor of the risks of artificial hormone replacement. Hysterectomy risks include lessened sexual desire, loss of erotic sensation in the breast and elsewhere, and weaker orgasms in up to 40 percent of women. Hot flashes, depression, and hair loss may also occur. Following oophorectomy, additional effects include vaginal dryness, severe hot flashes, bone and joint pain, and premature osteoporosis. Despite scientific evidence, surgeons continue to assume sexual changes are psychological and prescribe mood-altering drugs or refer the patient to a psychiatrist (Boston Women . . . 1984).

Given the high rates of unnecessary surgery and the noticeable regional variations in rate (Roos 1984), every women needs to ask not only "Is this surgery necessary?" but also "What can I do to prevent the conditions that might require surgery?"

## Mental Health

Nowhere do the myths about mid-life and older women have such devastating effects as in the realm of mental functioning. The word *menopausal* is itself virtually a pejorative term in our society, implying irrationality and emotional instability if not outright craziness. At the very least it implies chronic depression to many people, often to menopausal women themselves. Research in progress in 1984 shows that whatever depression occurs in women at mid-life is associated not with menopause but with other stresses and losses (McKinlay 1984): divorce, illness or death of spouse, parental illnesses or deaths, personal illness, financial crisis, job loss, deaths of friends, financial obligations to children, poverty.

After menopause is well past and one is clearly older, a new set of myths and a deeper ageism take over. *Senile* is another pejorative word that is very much alive and feared in our culture, despite the fact that *senility* is not a precise scientific or medical term. The term *senility* should not be used for changes among older people in mental functioning or behavior, without distinguishing among different causes of those changes. Many behavior changes are reversible or preventable because they result from incorrect use of drugs (too high dosages or in combinations, "polypharmacy"), malnutrition, undiagnosed infections, abuse, neglect, or combinations of these. The major misdiagnosis is labeling treatable depression as senility.

Depression is more common for men in old age than for women if suicide rates are a marker for depression. Suicide may mean for very old people something very different from its meaning for younger people. More and more people are coming to old age with a different sense of themselves and their ability to control their lives. They may feel a strong wish to control the way they will die if they can no longer fully live.

Modern medicine now has the means to prolong life and nonlife for more of us almost indefinitely, giving rise to the idea of "living wills," already a legislated possibility in twenty-two states (Ramsey 1985). A living will is a written statement of intention through which people may decide in advance that they do not wish all possible means to be used to keep them alive in the event of accident or incurable illness. Groups have begun to raise the possibility that seriously ill people ought not be denied the right to end their own lives as a planned ritual of farewell rather than a secret, lonely act of desperation.

## Government's Response to a Growing Elder Population

Unlike almost all major industrial powers, the United States has no systematic commitment to provide comprehensive care for its elder citizens. Social Security benefits, Medicare, and Medicaid all have built-in disadvantages for or outright discriminations against women of all ages, both homemakers and those working outside the home. Pension and insurance programs do not protect women either as workers in the home or as breadwinners. Men designed them with woman-as-dependent, not woman-as-breadwinner, as the model, setting the stage for the creation of thousands of displaced homemakers, who are unable to support themselves.

The poorer a person, the greater the percentage of income that must be spent on medical care. For example, an income of $5,000 a year or less demands that about 21 percent be spent out-of-pocket, whereas those averaging $30,000 or more per year spend about 2 percent (Growing old . . . 1984). Medicare, the 1965 federal program which most people assume covers the medical care costs of the elderly, actually pays only about 40 percent, and after one hundred days, it does not pay for nursing home care at all. After ninety days of Medicare hospitalization, for example, if people over sixty-five do not have private insurance, they must use personal resources to pay for any further care, since only sixty additional days are allowed in a lifetime. As soon as they have exhausted their resources, they can declare themselves poor, which means joining the ranks of welfare recipients in order to receive care from those few providers or facilities willing to accept Medicaid.

Medicaid is a joint state-federal program that pays for health services for welfare clients. Beyond a core of federal requirements, eligibility and services vary widely from state to state, according to each state's judgments about who is eligible to be poor and what kinds of medical care it is willing to cover, even with some federal support. Despite escalating resistance of medical providers to accepting Medicaid, the largest percentage of funds expended for this program has always gone to medical institutions and to doctors (Boston Women . . . 1984; Kutza 1984).

In some states Medicaid pays for many services not covered by Medicare, but fully a third of those eligible for Medicaid never apply. Millions more might become entitled if standards of eligibility were made comparable from state to state at an adequate level. The rolls continue to grow as unemployment grows and particularly as more and more elderly, mostly women, fall through the cracks of the Medicare system. Only the Social Security–eligible may obtain Medicare services, and about a million people are *not* Social Security–eligible, most of them women. Millions more women may have to be declared "medically indigent," that is, not poor enough for welfare, but too poor to pay medical bills. Still more millions are struggling just above these arbitrary lines, only to be thrown into the category of poor or indigent as soon as they have exhausted their savings.

The current administration has systematically targeted social programs of all kinds, including Social Security and food stamps, in order to reduce federal expenditures, and in 1984, the administration proposed more cuts in Medicare and Medicaid. Since the Social Security Administration was reported to be on the verge of bankruptcy, controlling Medicare costs became the key to the program's sheer fiscal survival (Pear 1983). In 1983, a program called Diagnosis-Related Groups (DRGs) was created by the Health Care Financing Administration (HCFA) to stop escalating reimbursement of Medicare hospital costs (Inglehart 1984). Prospective reimbursement via DRGs, which would establish a fixed fee for treament of all conditions of a similar kind, is based on past audits of similar medical and surgical cases; this fee would be all any hospital could expect from the federal government for its Medicare patients. Only massive lobbying by the American Medical Association prevented the DRG principle from being applied to physician fees as well. Some states were granted waivers in order to test other cost-containment plans. The Kennedy-Gephardt bill, which was introduced but not passed in 1984, would subject both private insurance companies and physician fees to the DRG principle.

In its present form the DRG system does not distinguish between average patient needs and the special needs of the frail elderly. Hospitals are already curtailing admissions or encouraging early discharges of frail elders, most of whom are women. These effects, together with federal and state efforts to limit nursing home and home care costs, may result in lack of care for older women (Berenson and Pawlson 1984). They may, for example, be discharged on a Friday but not have home care services available until the following Monday. Women are reporting that the quality of care for the elderly is endangered (Somaini-Dayer 1985). The pressure for cost-containment with DRGs may also result in special hardships for women since more sweeping surgery (as in the case of hysterectomy-oophorectomy) is usually cheaper than the more delicate life-enhancing procedures (such as myomectomy, which removes a fibroid but leaves the uterus) (Smits and Watson 1984).

To further control Medicare costs, another proposal was passed in 1984 to enroll as many of the elderly as possible into existing (federally approved) Health Maintenance Organizations (HMOs) (Inglehart 1985). In effect, the original 1965 promise of Medicare—the freedom of the open medical market to consumers and guaranteed support of fee-for-service to providers—is finally being withdrawn. Despite growing concern in the medical community over this HMO trend, the plan has actually created an unexpected financial bonanza for some capital-poor HMOs, especially those run by hospitals, which are permitted to keep any excess over the HCFA-established capitation rates to further develop HMO services for the elderly (Inglehart 1985). Most HMOs have done exactly that.

One of the original fears about HMOs—that they would demonstrate their benefits, savings, and profits only through avoiding or undertreating potentially ill clients—has not proved true over time. In general, people with the same conditions have comparable outcomes with less (and less expensive) treatment and hospitalizations. In the HMOs that include around 200,000 Medicare beneficiaries, the tentative results appear to more than justify the original HMO premise: the elderly do just as well, perhaps better, in HMOs than in routine, fee-for-service care, and they do better with less hospitalization (Inglehart 1985).

Services such as home care are funded separately from Medicare and are not provided by HMOs. Four Social Health Maintenance Organizations (SHMOs), which combine social services with health and medical services on a prepaid basis, were ready to begin in 1984 but were stopped by David Stockman, director of the Bureau of Budget and Management. Congress rescued the project by attaching a provision granting the necessary permissions for three years to the 1984 Deficit Reduction Act, thus forestalling a presidential veto. The SHMOs will enroll 20,000 persons on Medicare, including some who are also on Medicaid, and the frail elderly. Women lobbied Congress for approval of these demonstration SHMOs in New York, Minnesota, Oregon, and California and should monitor them for outcomes for the older women enrolled.

## Older Women's Activism: 1984

Today, older women have begun to articulate their own needs in existing feminist and women's health groups as well as in elder activist groups. They have joined with other women to gather facts to present a clear, honest picture of the situation of older women, and they are beginning to speak on their own behalf in state and national legislative arenas. Older women are naming those health concerns unique to them and are beginning to fight for solutions to the problems created by our policymakers. They have created their own organization, the Older Women's League (OWL), which in four years established chapters in thirty-five states.

In 1984 OWL, reminding us that 16 million women are age sixty-five or older:

- Took the lead on the question of earnings sharing, a *Social Security reform*, by forming a coalition, the Citizen's Council, to watchdog the issue and by conducting a public education campaign around Mother's Day.

- Was instrumental in the passage by Congress of the Retirement Equity Act, an important first step in the direction of *pension equity*.

- Promoted its model bills on *access to health care insurance* and on the provision of *respite for caregivers* in several states.

- Helped defeat plans to scrap the Senior Community Service Employment Program, three-quarters of whose participants are poor older women (Older Women's League 1984).

Other examples of older women's activism include the National Women's Health Network, which organized two committees, one on mid-life women's health issues and another on older women's health issues. The *Network News* of March-April 1984 was devoted to these issues (Midlife and . . . 1984). In 1984 the American Association of Retired Persons (AARP) started the Women's Initiative, a project that will concentrate on long-term care problems and on the effects of proposed budget cuts on older women (Ramsey 1985). Women members of the American Public Health Association presented two policy statements to the membership in 1984, one on aging women's health issues and the other on the need for nondiscrimination in health and disability insurance (Policy statements 1984).

What does all this mean for older women? To maximize the quality of her life and survival, today's mid-life or older woman must take herself seriously and believe that she has a future worth fighting for. Despite enormous differences in social class and ethnicity, most women over forty-five are not prepared by their upbringing to survive on their own, except temporarily, or to believe in their worth as separate human beings. The challenge facing those older women who are already involved in organizing is to draw in the women who have never participated in any type of activism.

The current administration is deciding right now on critical new directions for health, social, and medical services in this country, and federal programs mandating consumer involvement have virtually been phased out. But it is not too late for older women to shape some of these decisions, at both the federal and the state levels, if they join with other women. It may be crucial for most women to join or form self-help groups and to work on a specific health problem affecting them personally before they can find the interest, entitlement, or enthusiasm to work as advocates for others. Most women need to experience firsthand the power of group support and a network of friends in order to break out of the discouragement and isolation that could so easily overtake them because of their worsening circumstances.

Elderly women predominate in nursing homes, chronic care facilities, and other institutions for older people. The quality of these settings varies enormously both in care given and in the expertise of medical personnel involved. Around 50 perent of those in nursing homes are there only because there is nowhere else for them to go. Women who have carried the caregiving load alone or with very little support are often the first to want to spare someone else the stress of caring for them.

The philosophy of self-help and mutual aid has influenced caregiving and housing arrangements. Elders can often avoid institutionalization and can live independently if there is someone to help with daily or specific tasks. More services are becoming available, such as home care, but some care could be exchanged among friends or roommates rather than being professionalized and medicalized. In some communities, "matchmaker" services already exist that help bring together elder women who need someone to live with or exchange tasks with. Innovation in housing and care alternatives results in a variety of group living arrangements. Some women are becoming more open to alternatives because they or their children have already tried group living.

Once mobilized, older women need to draw on the work of feminist and consumer critics in evaluating health and medical care. They need to work on the Equal Rights Amendment in their own states, as one of the quickest routes to equity in social programs. They need to take on the continuing scandal of nursing homes as part of their special agenda and keep up the pressure until permanent improvements are made. They need to monitor and fight the efforts to cut Medicare, Medicaid, and other vital health programs unless these cuts are preceded by a new national health program. They must realize how cost-of-living freeze proposals for Social Security will particularly affect the oldest women over age seventy-two and oppose these plans.

Older women will have to make sure that self-care and self-help programs are not controlled by professionals. The medical model of personal wellness is inadequate because so many wellness goals are impossible without community support. We need housing for elder independent living; bike paths and clear sidewalks; decent, safe, accessible public buildings, public transportation, gyms and swimming pools; safe neighborhoods. Profit-making nursing homes and health spas will eat up both public and private dollars unless nonprofit, community-controlled options are created. Aging will indeed be a disease if participation in life is cut off by declining access to the world. The make-believe world of television is still largely a distorted and distorting substitute for that world, but it is the only world to which many elderly women have any access. Age is a prison only if society makes it so. We must pledge the resources to keep the world open for the aging. Teaching these truths will increasingly be the new task of older women.

## Notes

[1] Numbness, pain, loss of strength in fingers owing to compression of the median nerve of the arm as it passes through the tunnel formed by the three wrist bones and the ligament in the wrist; it is most common among workers using their hands for long hours in repetitive tasks.

[2] Osteoporosis is a disease more common in women in which calcium loss from bones is great enough to cause spontaneous fractures or greatly increase general fracture risk. Conferences similar to this one are held regularly on controversial medical issues. A team of interdisciplinary experts assembles, reviews, and discusses all the available data and makes recommendations designed to guide practicing physicians and consumers.

## References

Berenson, Robert A., and L. Gregory Pawlson. 1984. The Medicare prospective payment system and the care of the frail elderly. *Journal of the American Geriatrics Society* 32, no. 11 (November):843–47.

Boston Women's Health Book Collective. 1984. *The new our bodies, ourselves*. New York: Simon & Schuster.

Brody, Elaine M. 1985. *Mental and physical health practices of older people*. New York: Springer Publishing Co., 25.

Brody, Jane. 1984. The nation grows older: Facts, projections, and gaps concerning data on aging. *Health and Medicine* 2, no. 4 (Summer-Fall):5–13, 16.

Butler, R.N. 1975. *Why survive? Being old in America*. New York: Harper/Colophon.

Butler, R.N., and Myrna I. Lewis. 1983. *Aging and mental health*. New York: New American Library.

*Cancer Facts & Figures 1985*. 1985. New York: American Cancer Society, 19–20.

Canellos. P. 1985. Ill-founded notions: Job discrimination against cancer patients. Boston: *Phoenix*, January 15, Lifestyle Section, 4–5.

Carlsberg, Florence. 1985. National Cancer Institute. Personal communication.

Chauncey, Caroline. 1984. Facing old age: "Golden years" promise poverty for women. *Dollars & Sense*, December.

Conrad, P., and R. Kern. 1981. *The sociology of health and illness: Critical perspectives*. New York: St. Martin's Press.

Daly, C.B. 1984. Project to test health plan for elderly. *Boston Globe*, 12 August.

DeLorey, Catherine. 1984. Health care and midlife women. In *Women in Midlife*, edited by G. Baruch and J. Brooks-Gunn. New York: Plenum Press.

Fisher, B., et al. 1985a. Five-year results of a randomized clinical trial comparing total mastectomy and segmental mastectomy with or without radiation in the treatment of breast cancer. *New England Journal of Medicine* 312 (14 March): 665–73.

Fisher, B., et al. 1985b. Ten-year results of a random clinical trial comparing radical mastectomy and total mastectomy with or without radiation. *New England Journal of Medicine* 312 (14 March):674–81.

Gelder, M. 1983. Medicaid: "We're on our way home, but it's a long journey." *Health and Medicine* 1, no. 4 (Winter-Spring):16, 24–25.

Gelein, J.L. 1982. Aged women and health. Symposium on women's health issues. *Nursing Clinics of North America* 17 (March) 17, 179–85.

Gorbach, Sherwood, et al. 1984. *The doctor's anti-breast cancer diet*. New York: Simon & Schuster.

Governor Lamm asserts elderly, if very ill, have "duty to die." 1984. *New York Times*, 29 March.

Greenberg, M. 1981. Hysterectomy, hormones and behavior: Letter to the editor. *Lancet* 449 (4 April):780–81.

Growing old in Reagan's America. 1984. *Staying Alive!* House Officer's Association [Boston City Hospital], October.

HIP (Help for Incontinent People, Inc.). 1984. *Resource guide of continence aids and services* (Union, S.C.), summer.

Homer, M.J. 1984. Outpatient needle localization and biopsy for non-palpable breast lesions. *Journal of the American Medical Association*. 252 (2 November):2452–54.

Howell, Mary 1974. What medical schools teach about women. *New England Journal of Medicine* 291, no. 6 (8 August):304–7.

Inglehart, J.K. 1985. Medicare turns to HMOs. Health policy report. *New England Journal of Medicine* 312, no. 2 (10 January):132–36.

Kasper, Anne S. 1977–78. Estrogens: Right-to-know scores one. *National Women's Health Network News*, December-January, 1.

Kenney, Charles. 1984. Battle on smoking intensifies in U.S. *Boston Globe*, 30 September.

Kushner, Rose. 1984. Is aggressive adjuvant chemotherapy the Halsted radical of the '80's? *CA-A Cancer Journal for Clinicians* 34, no. 6 (November-December): 345–51.

Kutza, Elizabeth Ann. 1984. Congress and the elderly. *Health and Medicine* 2, no. 4 (Summer-Fall):14.

Langer, Ellen. 1983. *The psychology of control.* Los Angeles: Sage.

Lazarus, B. 1984. A victim of cancer; then, of employers. *New York Times*, 31 March.

Lewis, Myrna. 1985. Older women and health: An overview. *Women and Health* 10, no. 2/3 (Summer/Fall).

Love, Susan. 1982. Fibrocystic "disease" of the breast—a nondisease. *New England Journal of Medicine* 307, no. 16 (14 October): 1010–14.

McCann, Jean. 1984. At five years lumpectomy seen as good as mastectomy: MNSABP. *Oncology Times*, October, 1.

McKinlay, John. 1981. From promising report to standard procedure: seven stages in the career of a medical innovation. *Milbank Memorial Fund Quarterly* 59, no. 3:374–411.

McKinlay, Sonja M. 1984. Papers presented at the 112th Annual Meeting of the American Public Health Association, 11–15 November.

Meyer, Deborah. 1985. 9 to 5. Personal communication.

Midlife and older women: Taking responsibility for our own health. 1984. *Network News*, March-April.

Mishler, Elliot, et al. 1981. *Social contexts of health, illness and patient care.* Cambridge: Cambridge University Press.

Moore, Athena. 1985. ASH (Action on Smoking and Health). Personal communication.

National Institutes of Health. 1984. Osteoporosis: Consensus development conference statement. 2–4 April.

National 9 to 5. 1980. *Vanished dreams: Age discrimination and the older woman worker.* Cleveland: National 9 to 5.

Notelovitz, Morris, and Marsha Ware. 1982. *Stand tall! The informed woman's guide to preventing osteoporosis.* Gainesville, Fla.: Triad Publishing Co.

Oakley, Ann. 1984. History of prenatal care. Paper presented at Pan-American Health Organization Conference on Appropriate Technology for Prenatal care, Washington, D.C., 26–30 November 1984.

Older Women's League. *Letter to members.* 1984.

Pear, Robert. 1983. Vast reform needed to save Medicare, study says. *New York Times*, 30 November.

Piven, Frances Fox. 1984. Women, poverty and politics. *Human SERVE Fund Update*, Spring.

Policy Statements. 1984. *American Journal of Public Health* 74, no. 3 (March):287–91.

Ramsey, Martha. 1985. American Association of Retired Persons. Personal Communication.

Roos, Noralou P. 1984. Hysterectomy: Variations in rates across small areas and across physician's practices. *American Journal of Public Health* 74, no. 4:327–35.

Scully, Diana. 1980. *Men who control women's health: The miseducation of obstetrician-gynecologists.* Boston: Houghton Mifflin Co.

Scully, Diana, and Pauline Bart. 1973. A funny thing happened on the way to the orifice: A study of women in gynecology textbooks. *American Journal of Sociology* 78, no. 4 (November):1045–50.

Smith, Sandy. 1984. Bill to extend DRGs to physicians opposed by medical societies. *OB/GYN News*, 1–14 June.

Smits, H.L., and R.E. Watson. 1984. DRGs and the future of surgical practice. *New England Journal of Medicine* 311, no. 25 (20 December):1612–15.

Somaini-Dayer, Pearl. 1985. How federal health policy is now backfiring locally. *Barre Vermont Times*, 30 January.

Women's Committee of the Massachusetts Coalition for Occupational Safety and Health (MassCOSH). 1983. *Our jobs, our health.* Boston: MassCOSH; Boston Women's Health Book Collective.

## Bibliography

Baruch, Grace K., and Jeanne Brooks-Gunn, eds. *Women in Midlife: Neither Young nor Old.* New York: Plenum Press, 1984. An excellent anthology including a chapter on "Health Care and Midlife Women."

Boston Women's Health Book Collective. *The New Our Bodies, Ourselves.* New York: Simon & Schuster, 1984. This rewritten edition contains a new chapter on "Women Growing Older."

Brody, Elaine. *Mental and Physical Health Practices of Older People.* New York: Springer Publishing Co., 1985.

Butler, Robert N. *Why Survive? Being Old in America.* New York: Harper-Colophon, 1975. Still essential reading.

Butler, Robert N., and Myrna Lewis. *Aging and Mental Health.* St. Louis: C.V. Mosby Co., 1982.

————. *Sex after Sixty: A Guide for Men and Women in Their Later Years.* New York: Harper & Row, 1976. New edition planned, to be called *Sex after Forty.*

Cohen, Leah. *Small Expectations: Society's Betrayal of Older Women.* Toronto: McClelland & Stewart, 1984.

Fonda, Jane. *Women Coming of Age.* New York: Simon & Schuster, 1984.

Gorbach, Sherwood, David R. Zimmerman, and Margo Woods. *The Doctors' Anti-Breast Cancer Diet.* New York: Simon & Schuster, 1984.

Greenwood, Sadja, *Menopause, Naturally: Preparing for the Second Half of Life*. San Francisco: Volcano Press, 1984.

Mace, Nancy L., and Peter V. Robins. *The 36 Hour Day*. Baltimore: Johns Hopkins University Press, 1981. A family guide to caring for persons with Alzheimer's disease, related dementing illnesses, and memory loss in later life.

Maddox, George, Lee N. Robins, and Nathan Rosenberg, eds. *Nature and Extent of Alcohol Problems Among the Elderly*. Research Monograph, no. 14. National Institute on Alcohol Abuse and Alcoholism. DHHS Pub. No. 84–1321, 1984.

Markson, Elizabeth, ed. *Older Women: Issues and Prospects*. Lexington, Mass.: Lexington Press, 1983. Academic in tone, but filled with useful information. The article on sexuality is especially useful.

McNeely, R.L., and John N. Colen. *Aging in Minority Groups*. Beverly Hills: Sage Publications, 1983.

Neugarten, Bernice L., ed. *Age or Need? Public Policies for Older People*. Beverly Hills: Sage Publications, 1982.

Notelovitz, Morris, and Marsha Ware. *Stand Tall! The Informed Woman's Guide to Osteoporosis*. Gainesville, Fla.: Triad Publishing Co., 1982.

Olson, Laura K. *The Political Economy of Aging*. New York: Columbia University Press, 1982.

Procino, Jane. *Growing Older, Getting Better: A Handbook for Women in the Second Half of Life*. Reading, Mass.: Addison-Wesley, 1983. Highly recommended.

Reitz, Rosetta. *Menopause: A Positive Approach*. New York: Penguin Books, 1979. Highly recommended.

Salber, Eva J. *Don't Send Me Flowers When I'm Dead: Voices of Rural Elderly*. Durham, N.C.: Duke University Press, 1983.

Secunda, Victoria. *By Youth Possessed: The Denial of Age in America*. Indianapolis and New York: Bobbs Merrill Co., 1984.

Shields, Laurie. *Displaced Homemakers: Organizing for a New Life*. New York: McGraw-Hill, 1981.

Silverman, Phyllis. *Helping Women Cope with Grief*. Beverly Hills, Sage Publications, 1981.

Slagle, Kate W. *Live with Loss*. Englewood Cliffs, N.J.: Prentice-Hall, 1982. Practical, compassionate techniques for coping with many kinds of loss and moving through grief to growth.

Voda, Ann M., Myra Dinnerstein, and Sheryl R. O'Donnell, eds. *Changing Perspectives on Menopause*. Austin: University of Texas Press, 1982. Anthology of current research.

Wilson, Emily, and Susan Mullally. *Hope and Dignity: Older Black Women of the South*. Phildelphia: Temple University Press, 1983.

Wolf, Deborah C. *Growing Older: Lesbians and Gay Men*. Berkeley: University of California Press, 1982.

Women's Research and Education Institute. *The Older Woman: The Economics of Aging*. Washington, D.C.: Women's Research and Education Institute, 204 Fourth St., S.E., Washington, D.C. 20003, 1984.

*Resources*

Films and Videotapes

Topics filmed in recent years include the need for privacy and affection in nursing homes, caring for aged parents, adaptive aids for older adults, and specific health topics. Films are available from university and public libraries, which will have evaluations by the Educational Film Library Association, and from the disease-oriented voluntary agencies. Catalogs are available from:

> Adelphi University Center on Aging
> Garden City, NY 11530
> (516) 486–4530
>
> American Association of Retired Persons
> Attn: Program Scheduler
> 1909 K St. NW
> Washington, DC 20049
> (202) 872–4700
>
> Multi-Focus, Inc.
> 1525 Franklin St.
> San Francisco, CA 94109
> (800) 821–1514 (films on sexuality)
>
> New Day Film Co-op, Inc.
> P.O. Box 315
> Franklin Lakes, NJ 07417
> (201) 633-0212
>
> Terra Nova Films, Inc.
> 9848 S. Winchester Ave.
> Chicago, IL 60643
> (312) 881–8491
>
> Women Make Movies, Inc.
> 19 W. 21st St. 2d Floor
> New York, NY 10010
> (212) 929–6477

## Organizations

American Association of Retired Persons, 1909 K St., NW, Washington, DC 20049; (202) 872–4700. Various publications; insurance and discounts for members; other services.

American Public Health Association, 1015 18th St., NW, Washington, DC 20036; (202) 789–5600. Various publications; list available.

Boston Women's Health Book Collective, 465 Mt. Auburn St., Watertown, MA 02172; (617) 924–0271. Responds to written requests for information on women's health issues; produces popular publications. Library open to the public.

*Broomstick,* c/o Options for Women over Forty, 3543 18th St., San Francisco, CA 94110; (415) 552–7460. Bimonthly periodical by and for women over forty. Free sample to any woman for her fortieth birthday.

Concern for Dying, 250 W. 57th St., New York, NY 10107; (212) 246–6962. Living-will registry, literature, and audiovisual materials available.

Gray Panthers, 3635 Chestnut St., Philadelphia, PA 19104. Intergenerational advocacy organization with local chapters.

Hysterectomy Educational Resources and Services, 501 Woodbrook Lane, Philadelphia, PA 19119; (215) 247–6232, (215) 461–6733. Provides hotline, information, workshops; publishes *HERS Newsletter.*

*Hot Flash,* c/o Dr. Jane Porcino, CED Rm. N239 Social and Behavioral Sciences, SUNY at Stony Brook, Stony Brook, NY 11794–4310; (516) 246–5936. Quarterly publication for mid-life and older women.

National Citizens Coalition for Nursing Home Reform. 1825 Conn. Ave., NW, Washington, DC 20009. Advocacy organization.

National Women's Health Network, 224 Seventh St., SE, Washington, DC 20003; (202) 543–9222. Consumer and provider group works on a variety of women's health issues. Publishes *Network News;* other publications available.

New Hampshire Feminist Health Center, 38 S. Main St., Concord, NH 03301; (603) 225–2739. Publishes *Womanwise* quarterly.

Older Women's League, 1325 G St., NW, Washington, DC 20005; (202) 783–6686. Advocacy for mid-life and older women. Provides educational materials on health care, pensions, welfare, Social Security, divorce. Publishes the *Owl Observer.*

Santa Fe Health Education Project, P.O. Box 577, Santa Fe, MN 87501–0577; (505) 982–3236. Publishes booklet on menopause and a newsletter series with subjects of interest to older women.

Senior Action in a Gay Environment, 208 W. 13th St., New York, NY 10011; (212) 741–2247. Services for older lesbians and gays.

Society for the Right to Die, 250 W. 57th St., New York, NY 10107; (212) 246–6973. Materials for the public and for health professionals supporting the patients' right to die.

# Humanities
## Women's Studies Scholarship: The Voice of the Mother

*Josephine Donovan*

> I want our day to come. I want women to take the lead. And I
> know, in the depth of my being and in all my knowledge of
> history and humanity, I know women will struggle for a social
> order of peace, equality, joy.
>
> Joan Kelly

Women may not have enjoyed a Renaissance in the quattrocento, as Joan
Kelly has convincingly argued (1977), but we are experiencing such a renaissance right now. The profusion of women's studies scholarship in the
humanities alone this year is extraordinary. It is not just the quantity that
is impressive. The theoretical challenge offered by this new scholarship on
women is forcing major reconceptualization in all the disciplines. New
imaginative reconstructions are in the process of being formulated in every
area.

To draw another analogy to the Renaissance, following Kelly (1984),
we may note that we are engaged in a major change in perspective. Just as
Galileo and others in early modern science said the earth is not the center
of the universe, so feminist scholars today are shifting perspective away
from the androcentric bias of the past. Leonardo da Vinci stated that: "anyone standing on the moon . . . would see this our earth . . . just as we see
the moon." In realizing the import of the feminist perspective, Joan Kelly
observed, "All I had done was to say, with Leonardo, suppose we look at
the . . . earth from the vantage point of the moon?"

Such a challenge to traditional conceptualization is necessarily revital-
izing the humanities. This year the Modern Language Association celebrated its centennial. In the commemorative issue of its journal, *PMLA*,
Carolyn G. Heilbrun (1984) commented on how the infusion of feminist

studies is helping to reanimate the discipline, bringing "gaiety and excitement to exhausted literary studies."

Because of the volume of feminist studies being produced, this chapter does not purport to be exhaustively comprehensive. Rather, I hope to indicate the principal theoretical trends, discussing a few works in some depth. Other major works published in the humanities last year are listed in the bibliography. I have defined humanities rather narrowly to include only secondary scholarly studies in the arts and letters, excluding all such primary works as fiction, poetry, autobiography, letters, and diaries.

In her remarks to the National Women's Studies Association in June 1984, Catharine R. Stimpson identified two major tendencies in feminist theory underlying current feminist scholarship. These she labeled the minimalist and the maximalist positions. To paraphrase and elaborate on her distinctions: the minimalist position, or what one could also call the liberal view, holds that women and men are minimally different and that what differences exist are due to socialization. Underneath we are all persons or androgynes. Feminism in this view should be dedicated to the eradication of difference, which is seen as the mainstay of inequality.

The maximalists, on the other hand, hold that there are important differences, that this is not necessarily a bad thing, and that women's traditional character and culture hold much of worth, much that indeed can be a redemptive source of political transvaluation. This position may be equated with cultural feminism, which has a long history, as I discuss in *Feminist Theory, The Intellectual Traditions of American Feminism* (Donovan 1985).

The two positions are intellectually at odds, because their theoretical premises are so divergent. It is clear, however, that the maximalist, or cultural, feminist position is becoming a dominant voice in women's studies scholarship in the humanities. In what follows I discuss the most recent manifestations of this tendency, as well as other theoretical developments, including those in Marxist feminist scholarship, which remains a vital and important field.

Probably the most important cultural feminist work to appear in 1984 was Nel Noddings, *Caring: A Feminine Approach to Ethics and Moral Education*. Following in the tradition of Carol Gilligan's *In a Different Voice* (1982) and Sara Ruddick's "Maternal Thinking" (1980), Noddings urges that traditional ethics has been dominated by "the language of the father"; the focus has been on abstract moral reasoning, on "principles and propositions, in terms such as justification, fairness, justice." Conversely, "the mother's voice has been silent." The feminine ethical response is, according to Noddings, rooted in the experience of caring and in the memory of having been cared for, principally by one's mother. Where the "approach through law and principle . . . is the approach of the detached one, of the father," the feminine response is "rooted in receptivity, relatedness and responsiveness." Following Gilligan, Noddings argues that women make their ethical decisions in a relational context.

Like many cultural feminists (see especially Kathryn Allen Rabuzzi, *The Sacred and the Feminine* [1982]), Noddings validates the daily world of the traditional woman, seeing it as a source of the feminine ethic. She urges that one "celebrate the ordinary, human-animal life that is the source of . . . ethicality and joy." This may mean delighting, say, in tending one's garden, in cooking, in feeding the cat, experiences that enhance one's sense of the immediate context and make one unlikely to betray it to abstract propositions.

Noddings exemplifies her contrast between a masculine and a feminine ethic by referring to the Abraham-Isaac story: "The father might sacrifice his own child in fulfilling a principle; the mother might sacrifice any principle to preserve her child." This proposition, as she acknowledges, over-simplifies but nevertheless states her thesis cogently. She recognizes that the weakness in her argument lies in the danger that ethical decisions will always be made according to an immediate, emotional, situational context and without regard to enduring principles of rightness. In this respect, Nodding's thesis recalls Joseph Fletcher's *Situation Ethics* (1966), although she distinguishes her approach from his. Nevertheless, she presents a number of intriguing hypothetical situations to specify how her approach might work in practice.

Some of her most noteworthy ideas occur in the chapter on education. Noddings argues that traditional schooling has been "a masculine project, designed to detach the child from the world of relation and project [her or him] . . . into a thoroughly objectified world." The traditional curricular purpose has been "to claim the child, to teach him or her to master the language, the rules, the games and the names of the father." "It is time," she urges, "for the voice of the mother to be heard in education." That voice would say that "the maintenance and enhancement of caring [must be] the primary aim of education." Noddings offers a number of practical suggestions as to how this might be accomplished. Boys, for example, should experience the apprenticeship in caring that girls now automatically receive.

Noddings is not interested in the liberal feminist agenda of integrating women into male activities, such as professional sports and the military, but in bringing men into harmony with traditional female practices and in transforming the public arena in accordance with a feminine ethic. This is an important, thoughtful, and far-reaching work.

Another paradigm of the patriarchal worldview—the Great Chain of Being—is challenged in Estella Lauter's outstanding study of contemporary women's art and poetry, *Women as Mythmakers* (1984). Lauter finds traditional binary and hierarchical categories blurred in the new feminine epistemology expressed in contemporary art and poetry. Boundaries between the human and the vegetative and animal world are erased. Hybrid forms appear: women transform into natural objects or merge with animal life. Lauter notes that contemporary imagery points to the formulation of a new myth in which "the affinity between women and nature [is] a starting point. . . . hybrid images [are melding] the old distinctions among the levels of the Great Chain of Being." What is emerging is "an image of relationships among orders of being that is extremely fluid." Susan Griffin's *Woman and Nature* (1978) is prototypical.

Lauter's discussion of imagery in contemporary women's art is fascinating; particularly intriguing is her analysis of Remedios Varo (1913–63), an obscure surrealist painter. She also discusses such major contemporary poets as Sexton, Atwood, Piercy, and Sarton whose works, she finds, reflect a high "degree of identification with nature." Not surprisingly, one of their primary gestures has been to resurrect and revalidate such ancient mythical figures as Demeter/Kore, Circe, Daphne, and Artemis/Diana, who express aspects of the woman-nature connection. Lauter theorizes somewhat as to why this identification seems so strong, but further speculations are needed. It is clear, however, as she points out, that what is involved is a renunciation of the "Apollonian bias of our scientific culture."

Jane Marcus (1984b) finds that British women writers of the 1920s created a myth similar to that described by Lauter. In "A Wilderness of One's Own," Marcus argues "there is a female version of pastoral which posits chastity as freedom in a wilderness presided over by Artemis." Marcus sees this Daphne/Diana impulse as "a flight into a pre-patriarchal magical world of trees and transformations, animals and plants, and proud inviolateness." "The anti-Apollonian discourse of feminist fantasy" reclaims a "prelapsarian world of preclassical feminine power." Marcus hypothesizes that this myth emerged because women felt frustrated in their attempts at political change, a motivation that may also be a factor in contemporary women's imaginings.

Another feminist study that reclaims a figure from classical myth is Lee Edwards's *Psyche as Hero* (1984). This work traces the figure of the female hero through two centuries of Western literature. Unlike the male warrior-hero, the female hero is, according to Edwards, motivated by love and a desire to establish community rather than to conquer and destroy. Although Edwards selects Psyche as the prototype of such heroism, I question whether this is an appropriate model. It is true that in Apuleius' version of the tale (which Edwards uses) Psyche is motivated by love, but it is erotic love for a specific man (or god, Cupid) and not for an ideal community. Also, she effects the deaths of her sisters in her attempt to reclaim Cupid.

Nevertheless, it is Edwards's idea of female heroism that matters, and in her discussion of twentieth-century fiction this idea illuminates particularly such varied works as *Gaudy Night, Mrs. Dalloway, Sula, Their Eyes Were Watching God*, and *The Dollmaker*. Here the protagonists do seem to be in search of a "new species of earthly communitas," and the works, to evince a "new symbolic mode that reflects a radicalized and feminized metaphysic." Edwards's study thus belongs in the cultural feminist tradition that honors a redemptive feminine principle.

Many cultural feminist scholars rely on Nancy Chodorow's *Reproduction of Mothering* (1978) for their ideas of female character; particularly persuasive has been her thesis that the female ego has more "fluid" boundaries than the male (an idea implicit in both Noddings and Lauter). Hanna Fenichel Pitkin provides a compelling reinterpretation of Machiavellian politics by use of Chodorow's ideas. In *Fortune Is a Woman: Gender and Politics in the Thought of Niccolò Machiavelli* (1984), Pitkin argues that the masculine need to establish autonomy against the maternal/feminine—the decisive event in the male maturation process, according to neo-Freudians like Chodorow—is at the root of Machiavelli's political theory and therefore of republican politics.

Seeing separation anxiety and fear of the engulfing mother as a quintessentially masculine experience, Pitkin posits that it was particularly acute in the Renaissance. This was partly because of the demise of traditional authority and the attendant compulsion to assert individual autonomy, but also she proposes (less persuasively) that women were making gains during the period and therefore were seen by men as something of a threat (Kelly, as noted, discounts that women made major progress in Renaissance Italy).

What is particularly original and interesting about Pitkin's study is her demonstration of how Machiavelli translated personal anxieties/fears about the feminine into a political theory that is built upon contempt for the feminine. "If *virtù* [which Pitkin translates as "manliness"] is Machiavelli's favorite quality, *effeminato* . . . is one of his most frequent and scathing epithets." Machiavelli sees the virtuous citizen as "stern, serious-minded," expressing a "courageous manliness that despises pleasure and playfulness." Women and the feminine—as *other*—are corrupting influences. "Civilization . . . history, culture . . . are . . . understood as male enterprises won from and sustained against female power. . . . The struggle to sustain civilization and republican liberty thus reflects the struggle of boys to become men."

In a particularly intriguing discussion that complements Lauter, Pitkin analyzes an unfinished poem by Machiavelli in which he posits Circe as the arch-witch-enemy of patriarchal civilization. "Juxtaposed to the masculine world of law and liberty [is] the forest world where men are turned into animals and held captive in permanent dependence." Another symbol of feminine power is the goddess Fortuna, who, Machiavelli stipulates in a celebrated passage in *The Prince*, must be battered into submission by the successful ruler. Pitkin's excellent study supplements Carolyn Merchant's discussion of Renaissance science in *The Death of Nature* (1980).

*Mothering the Mind*, (1984), edited by Ruth Perry and Martine Watson Brownley, is a collection of essays organized around the thesis that artists often have a mothering figure in their lives who provides psychic, emotional, and economic space that enables the artistic enterprise. It is the editors' hope that such studies will help to dispel the romantic myth of the artist as "individual genius toiling alone" and "to reinstate the value of connectedness," the emotional and sometimes intellectual collaboration that contributes to the creative effort. It is noteworthy that this nurturing role may be filled by men as well as women (Leonard Woolf and G. H. Lewes), by lesbian and gay lovers (Alice B. Toklas and Walter Watts-Dunton), and by aunts (Mary Moody Emerson) and sisters (Dorothy Wordsworth).

The most interesting section is, however, that devoted to mothers. Of particular importance is Mary Helen Washington's thesis (following Barbara Christian [1980]) that a primary motivation for black women writers has been to transcribe the oral histories, the stories of their mothers. Unlike the "anxiety of authorship" which Gilbert and Gubar (1979) claim affects the white woman writer, there is authorial continuity for the black woman because she posits her mother as her artistic predecessor. Paule Marshall, for example, said her mother "laid the foundation of [her] aesthetic." And Dorothy West observed, *"All my mother's blood came out in me. I was my mother talking."*

Virginia Woolf once noted that her mother's praise made her feel ecstatic, "like being a violin and being played upon." In her contribution to this collection Jane Marcus suggests that "this metaphor, with its consciousness of the mother-daughter erotic" is a "perfect figure to express the relationship between the woman artist and a mother-mentor." In another article in *Mothering the Mind*, Jane Lilienfeld analyzes the intense relationship Colette had with her mother, Sido. For Colette "Eden was embowered by her mother's nature." "Sido," the daughter wrote, "was a witch. She could make anything bloom."

Another study that sees women's fantasies as projecting Eden-like gardens is Annette Kolodny's *The Land Before Her* (1984). This work, based on a selection of American women's responses to the frontier, concludes that women were moved to transform the wilderness into gardens. "Massive exploitation and alteration of the continent do not seem to have been part of women's fantasies. They dreamed [instead] of locating a home and a familial human community within a cultivated garden."

The conflict between the world of the mothers or grandmothers and the world of patriarchal civilization is seen from a native American point of view in *American Indian Women: Telling Their Lives* (1984) by Gretchen M. Bataille and Kathleen Mullen Sands, a study of autobiographies. In these works the tension is between retention of native traditions and acculturation to white society. The authors posit an evolution in American Indian women's autobiographies that parallels somewhat the historical stages in black literature: from concern about assimilation (or "passing") to a return to and affirmation of tradition. As articulated in *This Bridge Called My Back* (1982), the traditional world may be seen as matrifocal and the white world as patriarchal. The Bataille and Sands study includes an extensive and valuable annotated bibliography.

One criticism I have of the book is the authors' putdown of feminism. Their claim is that Indian women hold considerable power in their community and therefore do not feel a "need" for feminism. However, the idea of the feminist presented by the authors is the erroneous media-perpetrated stereotype of the careerist isolate; were they to understand feminism as a broader vision that often validates traditional women's experience, they would see that it surely connects to the worlds of Indian women.

Fifteen contemporary black women writers are the subject of Mari Evans's collection, *Black Women Writers 1950–80* (1984). This work provides useful introductions to these writers; it includes short bibliographies and in most cases "Why I Write" statements by the authors themselves. As with the Bataille and Sands work, however, little attempt is made to develop ideas about a common aesthetic. More useful in this regard is *Black Literature and Literary Theory* (1984), edited by Henry Louis Gates, Jr., although this collection includes only three articles on women writers.

The lives of nineteenth-century black women are brought to life in Dorothy Sterling's massive collection, *We Are Your Sisters, Black Women in the Nineteenth Century* (1984). This is a wonderful book, full of rich, authentic, firsthand detail about specific lives culled from published and unpublished sources and including numerous photographs. The most interesting narratives are those drawn from the oral histories taken from ex-slaves, recorded in WPA projects in the 1930's. Sterling has done an excellent job of editing, piecing together fragments of narrative into a fabric that reads like an epic novel. Prepared primarily for the general reader, it is sufficiently annotated to be of value as well to the scholar. It should prove an invaluable resource for women's studies, American history, and black studies courses in both universities and high schools.

My only criticism of the Sterling book is that there is little on black lesbians or "romantic friendships" among black women or black and white women. The nature and extent of the intense female bonding that existed in nineteenth-century society is addressed in some of the articles in the lesbian issue of *Signs* (summer 1984). In particular, the role played by such sexologists as Krafft-Ebing and Havelock Ellis in determining lesbian identities is examined. Esther Newton looks at the creation of the "mannish lesbian" image and how it impinged upon early twentieth-century "new women," particularly Radclyffe Hall. Sharon O'Brien considers how Willa Cather was affected by some of the same ideology and how it emerged in her fiction. And Martha Vicinus examines unpublished autobiographical narratives by English boarding school girls, as well as relevant published materials, in an effort to further refine our understanding of adolescent smashes, raves and crushes, and to determine when and how the sexologists' views became current. It is clear that the latter question is a crucial one to which future studies will be dedicated.

A particularly valuable retrieval of lost women writers is Peter Dronke's *Women Writers of the Middle Ages* (1984). While his major purpose is not to develop an aesthetic but to survey major writings, Dronke does note that the women's works may be distinguished from men's writing by "a lack of apriorism, of predetermined postures: again and again we encounter attempts to cope with human problems in their singularity—not imposing rules or categories from without, but seeking solutions that are apt and truthful existentially." This tendency would, of course, be likely among unschooled writers, but it may also be a reflection of a fundamentally female epistemology. Such a thesis has been developed by Nancy Hartsock (1983a, 1983b), Sara Ruddick (1980), and myself (1984).

Dronke's most interesting speculations concern the eccentric vulgar Latin used by many of the women. Like women folk artists, medieval women writers, lacking training, created unusual "artless" figures drawn from their own experience. Here, as with the American Indian women, black women, and indeed all women writers to some degree, there was an implicit discordancy between the patriarchal standards imposed by the schools and an aesthetic derived from women's own culture and traditions.

Although this is an impressive scholarly work, it is clear that Dronke has touched only the tip of the iceberg; further studies of medieval women's writings are much needed. Particularly interesting are his discussions of Vibia Perpetua, a Christian martyr executed C.E. 203; Dhuoda, who wrote in the ninth century; the prodigious Hildegarde of Bingen (1098–1179), who remains, as Dronke notes, "an overpowering, electrifying presence"; and the obscure Marguerite Porete, whose work, scholars have recently acknowledged, is "of incomparable originality." She was burned to death as a heretic in Paris in 1310. Dronke includes extensive selections (in Latin and old French) from these writers' works.

A contemporary celebrant of heretics, witches, and now "proud Prudes and Nag-Gnostics" is feminist theologian Mary Daly. In her sequel to *Gyn-Ecology* (1978), entitled *Pure Lust* (1984), Daly continues "the other-world journey of Exorcism and Ecstasy" begun in the previous work. Both books are structured upon a Gnostic myth of the soul's voyage past "the demons of patriarchy" who are exorcised and transcended through the use of magical new words, which express new ways of being. "Our creation involves striving for biophilic participation in Be-ing, transcending the forces of necrophilic negation."

The demons represent the "Seven Deadly Sins of the Father" plus one (deception). *Gyn/Ecology* dealt with the first three. *Pure Lust* concerns aggression and obsession, which correspond to the deadly sins of anger and lust. Here again Daly uses a witty, iconoclastic, antinomian style to considerable effect. Her deconstructive word-play does not have the shock-value it had in *Gyn/Ecology*, but it has an element of lightness and humor, qualities that were lacking in the earlier book.

Daly, like the artists Lauter and Marcus studied, seems to be developing a consciousness that is in tune with natural rhythms, with animal and vegetative life. It is a matter, she says, of developing a "metapatriarchal consciousness . . . that is in harmony with the Wild in nature and in the Self." *Pure Lust*, she maintains, is a work of "conjuring" that "conjoins women with our Selves and our Sisters, and with earth, air, fire and water. It connects us with the rhythms of the farthest stars and of our own sun and moon. It mends our broken ties with the Witch within our Selves, who spins and weaves the tapestries of Elemental creation." While one may not agree with all of Daly's theories, one must nevertheless honor her continuing intellectual brilliance and moral courage.

Another work that expresses the postmodernist deconstructive approach in feminist theory is Teresa de Lauretis's *Alice Doesn't: Feminism, Semiotics, Cinema* (1984). This work belongs in the rarified intellectual strata of European postmodernist theory and therefore is likely to appeal only to those well versed therein. Her primary challenge is to the theories of Lacan, Derrida, and others who pose women as an absence in the patriarchal cultural fabric. Most interesting to the common reader will be her chapter "Desire in Narrative." Here she poses stimulating suggestions about the nature of patriarchal narrative structure, which reflects, she contends, an Oedipal project. Traditional story "demands sadism, depends on making something happen, forcing a change in another person, a battle of will and strength, victory/defeat, all occurring in a linear time with a beginning and an end." And all are accomplished by male subjects "independent of women's consent."

Sadomasochism, pornography and other fringe sexual practices are defended in *Pleasure and Danger* (1984), edited by Carole S. Vance, a compendium of the papers presented at the celebrated 1982 Feminist IX Conference held at Barnard. This work presents the view primarily of the "liberation feminists," so labeled by Ann Ferguson in a useful article, which appeared in the autumn 1984 issues of *Signs*. (Whether the libertarian feminists are feminist at all is a further question. Mary Daly, taking the radical feminist view in *Pure Lust*, argues otherwise. Calling their position "pseudofeminist masosadism," Daly says, "women who practice such politics support the State by diverting energy into female self-destruction and by blocking woman-identified creativity.")

The liberationists contend that the radical feminists are "prudes" (which is, presumably, why Daly has revalidated the term in *Pure Lust*), who dwell too much on the dangerous side of sexuality; they see themselves as focusing on its pleasurable aspects; for the liberationists, however, this seems to mean primarily indulging in practices now considered taboo. To date, there has been more heat than light generated in the so-called sexuality debates; the liberationists continually misrepresent radical and cultural feminism, and have yet to articulate persuasively their own position. *Pleasure and Danger*, although an effective plea for tolerance (Hortense J. Spillers cautions against the "deadly metonymy" of seeing all women as extensions of oneself), unfortunately adds little enlightening theory.

The final area in which theoretical activity continued in 1984 was in Marxist feminist or socialist feminist theory. The principal contribution was Lise Vogel's *Marxism and the Oppression of Women*, subtitled *Toward a Unitary Theory* (1984). In order to properly situate Vogel's work it is necessary to briefly review recent socialist feminist theory.

A central theoretical concern among socialist feminists has been to determine a material or economic basis for women's oppression, to find a relation between the world of production and women's status. Since women's place has been principally in the home and her connection to the economy that of the unpaid labor of housework, much discussion has focused on the role housework plays in the capitalist economy. Housework is often referred to by Marxists as reproductive labor, on the idea that it "reproduces" workers for the system by refueling them, so to speak, with food, clothes, and so on. This unpaid reproductive labor is done mainly by women. Marxist theorists have generally concluded that this labor is functional to the continuation of capitalism. The problem with this theory is that while it shows how house laborers may be functional to capitalism, it does not explain why women are oppressed, why women are chosen for the reproductive role.

Consequently, there has been an inherent dualism in many socialist feminist approaches to date, a dualism that has been referred to by Heidi Hartmann and others as the "unhappy marriage of Marxism and feminism" (1981). The unhappiness resides largely in the fact that feminists insist that women's oppression is not fully explained by material factors, that male domination or patriarchy seems to transcend economic and social systems. The problem for socialist feminists is how to connect the essentially ideological, psychological, and sometimes biological dimension underscored by radical feminists with the material, economic aspect emphasized in the Marxist view. One recent attempt to establish a feminist historical materialism is Nancy Hartsock's *Money, Sex, and Power* (1983b).

Lise Vogel's new work takes another tack. Her thesis is that women's oppression is rooted in a biological fact, that they are the childbearers. In particular, the fact that men must provide "subsistence to women during the childbearing period . . . forms the material basis for women's subordination in class society." This is because the provision of subsistence during that period establishes the division of labor that assigns women to the role of reproduction and men to production, which itself establishes male dominion. (Here Vogel presumably relies on Engels's and subsequent Marxist theory that whoever controls the purse strings controls the household, that power resides in money.) Vogel, therefore, believes that domestic labor must "wither away" if women are to be liberated. Her thesis, although a useful contribution to Marxist feminist theory, is not likely to be definitive.

Joan Kelly's attempt to wrestle with the problem of dualism in Marxist feminist theory was reprinted in her posthumous collection of essays, *Women, History, and Theory.* In an article entitled "The Doubled Vision of Feminist Theory" (1979), Kelly also sees women's domestic labor as functional to the reproduction of labor and therefore contributive to surplus value in capitalism. She urges, therefore, that we not think of women historically as existing in a "separate sphere" but rather as an integral economic unit that exists in dialectical relationship with the rest of society. Moreover, Kelly adumbrates an idea developed more fully by socialist feminists in the 1980s (notably Hartsock) that their differing economic functions impress upon "women and men differently, making 'women' and 'men' social categories, just as worker and bourgeois are, and black and white."

Delores Hayden's *Redesigning the American Dream: The Future of Housing, Work and Family Life* (1984), an important new study of American architecture and urban design, relies in part on socialist feminist theory and in part on materialist feminist theory developed in the nineteenth century (and treated in her earlier work, *The Grand Domestic Revolution* [1981]). Hayden observes that historically in the industrial world there have been three kinds of housing. One, the haven model, first articulated by Catharine Beecher, which remains predominant today, is that of the single-family suburban unit. Here the domestic site reflects a "pre-capitalist patriarchal structuring of reproduction." The post–World War II period saw the proliferation of this model in the suburban Levittowns built for the returning veteran and his wife.

The second strategy, favored by the Marxists, has been to socialize domestic labor and integrate women into productive labor. The architecture developed for this was "high-rise mass housing" that nevertheless did little to encourage socialization of domestic labor. Consequently, while in the American system women work twenty-one more hours per week than men, in the U.S.S.R. women work seventeen more hours than men. In both countries women bear primary responsibility for reproductive labor. Hayden argues that the architecture of gender must be changed if domestic labor is to be truly socialized and if women are to have effective access to the productive world. The third strategy, developed by such nineteenth-century feminists as Melusina Fay Pierce, provides the most promising model, according to Hayden. This design involves "low-rise multi-family housing treated aesthetically as a village with shared common, courtyards, arcades, and kitchens."

Hayden proposes a number of practical changes that can be done within existing town layouts; for example, portions of suburban backyards could be pooled to create village greens where public service buildings such as child-care centers, laundries, and solar greenhouses could be located and where collective community labor could occur. Conversely, Hayden argues for "domesticating urban space" on Frances Willard's idea of making "the whole world homelike" so that women and children may feel safe in public space. This, too, would help end the private confinement and isolation of women, children, and the elderly. Specific suggestions here include safe public transportation, safe houses for women, supervised play areas for children in banks and other public buildings, and the removal of woman-denigrating pornography from public space. Hayden therefore joins Noddings and others in urging that the situation and culture of women—"the voice of the mother"—be articulated and integrated in future architecture and urban design.

## References

Bataille, G.M., and K.M. Sands. 1984. *American Indian women: Telling their lives.* Lincoln: University of Nebraska Press.

Chodorow, N. 1978. *The reproduction of mothering: Psychoanalysis and the sociology of gender.* Berkeley: University of California Press.

Christian, B. 1980. *Black women novelists: The development of a tradition: 1892–1976.* Westport, Conn.: Greenwood Press.

Daly, M. 1978. *Gyn/Ecology: The metaethics of radical feminism.* Boston: Beacon Press.

_____1984. *Pure lust: Elemental feminist philosophy.* Boston: Beacon Press.

DeLauretis, T. 1984. *Alice doesn't: Feminism, semiotics, cinema.* Bloomington: Indiana University Press.

Donovan, J. 1984. Toward a women's poetics. *Tulsa Studies in Women's Literature* 3, no. 1–2.

_____1985. *Feminist theory: The intellectual traditions of American feminism.* New York: Ungar.

Dronke, P. 1984. *Women writers of the Middle Ages: A critical study of texts from Perpetua (d. 203) to Marguerite Porete (d. 1310).* Cambridge: Cambridge University Press.

Edwards, L. 1984. *Psyche as hero: Female heroism and fictional form.* Middletown, Conn.: Wesleyan University Press.

Evans, Mari, ed. 1984. *Black women writers 1950–1980: A critical evaluation.* Garden City, N.Y.: Doubleday.

Ferguson, A. 1984. Sex war: The debate between radical and libertarian feminists. *Signs* 10, no. 1:106–12.

Fletcher, J. 1966. *Situation ethics: The new morality.* Philadelphia: Westminster.

Gates, Henry Louis, Jr., ed. 1984. *Black literature and literary theory.* New York: Methuen.

Gilbert, S., and S. Gubar. 1979. *The madwoman in the attic: The woman writer and the nineteenth-century literary imagination.* New Haven: Yale University Press.

Gilligan, C. 1982. *In a different voice: Psychological theory and women's development.* Cambridge, Mass.: Harvard University Press.

Griffin, S. 1978. *Woman and nature: The roaring inside her.* New York: Harper.

Hartmann, H. 1981. The unhappy marriage of Marxism and feminism. In *Women and revolution,* edited by Lydia Sargent, 1–42. Boston: South End Press.

Hartsock, N.C.M. 1983a. The Feminist standpoint: Developing the ground for a specifically feminist historical materialism. In *Discovering reality: Feminist perspectives on epistemology, metaphysics, methodology, and the philosophy of science*, edited by Sandra Harding and Merrill B. Hintikka. Dordrecht, Holland: Reidel.

———1983b. *Money, sex, and power: Toward a feminist historical materialism*. New York: Longman.

Hayden, D. 1981. *The grand domestic revolution: A history of feminist designs for American homes, neighborhoods and cities*. Cambridge, Mass.: MIT Press.

———1984. *Redesigning the American dream: The future of housing, work and family life*. New York: Norton.

Heilbrun, C.G. 1984. The profession and society, 1958–83. *PMLA* 99, no. 3:408–13.

Kelly, J. 1977. Did women have a renaissance? In Stimpson, ed. *Women, history, and theory*, 19–50.

———1979. The doubled vision of feminist theory. In Stimpson, ed., *Women, history, and theory*, 51–64.

———1984. Preface to Stimpson, ed., *Women, history, and theory*. xi–xiv.

Kolodny, A. 1984. *The land before her: Fantasy and experience of the American frontier*. Chapel Hill: University of North Carolina Press.

Lauter, E. 1984. *Woman as mythmakers: Poetry and visual art by twentieth-century women*. Bloomington: Indiana University Press.

Lilienfeld, J. 1984. The magic spinning wheel: Straw to gold—Colette, Willy, and Sido. In Perry, *Mothering the mind*, 164–78.

Marcus, J. 1984a. Virginia Woolf and her violin: Mothering, madness, and music. In Perry, *Mothering the mind*, 180–201.

Marcus, J. 1984b. A wilderness of one's own: Feminist fantasy novels of the twenties: Rebecca West and Sylvia Townsend Warner. In *Women writers and the city: Essays in feminist literary criticism*, edited by Susan Merrill Squier, 134–60. Knoxville: University of Tennessee Press.

Merchant, C. 1980. *The death of nature: Women, ecology, and the scientific revolution*. New York: Harper.

Moraga, C., and G. Anzaldúa. 1982. *This bridge called my back: Writings by radical women of color*. Watertown, Mass.: Persephone Press.

Newton, E. 1984. The mythic mannish lesbian: Radclyffe Hall and the new woman. *Signs* 9, no. 4:557–75.

Noddings, N. 1984. *Caring: A feminine approach to ethics and moral education*. Berkeley: University of California Press.

O'Brien, S. 1984. "The thing not named": Willa Cather as a lesbian writer. *Signs* 9, no. 4:576–99.

Perry, R., and M.W. Brownley, ed. 1984. *Mothering the mind: Twelve studies of writers and their silent partners*. New York: Holmes & Meier.

Pitkin, H.F. 1984. *Fortune is a woman: Gender and politics in the thought of Niccolò Machiavelli*. Berkeley: University of California Press.

Rabuzzi, K.A. 1982. *The sacred and the feminine: Toward a theology of housework*. New York: Seabury.

Ruddick, S. 1980. Maternal thinking. *Feminist Studies* 6, no. 2:343–67.

Sterling, D., ed. 1984. *We are your sisters: Black women in the nineteenth century.* New York: Norton.

Stimpson, C.R. 1984. Address to the National Women's Studies Association at New Brunswick, N.J., 24 June 1984.

Stimpson, Catharine R., ed. 1984. *Women, history and theory: The essays of Joan Kelly.* Chicago: University of Chicago Press.

Vance, C.S., ed. 1984. *Pleasure and danger: Exploring female sexuality.* Boston: Routledge & Kegan Paul.

Vicinus, M. 1984. Distance and desire: English boarding school friendships. *Signs* 9, no. 4:600–22.

Vogel, L. 1983. *Marxism and the oppression of women: Toward a unitary theory.* New Brunswick, N.J.: Rutgers University Press.

Washington, M.H. 1984. I sign my mother's name: Alice Walker, Dorothy West, Paule Marshall. In Perry, *Mothering the mind,* 142–63.

## Bibliography

Ascher, Carole, Louise DeSalvo, and Sara Ruddick. *Between Women: Biographers, Novelists, Critics, Teachers and Artists Write about their Work on Women.* Boston: Beacon Press, 1984.

Auster, Albert. *Actresses and Suffragists: Women in the American Theatre 1890–1920.* New York, Praeger, 1984.

Baxandall, Rosalyn. *Dreams and Dilemmas: An Introduction to Elizabeth Gurley Flynn's Writing on Women.* New Brunswick, N.J.: Rutgers University Press, 1984.

Brady, Kathleen. *Ida Tarbell: Portrait of a Muckraker.* New York: Seaview/Putnam, 1984.

Brownmiller, Susan. *Femininity.* New York: Simon & Schuster, 1984.

Buel, Joy Day, and Richard Buel, Jr. *The Way of Duty: A Woman and Her Family in Revolutionary America.* New York: Norton, 1984.

Bulkin, Elly, Minnie Bruce Pratt, and Barbara Smith. *Yours in Struggle: Three Feminist Perspectives on Anti-Semitism and Race.* Brooklyn: Long Haul Press, 1984.

Cameron, Averil, and Amélie Kuhrt, eds. *Images of Women in Antiquity.* Detroit: Wayne State University Press, 1984.

Campbell, D'Ann. *Women at War with America: Private Lives in a Patriotic Era.* Cambridge, Mass.: Harvard University Press, 1984.

Chambers-Schiller, Lee Virginia. *Liberty, a Better Husband: The Single Woman in America: The Generations of 1780–1940.* New Haven: Yale University Press, 1984.

Chase, Karen. *Eros and Psyche: The Representation of Personality in Charlotte Brontë, Charles Dickens and George Eliot.* New York: Methuen, 1984.

Clinton, Catherine. *The Other Civil War: American Women in the Nineteenth Century.* New York: Hill & Wang, 1984.

Drachman, Virginia, G. *Hospital with a Heart: Women Doctors and the Paradox of Separatism at the New England Hospital 1862–1969*. Ithaca: Cornell University Press, 1984.

Duby, Georges. *The Knight, the Lady and the Priest: The Making of Modern Marriage in Medieval France*. New York: Pantheon, 1984.

Eckhardt, Celia Morris. *Fanny Wright: Rebel in America*. Cambridge, Mass.: Harvard University Press, 1984.

Edmondson, Linda Harriet. *Feminism in Russia 1900–17*. Stanford: Stanford University Press, 1984.

Falk, Candace. *Love, Anarchy and Emma Goldman*. New York: Holt, Rinehart, 1984.

Ferguson, Kathy E. *The Feminist Case against Bureaucracy*. Philadelphia: Temple University Press, 1984.

Fraistat, Rose Ann C. *Caroline Gordon as Novelist and Woman of Letters*. Baton Rouge: Louisiana State Press, 1984.

*Frontiers* 7, no. 3 (1984). Special issue: Women and the Western Frontier.

Gelfant, Blanche H. *American Women Writing: Voices in Collage*. Hanover, N.H.: University Press of New England, 1984.

Grahn, Judy. *Another Mother Tongue: Gay Words, Gay Worlds*. Boston: Beacon Press, 1984.

Griffith, Elizabeth. *Elizabeth Cady Stanton*. New York: Oxford University Press, 1984.

Guest, Barbara. *Herself Defined: The Poet HD and Her World*. New York: Doubleday, 1984.

Hallett, Judith P. *Fathers and Daughters in Roman Society: Women and the Elite Family*. Princeton: Princeton University Press, 1984.

Halperin, John. *The Life of Jane Austen*. Baltimore: Johns Hopkins University Press, 1984.

Hewitt, Nancy A. *Women's Activism and Social Change: Rochester, New York, 1822–1972*. Ithaca: Cornell University Press, 1984.

Hill, Patricia R. *The World Their Household: The American Woman's Foreign Mission Movement and Cultural Transformation*. Ann Arbor: University of Michigan Press, 1984.

Hoff-Wilson, Joan, and Marjorie Lightman. *Without Precedent: The Life and Career of Eleanor Roosevelt*. Bloomington: Indiana University Press, 1984.

Honey, Maureen. *Creating "Rosie the Riveter": Class, Gender, and Propaganda during World War II*. Amherst: University of Massachusetts Press, 1984.

Hooks, Bell. *Feminist Theory: From Margin to Center*. Boston: South End Press, 1984.

Horn, Pierre L., and Mary Beth Pringle. *The Image of the Prostitute in Modern Literature*. New York: Ungar, 1984.

Hunter, Jane. *The Gospel of Gentility: American Missionaries in Turn-of-the-Century China*. New Haven: Yale University Press, 1984.

Kelley, Mary. *Private Woman, Public Stage: Literary Domesticity in Nineteenth-Century America*. New York: Oxford University Press, 1984.

King, Betty. *Women of the Future: The Female Main Character in Science Fiction.* Metuchen: Scarecrow, 1984.

Kornbluh, Joyce L., and Mary Frederickson, eds. *Sisterhood and Solidarity: Worker's Education for Women, 1914–84.* Philadelphia: Temple University Press, 1984.

Langer, Elinor. *Josephine Herbst: The Story She Could Never Tell.* Boston: Little, Brown, 1984.

Lebsock, Suzanne. *The Free Women of Petersburg: Status and Culture in a Southern Town 1784–1860.* New York: Norton, 1984.

Lewin, Miriam, ed. *In the Shadow of the Past: Psychology Portrays the Sexes, a Social and Intellectual History.* New York: Columbia University Press, 1984.

Lorde, Audre. *Sister Outsider: Essays and Speeches.* Trumansberg, N.Y.: Crossing Press, 1984.

Malcolm, Janet. *In the Freud Archives.* New York: Knopf, 1984.

Martin, Wendy. *An American Triptyche: Anne Bradstreet, Emily Dickinson and Adrienne Rich.* Chapel Hill: University of North Carolina Press, 1984.

Masson, Jeffrey Moussaieff. *The Assault on Truth: Freud's Suppression of the Seduction Theory.* New York: Farrar, Straus & Giroux, 1984.

Maynard, John. *Charlotte Brontë and Sexuality.* Cambridge: Cambridge University Press, 1984.

Moses, Clare. *French Feminism in the Nineteenth Century.* Albany: State University of New York, 1984.

Nagel, Gwen L. *Critical Essays on Sarah Orne Jewett.* Boston: G.K. Hall, 1984.

Newman, Louise M. *Men's Ideas/Women's Realities: Popular Science 1870–1915.* New York: Pergamon, 1984.

Nussbaum, Felicity A. *The Brink of All We Hate: English Satires on Women.* Lexington: University Press of Kentucky, 1984.

Patai, Daphne. *The Orwell Mystique: A Study in Male Ideology.* Amherst: University of Massachusetts Press, 1984.

Phillips, J.A. *Eve: The History of An Idea.* New York: Harper, 1984.

Pollak, Vivian R. *Dickinson: The Anxiety of Gender.* Ithaca, N.Y.: Cornell University Press, 1984.

Pomeroy, Sarah B. *Women in Hellenistic Egypt: From Alexander to Cleopatra.* New York: Schocken, 1984.

Pope, Deborah. *A Separate Vision: Isolation in Contemporary Women's Poetry.* Baton Rouge: Louisiana State University, 1984.

Rafter, Nicole Han. *Partial Justice: Women in State Prisons, 1800–1935.* Boston: Northeastern University Press, 1984.

Rothman, Ellen K. *Hands and Hearts: A History of Courtship in America.* New York: Basic, 1984.

Rudnick, Lois Palken. *Mable Dodge Luhan: New Woman, New Worlds.* Albuquerque: University of New Mexico Press, 1984.

Scott, Ann Firor. *Making the Invisible Woman Visible.* Urbana: University of Illinois Press, 1984.

Scott, Bonnie Kime. *Joyce and Feminism*. Bloomington: Indiana University Press, 1984.

Spencer, Samia I., ed. *French Women and the Age of Enlightenment*. Bloomington: Indiana University Press, 1984.

Spurling, Hilary. *Ivy: The Life of I. Compton-Burnett*. New York: Knopf, 1984.

Toth, Emily, ed. *Regionalism and the Female Imagination: A Collection of Essays*. New York: Human Sciences Press, 1984.

Trible, Phyllis. *Tests of Terror: Literary-Feminist Readings of Biblical Narratives*. New York: Fortress, 1984.

Van Wagner, Judy K. Collischan. *Women Shaping Art: Profiles in Power*. New York: Praeger, 1984.

Walsh, Andrea S. *Women's Film and Female Experience 1940–50*. New York: Praeger, 1984.

Warren, Joyce. *The American Narcissus: Individualism and Women in Nineteenth-Century Fiction*. New Brunswick, N.J.: Rutgers University Press, 1984.

Weidman, Judith, ed. *Christian Feminism: Visions of A New Humanity*. New York: Harper, 1984.

Wexler, Alice. *Emma Goldman: An Intimate Life*. New York: Pantheon, 1984.

Wilson, Katharina M., ed. *Medieval Women Writers*. Athens: University of Georgia Press, 1984.

Winter, Kate H. *Marietta Holley: Life with "Josiah Allen's Wife."* Syracuse: Syracuse University Press, 1984.

*Women's Studies* 11, no. 1–2 (1984). Special issue on women in the Middle Ages.

*Women's Studies International Forum* 7, no. 2 (1984). Special issue on Orwell and feminist science fiction.

*Women's Studies International Forum* 7, no. 5 (1984). Pilot issue of *Hypatia*, a journal of women and philosophy edited by Azizah al-Hibri.

Yates, Gayle G., ed. *Harriet Martineau on Women*. New Brunswick, N.J.: Rutgers University Press, 1984.

# Law

## *Lynn R. Holmes*

The year 1984 will be remembered as a watershed in bringing to the forefront, both in Congress and the courts, several issues that affect the rights of women in the United States. There were various reasons for the increased focus on legislation of particular concern to women. The most apparent factor was the 1984 presidential election. The 1984 campaign season, for the first time, included discussions about the increased influence of women voters who now make up a majority of the electorate. This was the campaign that revived the phrase *gender gap*—the notion that women give less support than men to the Republican party and President Reagan—in the political vocabulary. This notion motivated both political parties to pursue the women's vote in 1984. In Congress, this phenomenon was manifested by an increased flurry of legislative activity on issues pertaining to women.

Another significant factor in the heightened level of attention to women's issues was the continued shift in focus by women's advocates on the type of issue to be pushed by Congress. There had been a move during the Ninety-seventh Congress (1981–82) toward consideration of the economic concerns of women. Thus an economic equity legislative package was introduced, and several provisions were passed in that session. The shift was even more dramatic in the Ninety-eighth Congress. The time devoted to "traditional" women's issues, such as abortion and the Equal Rights Amendments, decreased markedly in comparison to bread-and-butter issues. A major reason for the reordering of priorities was a probable conclusion by women's leaders that a change in legislative strategy was needed in the environment of the Reagan presidency. The change was fueled also by the defeat in the House of Representatives of a new Equal Rights Amendment. Moreover, the prioritizing of legislative goals reflected a realization that there must be broader issues around which women could rally and gain support in Congress as well.

## Legislation Signed Into Law in 1984

In keeping with the trend toward focusing on issues that affect the economic well-being of women, women's groups were successful in gaining passage of two measures that were signed into law in 1984. In August, Congress passed and the president signed the Retirement Equity Act, which was designed to correct inequities in the pension system. Although ten years earlier Congress had enacted the Employee Retirement Income Security Act of 1974, a law that provided standards for private pension plans, statistics showed that women generally receive lower pension benefits than men. There have been several reasons for the disparities that exist between men and women in the retirement system. Historically, women have not participated in the labor force to the extent men have. Moreover, women generally earn less than men. Therefore, since pension benefits are tied to length of job service and earnings, it is not surprising that women's pension benefits are lower than those of men.

The 1984 Retirement Equity Act makes the following changes in the current pension law: (1) it lowers from twenty-five to twenty-one the minimum age for participation in private pension plans and the minimum age from which service must be counted for pension benefits; (2) it allows employees to leave a job for up to five years without losing any time accrued for pension participation and vesting; (3) it allows employees on maternity or paternity leave to earn limited pension credits in order to prevent a break-in-service; (4) it provides that pension benefits may be assigned to an ex-spouse in case of divorce; (5) and it allows a spouse to receive pension benefits if a wage earner with ten years on the job dies before retirement age but after reaching age forty–five (U.S. Library of Congress, 1984c). Even though the Retirement Equity Act treats both male and female workers equally, it is clear that women stand to benefit more from the new law, particularly from the provisions for credit for breaks-in-service since women are more likely than men to take time off for child care.

Women's advocates have targeted several additional pension reforms for consideration in the Ninety-ninth Congress. Their aim is to expand pension coverage for women who are already in the workplace. Among the ideas being discussed are a reduction in the number of years an employee must work before becoming entitled or vested in a plan and an increase in coverage for part-time workers.

The second legislative proposal passed in 1984 stengthened the laws with respect to the speedy collection of child support payments. According to Census Bureau data, child support payments due for the year 1981 amounted to $9.9 billion of which $6.1 billion, or 62 percent, was paid (U.S. Library of Congress 1984a). Because of this problem, the federal government, particularly Congress, has taken an increased interest in the issue of child support enforcement. Historically, the responsibility for this matter has rested with the state governments, and until 1975, the federal government confined its collection efforts to those children of families that received Aid for Dependent Children (AFDC) payments. In 1974, however, Congress passed legislation (signed by President Ford the next year) that established a federal child support enforcement program requiring states to provide a mechanism for collection for both welfare and nonwelfare families. But because of the lack of uniformity in enforcing the 1975 law at the state vel, Congress, motivated by a 1983 Department of Health and Human Services study, reopened the matter. The child support issue gained overwhelming support as twenty-three bills were introduced during the Ninety-eighth Congress. During the first session, the House passed the bill unanimously, as did the Senate in 1984.

The new law, signed by President Reagan in August of 1984, made major changes in the earlier child support law. The revisions include (1) a requirement that states devise procedures to withhold past-due support from a parent's income; (2) provisions for states to seize state income tax refunds, place liens against the property of a parent, and report child support delinquencies to consumer credit agencies; and (3) an incentive mechanism that bases federal payments to states on the number of collections on behalf of both AFDC and non-AFDC families. (U.S. Library of Congress 1984a).

## Legislation Introduced or Considered

In addition to the proposals that were signed into law, Congress considered other legislative matters in 1984 of interest to women. Most of the items, whether they were merely "dropped in the hopper" or debated at the committee level, reflected the trend among women's groups to advance economic issues rather than traditional women's issues.

### Insurance Equity

Both the House and the Senate looked at the question of gender-based actuarial rating systems in the insurance industry. Both proposals—the Nondiscrimination in Insurance Act (H.R. 100) and the Fair Insurance Practices Act (S. 372)—would have required insurers to develop a single rate table for both sexes for life, auto, disability, health, and pension insurance. In the House, the Energy and Commerce Committee passed a substitute that was supported by the insurance industry, which would have extended protections only to group employee plans, thus exempting many life and health plans and most automobile insurance plans. In the Senate, the Commerce Committee in 1973 had commissioned a study by the General Accounting Office on the matter. The report, "Economic Implications of the Fair Insurance Practices Act" was submitted to the committee in 1984; it concluded that the legislative proposals would have "substantial" economic effects that could ultimately lead to insolvency in some insurance companies and pension plans (U.S. General Accounting Office, 1984).

Because of Congress's unwillingness to move on this issue, women's groups have begun to target their actions on activity at the state level. In September 1984, the Pennsylvania Supreme Court ruled that gender-based automobile rates violated the Equal Rights Amendment in the state's constitution. As a result of the outcome in Pennsylvania, the first major test case was filed in the District of Columbia by the National Organization of Women against Mutual of Omaha Insurance Company (Hook and Cohodas 1985). In the final analysis, success on this issue will depend on the ability of women's advocates to outmaneuver the powerful insurance industry lobby.

## Equal Rights

The states' failure to ratify the Equal Rights Amendment has forced women's groups to reexamine their legislative strategy with respect to this issue. One alternative approach has been a proposal to "neutralize the U.S. Code. Two measures were introduced in the Ninety-eighth Congress. The Senate bill (S. 501) proposed to revise approximately a hundred existing federal laws that discriminate on the basis of sex by removing from the code certain statutes ruled unconstitutional and amending the law to conform with current legal practices. Typically, such a revision would replace single-sex language with neutral terms such as *persons* instead of *males*. The bill, viewed by some as only an interim step to a more comprehensive revision of the code, passed the Senate in April. The companion bill died in the House.

Another measure, part of the Economic Equity Act, would require revision of all federal statutes and regulations to make them sex-neutral. The legislation would require the head of each federal agency to review its regulations and policies that result in sex-based distinctions and to report to Congress proposals to make those regulations neutral as to sex.

## Comparable-Worth Pay Equity

Several proposals were introduced in the Ninety-eighth Congress on the issue of comparable worth—the idea that jobs of equal value to an employer should be equally compensated, whether or not they are similar in content and regardless of wage levels in the marketplace. The two principal House proposals were introduced by Congresswoman Mary Rose Oakar. The Pay Equity Act of 1984 (H.R. 5092) would have required federal agencies responsible for enforcing equal employment opportunity laws to submit detailed reports periodically to the president and Congress. The Federal Employees Pay Equity Act of 1984 (H.R. 4599) was designed to promote the concept of pay equity and eliminate discriminatory practices based on sex, race, or ethnicity in federal government agencies.

Hearings were held on both proposals in 1984 in the Subcommittee on Compensation and Employee Benefits of the House Post Office and Civil Service Committee. In addition, the Joint Economic Committee held hearings on the issue of women in the labor force, which included testimony on pay equity. One pay equity proposal, H.R. 5680, passed the House in June by a vote of 413 to 6 and would have required a study of the Federal Civil Service job and wage classification system. That proposal met opposition in the Senate, however, and died at the end of the Ninety-eighth Congress.

## Developments in the Legal Arena

Although Congress is certain to reconsider these proposals in the Ninety-ninth Congress, most of the activity will continue to be focused in the courts and at the state level. The comparable worth doctrine has been a thorny issue for the courts. In 1981, the Supreme Court ruled in *County of Washington, Oregon, v. Gunther* that women bringing sex-based wage discrimination claims under Title VII are not required to satisfy the equal work standard of the Equal Pay Act. The Court hastened to point out that the case was not a ruling on the issue of comparable worth. The *Gunther* case has been used as a starting point in sex-based wage discrimination cases; however, the courts have been increasingly reluctant to rule on the comparable value of different jobs held by males and females.

In a recent case, the nursing faculty at the University of Washington contended that they should be paid comparably to male teachers in the univeristy's other schools and colleges. They argued, also, that the nursing school's lower pay scale was evidence of the university's discrimination against its female employees. The Ninth Circuit Court of Appeals rejected the nurses' argument and ruled that Title VII discrimination suits may not be brought if disparities in salary reflect market conditions. Moreover, the judge remarked that acceptance of the nurses' premise "would plunge us into uncharted and treacherous areas." It appears that the 'market-forces' argument may be the one to use to allow judges to get around the controversial nature of comparable worth.

## Grove City Case

Perhaps the most significant decision handed down by the Supreme Court in 1984 was *Grove City College*, v. *Bell*. In February, the Court ruled that Title IX of the Education Amendments of 1972 applies to colleges and universities through federal student financial aid programs. More important, the Court also ruled that Title IX applies only to the particular program or activity receiving federal financial assistance and not necessarily to institutions as a whole.

The case involved Grove City College, a small coeducational school in Pennsylvania, which had never received direct government funds. The dispute arose in 1977 when administrators at the college refused to sign a federal form assuring that they operated in compliance with Title IX, a form the U.S. Department of Education requires all recipients of federal aid to sign. Grove City College officials contended that the school had never accepted federal aid directly and thus was not a "program or activity" and subject to coverage by Title IX. Moreover, the college claimed that the federal financial aid that its students received—Pell Grants in this case—was not aid to the college. The Department of Education rejected the college's arguments and cut aid to the Grove City students, which prompted the college to sue.

In 1982, the U.S. Court of Appeals for the Third Circuit supported the department's aid termination, holding that the college was a "recipient" for purposes of Title IX. The Court of Appeals ruled, also, that when federal aid is indirect or not earmarked the "program" under the language of Title IX refers to the institution. In its 6–3 decision, the Supreme Court overturned that part of the Third Circuit's decision. Justice Byron White, who wrote the majority opinion, said that the Court had "formed no persuasive evidence suggesting that Congress intended that the department's regulatory authority follow federally aided students from classroom to classroom, building to building, or activity to activity."

The Court's narrow interpretation of Title IX caused civil rights groups as well as women's advocates great concern, particularly since the "program or activity" language appears in Title VI of the 1964 Civil Rights Act, which prohibits discrimination on the basis of race, and in Section 504 of the Rehabilitation Act of 1973, which prohibits discrimination against the handicapped. Because of this concern, several bills were introduced in Congress in response to the *Grove City* decision.

The legislation that was considered, the Civil Rights Act of 1984, was introduced by Congressman Simon in the House and Senator Kennedy in the Senate and proposed to broaden the enforcement provisions to prohibit discrimination by "recipients" of federal financial assistance. The bill also extended the same coverage to Title VI of the Civil Rights Act of 1964 and Section 504 of the Rehabilitation Act of 1973. The Simon bill passed the House in June by a vote of 375 to 32 with an amendment to apply the antidiscrimination laws for the first time to Congress and the judiciary. The companion bill ran into stiff opposition from conservatives in the Senate. The opponents felt that the term *recipient* in the language of the proposal was much too broad and did not reflect the intent of Congress when it passed Title IX. Because the Senate failed to act on the legislation, the Civil Rights Act of 1984 died in the Ninety-eighth Congress.

What effect the *Grove City* decision will have on future Title IX enforcement is difficult to assess. According to the National Women's Law Center, the Department of Education has ended or restricted the focus of approximately sixty antidiscrimination law-suits. The *Grove City* Title IX precedent has not yet been tested in other Title VI and Section 504 cases. Congress is sure to return to the issue in the Ninety-ninth Congress.

## Women In The Legal Profession

The American Bar Association (ABA) in late 1983 released the results of a survey it commissioned on women lawyers. According to the ABA, the survey's random interview confirmed an "overwhelming acceptance of women lawyers by their male colleagues and a corresponding satisfaction among women with their lot in a male-dominated profession." Interestingly, the conclusions drawn from the survey were somewhat paradoxical as highlighted by the title of the *ABA Journal* article that reported the poll: "Women Lawyers Work Harder, Are Paid Less, but They're Happy." Although the survey respondents noted an "overwhelming acceptance" of women lawyers in the profession, the same ABA poll showed that 65 percent of male lawyers have no women colleagues at work. Moreover, the poll highlighted the difference in the median income of male and female lawyers: $33,000 for women compared to $53,000 for men. According to the report, the wide disparity in median income is due to the fact that women lawyers are concentrated in the younger and less experienced ranks of the legal profession (Survey . . . 1983).

Despite the American Bar Association's report that most women lawyers were satisfied with their jobs, the Supreme Court provided a forum in 1984 for a lawyer who was dissatisfied with her treatment in a major law firm. Elizabeth Hishon sued the Atlanta firm of King and Spalding after she was not selected as a partner. The Supreme Court, in a unanimous decision, ruled that Title VII of the Civil Rights Act of 1964 prohibits a law firm from denying partnership status on the basis of sex to an associate employed by the firm. It is unclear what the impact of the *Hishon* decision will be. Hishon's case was remanded to the lower courts for relief, and major firms will watch for the final outcome. Most small firms will not be affected by *Hishon* (Zarefsky 1984).

Women lawmakers did not increase their ranks during the 1984 election. There are still twenty-four members in Congress—twenty-two in the House of Representatives and two in the Senate. On the Republican side in the House, two of the women legislators are among the leadership. With respect to women in the federal judiciary, the number appointed to district and appeals courts decreased under President Reagan. In fact, a recent study estimated that only 9.3 percent of district court appointments and 3.2 percent of appeals court appointments were female during the president's first term (as compared to 14.4 percent and 19.6 percent, respectively, during the Carter administration). If the trend under Reagan continues, the number of women on the federal bench, currently 10 to 12 percent, will be reduced substantially. (Kamen 1985).

## Conclusion

It is difficult to predict whether the flurry of activity that occurred in 1984 on women's issues will continue. Although women represent a majority of voters, it is unclear whether Congress will focus on matters of concern to women in a nonelection year. One trend that is likely to continue will be the attention given by women's advocates to more broadly based concerns. It is unlikely, particularly during the Reagan years, that very much political capital will be spent on abortion and the Equal Rights Amendment. Moreover, women's groups are channeling their forces to a larger degree at the state and local level. Given the views of the current administration with respect to women's issues, the strategy to target state government and the judiciary is a good one politically. In fact, it has been suggested that the skirmishes that have taken place over abortion and the ERA have, in effect, forced women's groups to revise and decentralize their strategy.

This notion was discussed recently by Eleanor Holmes Norton, former chairperson of the Equal Employment Opportunity Commission, in an article "Goodbye ERA . . . Hello Equality" on the defeat of the ERA:

> The impressive majority for equality for women—assembled in less than a decade—fell short of the consensus required by the Constitution. . . . Women had decentralized their strategies in any case. The magnitude of change necessary to fully transform their status required much. . . . Already it is clear that the constitutional defeat of the ERA is having the opposite effect. Undaunted, women continue to seek equality through whatever means the law affords. No section of society is immune from revision in terms of equality. (Norton 1984)

The challenge for advocates of women's issues will be to continue the election-year momentum and interest that peaked in 1984.

## References

Hook, Janet, and Cohodas, Nadine. 1985. Women renew drive for "economic equity." *Congressional Quarterly*, 26 January 146–149.

Kamen, Al. 1985. Wealthy white males predominate among Reagan judicial appointees. *Washington Post*,14 February.

Norton, Eleanor Holmes. 1984. Goodbye ERA . . . hello equality. *Human Rights*, no. 12 (Spring): 14–50.

Survey: Women lawyers work harder, are paid less, but they're happy. 1983. *ABA Journal*, October.

U.S. Commission on Civil Rights. 1984. *Comparable worth: Issue for the 80's*. Washington, D.C.: U.S. Government Printing Office, 6–7 June.

U.S. General Accounting Office. 1984. *Economic implications of the Fair Insurance Practices Act*. GAO report no. OCE–84–1. Washington, D.C.: U.S. Government Printing Office, 6 April.

U.S. Library of Congress, Congressional Research Service. 1984a. Child support enforcement (by) Carmen D. Soloman. 13 September. Washington, D.C. Mimeo.

————. 1984b. Legal analysis of *Grove City College v. Bell* and its implications concerning enforcement of other civil rights statutes (by) Karen Lewis. Washington, D.C. Mimeo.

————. 1984c. Women's pension equity (by) Ray Schmitt. Washington, D.C. Mimeo.

Zarefsky, Paul. 1984. How the Hishon decision will affect your firm. *ABA Journal*, September.

## Bibliography

"An Insurer's Rates under Feminist Fire." *Newsweek*, 27 August 1984, 58.

Berry, Mary Frances. "Turning Back the Clock On Women and Minority Rights." *Negro History Bulletin* 46 (July-September 1983): 82–84.

Bittman, M. "Comparable Worth is Put to Test at Yale." *Business Week*, 26 November 1984, 92.

Campbell, Nancy Duff, Marcia Greenberger, Margaret Kohn, and Shirley Wilcher. *Sex Discrimination in Education: Legal Rights and Remedies*. 2 vols. National Women's Law Center, 1983.

Couric, Emily, ed. *Women Lawyers: Perspectives on Success*. New York: Law & Business/Harcourt Brace Jovanovich, 1984. Information and advice about every professional avenue a female lawyer may pursue in private, public, and political sectors from the perspective of fifteen successful women.

"Criminal Justice Politics and Women: The Aftermath of Legally Mandated Change," *Women and Politics* 4; no. 3 (Fall 1984). A whole issue of articles on women prisoners, domestic violence, sexual assault, and prostitution law.

"Election Year Focuses on Women's Issues." *U.S. News and World Report*, 18 June 1984, 73.

Gold, Michael Evan. *A Dialogue on Comparable Worth*. Ithaca, N.Y.: ILR Press,

1983. Using the format of debate between opposing viewpoints, Gold presents and analyzes the arguments for and against comparable worth standards of pay.

Kamerman, Sheila B., Alfred J. Kahn and Paul Kingston. *Maternity Policies and Working Women.* New York: Columbia University Press, 1983. This review of policy development and implementation in business and industry considers company policies on health insurance, leave, and income protection and job security for employees having babies. Although the effect of legislation may be to reduce benefits in some companies, the authors endorse state legislation as a means of providing at least a minimum of temporary disability insurance.

"Law firms Not Exempt from Title VII (Supreme Court Decision on Partnerships and Sex Discrimination)." *Monthly Labor Review* 107 (July 1984): 46–47.

O'Connor, Karen, and Lee Epstein. "Beyond Legislative Lobbying: Women's Rights Groups and the Supreme Court." *Judicature* 67 (September 1983): 134–43.

Remick, Helen, ed. *Comparable Worth and Wage Discrimination.* Philadelphia: Temple University Press, 1984. Lawyers, industrial relations experts, psychologists, economists, and others examine comparable worth as a social policy and explore possibilities for implementation.

Selden, Catherine, Ellen Mutari, Mary Rubin, and Karen Sacks. *Equal Pay for Work of Comparable Worth: An Annotated Bibliography.* Chicago: American Library Association, Office for Library Personnel Resources, 1982. A review essay and bibliography covering the literature through 1981.

Tong, Rosemarie. *Women, Sex and the Law.* Totowa, N.J.: Rowman & Allenheld, 1984. Considers the role of law in controlling or effecting change in five areas: pornography, prostitution, sexual harassment, rape, and wife battering.

White, T.H. "New Powers, New Politics." *New York Times Magazine*, 5 February 1984, 22–28.

## Government Reports and Documents

U.S. Bureau of the Census. *Child Support and Alimony: 1981* (advance report). Current Population Reports, special studies, series p-23, no. 124. Washington, D.C.: U.S. Government Printing Office (hereafter GPO), 1983.

U.S. Congress. Conference Committee. *Child Support Enforcement Amendments of 1984;* conference report to accompany H.R. 4325. 98th Cong., 2d sess. H. Rep. no. 98–925. Washington, D.C.: GPO, 1984.

U.S. Congress. House Committee on Ways and Means. *Child Support Enforcement Amendments of 1983;* report to accompany H.R. 4325. 98th Cong., 1st sess. H. Rep. 98–527. Washington D.C.: GPO, 1983.

U.S. Congress. Senate. Committee on Finance. *Child Support Enforcement Amendments:* Report to accompany H.R. 4325. 98th Cong., 2d sess. S. Rep. 98–387. Washington, D.C.: GPO, 1984.

U.S. Congress. Senate. Committee on Labor and Human Resources. *Women in Transition, 1983: Hearing November 8, 1983, and Examination of Problems Faced by Women.* S. Rep. 98–624.

U.S. Congress. Senate. Committee on the Judiciary. *Sex Discrimination in the United States Code Reform Act of 1983: Report on S. 501 Together with Additional Views.* 98th Cong, 2d sess. S. Rep. 98–390. Washington, D.C.: GPO, 1984.

U.S. Congress. Senate. *Retirement Equity Act of 1984: Report to Accompany H.R. 4280, including Cost Estimate of the Congressional Budget Office.* 98th Cong. 2d sess. S. Rep. 98–575. Washington D.C.: GPO, 1984.

U.S. Congress. House. Committee on Education and Labor. *Civil Rights Act of 1984. June 7, 1984.* 98th Cong., 2d sess. H. Rep. 98–829, pt. 2. Washington, D.C.: GPO, 1984.

U.S. Congress, House. Committee on the Judiciary. *Civil Rights Act of 1984. June 7, 1984.* 98th Cong. 2d sess., H. Rep. 98–829 pt. 1. Washington, D.C.: GPO, 1984.

## *Resources*

National Women's Law Center, 1751 N Street NW, Washington, DC 20036; (202) 872–0670.

Women's Equity Action League, 805 15th Street NW, Washington, DC 20005; (202) 638–1961.

Federally Employed Women, 1010 Vermont Avenue NW, Washington, DC 20005; (202) 638–4405.

NAACP Legal Defense and Educational Fund, 806 15th Street NW, Washington, DC 20005; (202) 638–3278.

Wider Opportunities for Women, 1325 G Street NW, Washington, DC 20005; (202) 638–3143.

Federation of Organizations for Professional Women, 1825 Connecticut Avenue NW, Washington, DC 20009; (202) 328–1415.

National Federation of Business and Professional Women's Clubs, 2012 Massachusetts Avenue NW, Washington, DC 20036; (202) 293–1100.

National Organization for Women (NOW), National Action Center, 425 13th Street NW, Washington, DC 20004; (202) 347–2279.

National Right to Life Committee, 419 7th Street NW, Washington, DC 20004; (202) 638–7936.

National Women's Political Caucus, 1411 K Street NW, Washington, DC 20005; (202) 347–4456.

National Association of Military Widows, 4023 North 25th Road, Arlington, VA 22207; (703) 527–4565.

Pension Rights Center, Women's Pension Project, 1346 Connecticut Avenue, Washington, DC 20036; (202) 296–3778.

Women's Legal Defense Fund, 2000 P Street NW, Washington, DC 20036; (202) 887–0364.

Older Women's League, 1325 G Street NW, Washington, DC 20006; (202) 783–6686.

National Council of Negro Women, 1819 H Street NW, Washington, DC 20006; (202) 293–3902.

National Committee on Pay Equity, 1201 16th Street NW, Washington, DC 20006; (202) 822–7304.

# Philosophy
## The Feminist Theory: The Franco-American Conversation

### Elissa Gelfand

Comparing intellectual feminism in the United States and France raises red flags in several quarters: American readers not fully familiar with the roots and goals of French feminist thought are, justifiably, wary of its abstractness and inaccessibility; American-based scholars of French women's studies correctly expect any such comparison to be attentive to its own assumptions and to its author's own culture-bound perspective; and many French theorists, also rightly, regard any dichotomizing structure as a dangerous perpetuation of traditional masculine ways of thinking. These reservations have, over the past decade, produced a number of examinations of what Domna Stanton (1980) called Franco-American "connections" and "disconnections," studies that first sought to delineate ideological divisions among French feminists and between American and French thinkers but that went on to argue for a dialogue across those cultural divergences. Dialogue was considered possible only if each side probed the interpretive context of the other. This effort was and still is hampered by the absence in both countries of translations of important and representative texts. The question remains, however, whether translations would suffice to make bridges between two such diverse modes of feminist thought.

The comparison of American and French feminism that follows will look primarily at the intellectual issues that have concerned women in both cultures, even while acknowledging that the isolation of intellectual activism from political activism is artificial. All feminist reevaluations here and abroad emerged in the late 1960s in the aftermath of other political events, in particular the civil rights and antiwar unrest in America, the students and workers' revolt in France, and the Quebec separatist movement in Canada. The first feminist calls for change shared the same high visibility and flowering of rage and excitement, but these similarities were also tempered by each country's specific historical oppression of women. It must, for example, be remembered that "French" women's studies refers to France, Belgium, Quebec, and some of French-speaking Africa. For the sake of coherence, "French" in this discussion will signal that body of research whose shared intellectual underpinnings are the Continental modern tradition that formed in France. The important "Introduction III" in Elaine Marks and Isabelle de Courtivron's *New French Feminisms* (1980, 28–38) and Carolyn Greenstein Burke's (1978) brief but informative history of the French women's movement outline pre- and post-1968 French women's activism and survey its chief ideological currents.

The institutional conditions under which women's studies have been pursued in France and the United States are very different: "American women scholars function primarily within an academic environment which has (at least recently) encouraged and supported their feminist activities . . . [but] neither American nor French feminism is studied or researched in any systematic context in France" (Finel-Honigman 1981, 320). Academic receptivity to women's studies was the subject of two important early articles, Stanton's sobering description (1977) of the deeper obstacles American scholars, despite apparent encouragement, must face, and Christiane Makward's more positive view (1977) of the American university climate that has fostered the development of women's studies here. These dissimilarities in administrative attitudes and in real possibilities for on-campus research have persisted, as documented by Burke (1978) and again by Makward (1980a).

Both the cause and the consequence of the differing receptiveness to women's studies of the French and American academies are, in part, the women who are engaged in feminist inquiry in both countries. If, in the United States, virtually all women's studies literature has been produced by affiliated academics or independent scholars, it is professional specialists—philosophers, psychoanalysts, novelists, poets, linguists, journalists—who have provided the principal French feminist reflections. This sharp contrast in intellectual and professional orientation explains to some degree the radically divergent goals, approaches, and styles of French and American texts. It also accounts for the different audiences to whom feminist writing is addressed—students and scholars in the United States and an informed but not necessarily academic intelligentsia in France.

American and French feminisms struggled and continue to struggle to improve women's material lives, addressing similar issues such as economic discrimination, reproductive rights, and civil and legal injustices. It is in the intellectual arena, however, that powerful differences appeared, differences rooted in each culture's noetic legacy. The American tradition of empirical research, coupled with the relatively minor influence of Marxist critique in this country, contrasts keenly with the long-standing French penchant for theory and the highly politicized character of French thought. The greatest single disjunction between the two countries' feminist perspectives results from these intellectual antecedents and national turns of mind: for French women, the central problem under investigation is language, whereas American women tend to focus on specific social, historical, political, or literary contexts. Whatever their disputes—and they are profound—French women share the belief that language, in the broad sense of all cultural systems or "discourses," is at the heart of the feminist enterprise. They argue that only a radical change in the structures of thought that underlie all forms of human organization can effect true social transformation. American feminists, although they have examined language as a behavioral phenomenon, have been more concerned to expose and change women's material situation.

Pursuing such different questions as the structure of language or thought and the material situation of women has made for nearly antithetical methods of analysis. Makward (1977) describes American feminists' tendency to amass data and textual exegeses prior to their formulation of theory, in contrast with French women's initial elaboration of theory, to be followed, in principle, by application. If, as Heather McClave put it, American scholars view "literal evidence as the base of believable truth" (1982–83, 206), French women see such evidence as merely one representation of larger systems of meaning at work, systems they seek to elucidate. In her excellent discussion of the nature of French theory, Alice Jardine (1982) says French feminists have focused on "process" rather than on "product".

To understand why French feminist intellectuals have looked to language as the source and perpetuator of women's estate, it is necessary to know something about the issues of their education. All the principal women theorists were marked by the French experience of modernity, that is, the crisis of truth and certainty that has occurred in twentieth-century European thinking. The pillars of the Western tradition—reason, monotheism, capitalism, clear hierarchies of value, and absolute truth—have been steadily crumbling in France under the blows of Marx, Nietzsche, Saussure, Freud, Lévi-Strauss, Lacan, Foucault, Derrida, and the whole line of other structuralist and poststructuralist thinkers. By bringing to light alternate realities like the unconscious, the divided self, communism, and polytheism—other realities that coexist with the accepted one—these critics introduced ambiguity into a previously unified conception of the world. Whereas philosophical, psychoanalytic, and political thought in the United States did not undergo this assault on logic and coherence, thus maintaining its belief in human authority and social order, French intellectual forces systematically shattered what they deemed the "myths" of Western culture by insisting on the problematics of "alterity." It was no longer possible to speak of a single, verifiable truth, a consistent, knowable human subject, or an adequate, meaningful language, since all were cultural fictions. In the place of absolute unity, there was now irremediable heterogeneity or difference.

It is against this backdrop that French feminist thought must be seen. The intellectual "fathers" mentioned above laid the groundwork for the continued reevaluation of all social structures, including sexual ones; the truly problematic and unstable status of the previously fixed entities "man"/"woman" and "masculine"/"feminine" was exposed. Far from the discrete, self-sufficient unities they had always been presumed to be, these sexual terms were determined to be in dynamic relation to each other and to depend ontologically on each other's existence. This belief that fundamental relational processes are always what make meaning emerge, a "structuralist vision," is at the core of French ideas on sexuality, ideas elaborated most often in a linguistic, philosophical, or psychoanalytic framework.

The centrality of sexuality for contemporary French theory in general, and feminist postulations in particular, cannot be overstressed. For most French thinkers, sexual difference, a complex and multilayered concept, exists and is irremediable. This "difference" includes the conventional Beauvoirian idea of a dialectical relationship between men and women, self and other, but has also come to signify the division, the dissidence within individuals, both female and male, themselves. For critics who consider sexual dichotomies as the basic relational structure upon which all other oppositional analogies have been built, "feminine" and "masculine" have ceased to have a one-to-one coincidence with biological or historical human entities, but have instead acquired metaphorical dimensions, as signifiers of the irreconcilable fragmentation and ambiguity of reality. American feminists, who most often study real biosocial women, are more apt to view difference as existing between women and men and thus as the locus of sexual inequality; seeking to eradicate inequality, they affirm women. For many French women, on the other hand, equality is a mythical goal. Sexual difference is ineradicable, and therefore they affirm abstract "woman."

It is worth noting that one consequence of this disparity between American "literalism" and French abstraction was to see feminism in the United States as being resolutely nontheoretical and, according to some, antitheoretical. It would be far more accurate, however, to speak of a different relationship to theory among women in the two cultures, stemming from the questions they ask and the analytic tools they adopt. Because American feminists, working from and with actual women, have sought primarily to establish the authority of the female experience, they have been most at home with methods that explore cultural identity and social and political power. They naturally turned to those fields with models for such investigation: politics, history, popular culture, sociology, psychology, and applied literary criticism. It is not a coincidence that what is called "feminist theory" in the United States, in its multiple radical, liberal, cultural, and lesbian forms, is generally congruent with the broad notion of political theory. In France, theorizing has served to undermine the whole concept of "authority" itself, the underlying chimera of masculine culture. Those areas most compatible with the feminist disruption of the stable, unitary structures in place, collectively called by French feminists the "Law," were psychoanalysis, linguistics/semiotics, philosophy, and Marxist politics. Although feminist study in both countries is comparably interdisciplinary, close examination reveals the very different directions each takes.

It is evident that if the issues being addressed in France and the United States are different, so too will be the ways of writing about them. All forces, in any academic branch in America, militate for solving problems and for working toward conceptual synthesis, integrity, and control. The author's authority is assumed and is necessary to validate the explication offered; likewise, the language of exposition is considered adequate and transparently useful. The French make no such optimistic assumptions. The author's mastery, like any other hierarchical fiction, is illusory, and language, itself highly problematic, can reflect the only authenticity possible, ambiguity. As a result, French feminist texts are usually more self-conscious, at times playful, in their expression. This same mistrust of language among many French-speaking feminists has also served to break down traditional barriers between analysis and fiction, between the expository and the imaginative, making their critiques freshly poetic—and often extremely difficult to read.

Some French women have addressed the problem of language head-on in calling for a specifically "feminine" speaking and writing (*l'écriture féminine*), an enormously controversial issue among feminists. For these women, it is precisely the feminine voice that has been repressed by and is absent from the "master's discourse." Making various connections between the female unconscious and language, these women, literally or metaphorically, locate a feminine discourse in the body, the psyche, or both. Linking the formation of language to processes in the unconscious, while at the heart of psychoanalytic principles in France, is alien to American psychological and linguistic apprehensions. Most American as well as nonpsychoanalytic French feminists have construed language more concretely and have rejected this unverifiable link. Materialist feminists in France have been particularly hostile to the idea of an écriture féminine, on the grounds that it reinforces the destructive biologizing view of women. Good elucidations of the nature and implications of a feminine discourse can be found in de Courtivron (1979), Makward (1980b), Jones (1981), and Makward and Weil (1982).

There are several fine overview articles that illuminate the intellectual heritage of feminist inquiry in France. Elaine Marks's now-standard text (1978) on the theoretical perspectives that inform avant-garde feminist thought elaborates with brilliant clarity on the role of "linguistic and structuralist theory, Marxian culture, psychoanalytic theory, and deconstruction strategies" (835). Isabelle de Courtivron (1979) cogently connects feminist inquiry to France's heritage of a traditionally politicized intelligentsia, focusing on women's use and subversion of the "master's discourse" in the service of radical analysis. In yet another excellent introduction to French feminism, Makward (1980a) explains the essential distinction between the conventional biological use of the terms *masculine* and *feminine* and their renewed sense in France as internalized "difference" that affects the imagination, speaking, and writing. And the French section in Eisenstein and Jardine's (1980) important collection of essays on sexual difference presents the central issues of French feminism: its critique of "Logos" or the entire system of language and meaning that has repressed female sexuality (Stanton 1980); the French refusal of women's "difference" as traditionally defined to suit male needs, in favor of recognizing the heretofore silenced female unconscious (Féral 1980); the French feminist celebration of a feminine principle which, at the same time, is in danger of reaffirming essentialist views of women (Makward 1980b); and the centrality of psychoanalysis for French feminists who, unlike many Americans, see its revolutionary potential (Gallop and Burke 1980).

This last essay articulates clearly the different shapes post-Freudian psychoanalysis has assumed in both countries: the American interpretation, which the authors criticize, focuses on curative ego psychology and the authority of the individual, whereas the French reading, far "bolder," stresses the power of the unconscious. An equally enlightening discussion of these conflicting readings of Freud is Sherry Turkle's introduction to her study of psychoanalysis and French culture (1978). The work of the most articulate American exponent of French psychoanalysis, Jane Gallop (1982), inventively engages French feminists in dialogue with their intellectual "fathers" and goes far in educating American readers about the radical implications for feminism of Lacan's rethinking of Freud. In sum, from the American psychoanalytic interpretation arose women's concern to achieve unity of self, autonomy, and authenticity; the French standpoint saw these desiderata as unreachable and, worse, as goals that perpetuated the myths that have been most detrimental to women.

Several pieces on current French feminist theory, in addition to defining central issues, enlarge the framework of discussion as well. Ann Jones's rendering (1981) of the French view of women's repression not only is eminently readable but is also engaged and persuasive in its effort to reconcile feminist theory with material practice. A special issue of *Yale French Studies* (1981) contains an introduction that compares American and French feminist ideas: using the original format of a conversation among scholars in French and American women's studies, this piece itself enacts the possibilities and limitations of cross-cultural exchange. And Gayatri Spivak's article in this issue (1981) brings a unique and vital perspective to feminist criticism by asking, "What is the constituency of an international feminism?" (155) and by showing the incompatibilities between Western assumptions about sexuality and Third World women's experience.

The nonspecialist seeking a truly comprehensive entry into the labyrinthine world of French feminist inquiry would do well to consult three works deserving special mention. Probably the single most important publication for English-speaking feminists interested in French women's studies is Marks and de Courtivron's anthology, *New French Feminisms* (1980). The translated texts are organized to provide both a historical picture of post-1968 feminist thought and an understanding of key issues. Two outstanding introductions trace the feminine and feminist traditions in France, up to and after Beauvoir's revolutionary *Second Sex* (1949). Makward and Weil (1982) reviewed the status of French women's studies for the Modern Language Association, and their commentary is a useful bibliographical resource, as well as a necessary assessment of the quality and availability of pedagogical materials in comparative women's studies. Lastly, an annotated bibliography of French feminist criticism, prepared by Virginia Hules and myself (to appear 1985), lists virtually all books and articles by and about French theorists who have investigated women's relation to language. Of particular note here is Hules's introductory essay on sexual difference. She traces thoroughly and concisely the connections and disconnections between French feminists and their paternal "masters" and goes on to examine the obstacles to cross-cultural feminist dialogue.

Americans who wish to pursue French reflections on gender and language more directly and who read French can tackle the most accessible works of the major theoreticians. It is necessary to consult texts spanning the past fifteen years not only because of the gradual evolution within many of the authors' projects but also because of the relative theoretical silence in France during recent years. At the same time American feminists have been pushing hard for more theory, French women have been experimenting with fictional forms. My purpose in presenting these French thinkers is somewhat paradoxical, for in trying to make them more familiar to an anglophone public, I also suggest the limitations to our intellectual intimacy with them.

The most prolific figure in French feminist thought, Julia Kristeva, began by studying avant-garde literature as manifestations of social disruption, a concept she went on to sexualize. Her training in linguistics and psychoanalysis led to her elaboration of the divided "speaking subject" and, thus, to the view of sexual difference as lying within the individual bisexual psyche. While for Kristeva the "feminine" and the "masculine" are eminently metaphorical terms, she has been careful in her work to maintain links between abstract and material sexual strutures. It is not surprising that American critics have generally found Kristeva's ideas the most assimilable and usable. The best presentation of Kristeva's ideas is Leon Roudiez's edition of important essays in translation, *Desire in Language* (1980). Roudiez's introduction offers valuable keys to the Kristevan universe, though it does not illuminate her feminism in detail. It is Alice Jardine, her principal American exegetist, who has provided the most edifying analyses of Kristeva's sexual theory and politics (Jardine 1980, 1981a, 1981b). Among the hundreds of books and articles Kristeva has produced, those most closely concerned with women's issues are *About Chinese Women* (1977a) and various essays from the past ten years (Kristeva 1974, 1977b, 1981). A number of interviews with her also give entry into Kristeva's views on female identity and feminine creation (Féral 1976; van Rossum-Guyon 1977b; "Woman can never . . ." 1980).

Almost at the opposite pole from Kristeva in terms of sexual difference is Annie Leclerc, best known for her controversial book, *Parole de femme* (1974). Propounding the physiological antinomies between women and men, Leclerc praises the "superior" female body. *Parole de femme*'s unequivocal belief in feminine specificity sparked further postulations of an écriture féminine arising from women's sexuality. "The Love Letter" (1980) also affirms women's special relationship to pleasure and creativity.

Somewhere between the antipodes of abstract bisexuality and literal biological difference are the important theorists Luce Irigaray and Hélène Cixous. Irigaray has played a central role in the French feminist critique of traditional psychoanalysis: *Speculum de l'autre femme* (1974) explores the "masculine imagination" at work in Freud's, Lacan's, and Plato's construction of "woman," and early essays from 1974–75 (some of which were reproduced in the collection, *Ce sexe qui n'en est pas un* [1977]) as well as the more poetic *Passions élémentaires* (1982) contain a probing scrutiny of and challenge to "phallogocentric" precepts. Irigaray exalts feminine desire, though she continually undoes fixed sexual designations and makes ambiguity and subversion the markers of her feminist reevaluation. She also argues for a feminine language (1977, 1980) even while she rejects codification of this potentially limitless discourse. Lately, Irigaray has focused on the repressed mother-daughter relationship (1981a, 1981b), and her call for the expression of the "maternal" has inspired many American critics to pursue this research approach. The inheritor of deconstructionist strategies that oppose fixed principles, Irigaray has given French feminist thought a provocative but formidable richness. Three interviews with her provide good overviews of her theories ("Pouvoir . . ." 1975; "Questions" 1977; and the particularly informative "Women's Exile" 1977). Her principal American interpreter, Carolyn Burke, has written a useful summary of Irigaray's analogical view of sexuality and language (Burke 1981).

Hélène Cixous, the only major feminist theorist to have taught women's studies in a French university, has also been a prolific critic. Like Kristeva, her early work consisted of analyses of "subversive" texts and, like Irigaray, her approach has been a deconstructive one that focuses on their multiple, unstable meanings. Cixous urges women to rethink and reclaim femininity both by exposing the mythical hierarchized oppositions (e.g., masculine/feminine) upon which Western culture is based and by expressing their heretofore repressed desire. Affirming feminine specificity, Cixous, like Irigaray, exhorts women to write from their unconscious and their (metaphorical) bodies; but Cixous ascribes a repressed feminine component to men as well, thus making her use of sexual terms a figurative one.

Paradoxically, while Cixous's theses overall are the hardest to classify, she does come the closest of any of the writers to actually describing the elusive écriture féminine: for her, it is multiple, irreducible, generous, moving, limitless. Two of Cixous's texts on sexuality and imaginative production, "The Laugh of the Medusa" (1976) and "Sorties" (1975), are now classics on the inscription of female desire. Cixous has also been important for her own plenteous output of unorthodox, incantatory fictions. There are several useful pieces on the creative and political implications of Cixous's ideas (Makward 1978; Andermatt 1979, and Conley's comprehensive study, 1984, whose writing mimetically evokes Cixous's own.) It is also in interviews that one can gain access to Cixous's feminist project ("Echange" in Clément and Cixous 1975, 247–96; Makward 1976; and especially van Rossum-Guyon 1977a).

There are other French-speaking women whose contributions are distinctive and noteworthy. Sarah Kofman's dense and illuminating rereading of Freud (1980a, 1980b) critiques his obsessional "explanation" and neutralization of female sexuality and locates symptomatic points in his texts where women's "frightening" power nonetheless comes through. As refreshing as Kofman's startling insights are Madeleine Gagnon's passionate poem-essays. A Québecoise committed to both national and feminist liberation, Gagnon has written several compelling exhortations to women to leave their silence (1974, 1977). The proteiform work of Catherine Clément is impressive for its intellectual breadth and notable for its unswerving commitment to Marxist political action. Along with psychoanalysis (1978, 1983) and structural anthropology, Clément has written on witchcraft, hysteria, and women's need for reasoned discourse (1975a, 1980) and on women and communism (1975b). Finally, the author Monique Wittig has been an eloquent spokeswoman for lesbian feminism and has enlarged the feminist analytic framework by giving primacy to homosexuality. Her complex conceptualization of lesbianism as the key force in the subversion of the sexual order enriches feminist visions of an alternative, nonrepressive culture (1980a, 1980b, 1980c, 1982).

Although this discussion of French feminist inquiry has concerned itself with those explorations whose grounding is philosophy, psychoanalysis, and linguistics, I must emphasize that a large and vocal materialist and Marxist feminist constituency has attacked their contentions. Two of the women mentioned, Wittig and Clément, give precedence to a feminist critique that addresses the cultural arrangements that oppress women. They are joined by others, including Beauvoir, for whom theory is a "feminist science" that ought to examine women's real material coL dition and who view speculations on sexual specificity as essentialist and retrogressive positions ("Variations . . . " 1980; Delphy-Dupont 1975, 1980; Guillaumin 1982). These women are hostile to what they consider obscure and elitist postulations which, by unmooring sexuality from real power relationships, absolve men from responsibility for women's oppression. While the stance of French Marxist and materialist feminists, by its insistence on historical and economic factors, is much more familiar to Americans than that of philosophically or psychoanalytically oriented theorizers, it is also true, ironically, that the entrenched leftist tradition from which French feminism arose is antithetic to the American experience.

The strongest push for international dialogue has come from feminist scholars themselves, though, initially, American university language and philosophy departments that disseminated developments in male Continental thought helped foster exchange. The idea that *texts* can refer not just to books or established canons but to all symbolic systems is gaining currency in the United States. Concomitantly, Americans are more willing to see linguistic, and not just political subversion, as a revolutionary act. And American feminists have realized women's studies is becoming too insular and have therefore encouraged the elaboration of more generally applicable theory. There is evidence of the American incorporation of French positions in the sheer number of French authors who appear in anthologies and special issues here (Eisenstein and Jardine 1980; Abel 1980–82; Keohane et al. 1982; and various journal special issues). In addition, translations of the more expository works of Kristeva, Cixous, Irigaray, and Wittig are slowly appearing. Finally, a growing number of American-based scholars are using French feminist discoveries in their own research, inspired by the work of such important critics as Shoshana Felman, Jane Gallop, Nancy Miller, Naomi Schor, and others.

It is not clear, however, that French receptivity to American viewpoints has been entirely equal. Although it appears that some French feminists, influenced by the American mode, see the need for making connections between theory and women's lived experience, few actually use American analytic methods. In keeping with their general turn to experimentations with fiction, French feminists concerned with language have greeted most enthusiastically those English and foreign-language novels they consider radical challenges to conventional logic and discourse (Makward 1981, 349).

The welcome and unprecedented outpouring of works that seek both to speak from women's experience and to generate new modes for women's expression have nonetheless created dilemmas for American feminist critics. In our efforts to explain and categorize avant-garde texts that challenge masculinist discourse, we risk reducing the richness and vitality of those texts. In addition, American women who have been made irrevocably self-conscious about language through their engagement with French feminist thought can find themselves torn between reproducing traditional male discourse and venturing into the frightening and exhilarating wilderness of new writing. Finally, those of us who respect the French feminist insistence on difference and thus accept the incompatibility of French and American approaches are still impelled to reconcile the two in the hope that, together, they will achieve more profound social change. The Franco-American conversation is likely to continue unsettling feminist scholarship and, in this unsettling, will do what criticism does at its best.

## References

Abel, Elizabeth, ed. 1980–82. *Writing and sexual difference*. Chicago: University of Chicago Press.

Andermatt, Verena. 1979. Hélène Cixous and the uncovery of a feminine language. *Women and Literature* 7, no. 1:38–48.

Burke, Carolyn Greenstein. 1978. Report from Paris: Women's writing and the women's movement. *Signs* 3, no. 4:843–55.

_____1981. Irigaray through the looking glass. *Feminist Studies* 7, no. 2:288–306.

Cherchez la femme. 1982. *Diacritics* 12, no. 2.

Cixous, Hélène. 1975. Sorties. In Clément and Cixous, *La jeune née*, 114–246. Partially translated in *Diacritics* 7, no. 2 (1977):64–69.

_____1976. The laugh of the Medusa. *Signs* 1, no. 4:875–93. A translation of "Le rire de la Méduse." *L'arc* 61 (1975):39–54.

Cixous, Hélène, Madeleine Gagnon, and Annie Leclerc. 1977. *La venue à l'écriture*. Paris: UGE.

Clément, Catherine. 1975a. La coupable. In Clément and Cixous, *La jeune née*, 10–113.

_____1975b. La femme dans l'idéologie. *La nouvelle critique* 82:41–46.

_____1978. *Les fils de Freud sont fatigués*. Paris: Grasset.

_____1980. Enslaved enclave. In Marks and de Courtivron, *New French feminisms*, 130–36. A translation of "Enclave esclave." *L'arc* 61 (1975): 13–17.

_____1983. *The lives and legends of Jacques Lacan*. New York: Columbia University Press. A translation of *Vies et légendes de Jacques Lacan*. Paris: Grasset, 1981.

Clément, Catherine, and Hélène Cixous. 1975. *La jeune née*. Paris: UGE.

Conley, Verena (Andermatt). 1984. *Hélène Cixous: Writing the Feminine*. Lincoln: University of Nebraska Press.

Courtivron, Isabelle de. 1979. *Women in movement(s): 1968–1978*. French Literature Series. Columbia: University of South Carolina.

Delphy-Dupont, Christine. 1975. Pour un féminisme matérialiste. *L'arc* 61:61–67. Partially translated as "For a materialist feminism," in Marks and de Courtivron, *New French feminisms*, 197–98.

_____. 1980. A materialist feminism is possible. *Feminist Review* 4:79–105.

Eisenstein, Hester, and Alice Jardine, eds. 1980. *The future of difference*. Boston: G.K. Hall.

Feminist readings: French texts, American contexts. 1981. *Yale French Studies* 62.

Féral, Josette. 1976. China, women and the symbolic: An interview with Julia Kristeva. *Sub-Stance* 13:9–18.

———. 1980. The powers of difference. In Eisenstein and Jardine, *Future of difference*, 88–94.

Finel-Honigman, Irene. 1981. American misconceptions of French feminism. *Contemporary French Civilization* 5, no. 3:317–25.

The French connection. 1981. *Feminist Studies* 7, no 2.

French feminist theory. 1981. *Signs* 7, no 1.

French issue. 1979. *Women and Literature* 7, no 1.

Gagnon, Madeleine. 1974. *Pour les femmes et tous les autres*. Montreal: Ed. de l'Aurore.

———. 1977. Mon corps dans l'écriture. In Cixous, Gagnon, and Leclerc, *La venue à l'écriture*, 63–116. Partially translated as "Body I" in Marks and de Courtivron, *New French feminisms*, 179–80.

Gallop, Jane. 1982. *The daughter's seduction: Feminism and psychoanalysis*. Ithaca: Cornell University Press.

Gallop, Jane, and Carolyn Burke. 1980. Psychoanalysis and feminism in France. In Eisenstein and Jardine, *Future of difference*, 106–21.

Gelfand, Elissa, and Virginia Hules, eds. 1985. *French feminist criticism: Women, language, and literature*. New York: Garland Publishing. Forthcoming.

Guillaumin, Collette. 1982. The question of difference. *Feminist Issues* 2, no 1:33–52. A translation of "Question de différence." *Questions féministes* 6 (1979):3–22.

Hules, Virginia. 1985. A topography of difference. In Gelfand and Hules, *French feminist criticism*.

Introduction. 1981. *Yale French Studies* 62:2–18.

Irigaray, Luce. 1974. *Speculum de l'autre femme*. Paris: Minuit. Translated as *Speculum of the other woman*. Ithaca: Cornell University Press, 1985.

———. 1977. *Ce sexe qui n'en est pas un*. Paris: Minuit. Translated as *This sex which is not one*. Ithaca: Cornell University Press, 1985.

———. 1980. When our lips speak together. *Signs* 6, no. 1:69–79. A translation of "Quand nos lèvres se parlent." *Les cahiers du GRIF* 12 (1976):23–28.

———. 1981a. And one doesn't stir without the other. *Signs* 7, no 1:60–67. A translation of *Et l'une ne bouge pas sans l'autre*. Paris: Minuit, 1979.

———. 1981b. *Le corps-à-corps avec la mère*. Ottawa: Ed. de la Pleine Lune.

———. 1982. *Passions élémentaires*. Paris: Minuit.

Jardine, Alice. 1980. Theories of the feminine: Kristeva. *Enclitic* 4, no. 2:5–15.

———. 1981a. Introduction to Julia Kristeva's "Women's time." *Signs* 7, no. 1:5–12.

———. 1981b. Pre-texts for the trans-Atlantic feminist. *Yale French Studies* 62:220–36.

———. 1982. Gynesis. *Diacritics* 12:54–65.

Jones, Ann Rosalind. 1981. Writing the body: Toward an understanding of l'écriture féminine. *Feminist Studies* 7, no. 2:247–63.

Keohane, Nannerl O., Michelle Z. Rosaldo, and Barbara C. Gelpi. 1982. *Feminist theory: A critique of ideology.* Chicago: University of Chicago Press.

Kofman, Sarah. 1980a. Ex: The woman's enigma. *Enclitic* 4, no. 2:17–28.

————. 1980b. The narcissistic woman: Freud and Girard. *Diacritics* 10, no. 3:36–45. This entry and Kofman 1980a are translated portions of *L'énigme de la femme: La femme dans les textes de Freud.* Paris: Galilée, 1980.

Kristeva, Julia. 1974. Pratique signifiante et mode de production. *Tel Quel* 60:21–33.

————. 1977a. *About Chinese women.* New York: Urizen Books. A translation of *Des Chinoises.* Paris: Ed. des femmes, 1974. Also partially translated as "On the women of China" in *Signs* 1, no. 1 (1974):57–81.

————. 1977b. Héréthique de l'amour. *Tel Quel* 74:30–49.

————. 1980. *Desire in language: A semiotic approach to literature and art.* Edited by Leon S. Roudiez. New York: Columbia University Press.

————. 1981. Women's time. *Signs* 7, no. 1:13–35. A translation of "Le temps des femmes." *34/44,* no. 5 (1979):5–19.

Leclerc, Annie. 1974. *Parole de femme.* Paris: Grasset.

————. 1977. La lettre d'amour. In Cixous, Gagnon, and Leclerc, *La venue à l'écriture,* 117–52. Partially translated as "The love letter" in Marks and de Courtivron, *New French feminisms, 237.*

McClave, Heather. 1982–83. Scholarship and the humanities. In *The women's annual: Number 3,* 205–29. Boston: G.K. Hall.

Makward, Christiane. 1976. Interview with Hélène Cixous. *Sub-Stance* 13:19–37.

————. 1977. La critique féministe, éléments d'une problématique. *Revue des sciences humaines* (December):619–24.

————. 1978. Structures du silence/du délire. *Poétique* 35:314–24.

————. 1980a. Nouveau regard sur la critique féministe en France. *Revue de l'Université d'Ottawa/University of Ottawa Quarterly* 50, no. 1:47–54.

————. 1980b. To be or not to be . . . a feminist speaker. In Eisenstein and Jardine, *Future of difference,* 95–105.

————. 1981. Les éditions des femmes: Historique, politique et impact. *Contemporary French Civilization* 5, no. 3:347–54.

Makward, Christiane, and Sylvie Weil. 1982. Directions in French women's studies. In *Women in print: Opportunities for women's studies research in language and literature,* 173–86. New York: Modern Language Association.

Marks, Elaine. 1978. Women and literature in France. *Signs* 3, no. 4:832–42.

Marks, Elaine, and Isabelle de Courtivron, eds. 1980. *New French feminisms: An anthology.* Amherst: University of Massachusetts Press.

Pouvoir du discours/Subordination du féminin: Entretien. 1975. *Dialectiques* 8:31–41. Reprinted in L. Irigaray, *Ce sexe . . .,* 65–82.

Questions. 1977. In L. Irigaray, *Ce sexe . . .,* 117–63.

Special feminist issue. 1980. *Enclitic* 4, no. 2.

Spivak, Gayatri Chakravorty. 1981. French feminism in an international frame. *Yale French Studies* 62:154–84.

Stanton, Domna. 1977. Parole et écriture: Women's studies, USA. *Tel Quel* 71–73:119–35.

_____. 1980. Language and revolution: The Franco-American dis-connection. In Eisenstein and Jardine, *Future of difference*, 73–87.

Textual politics, feminist criticism. 1975. *Diacritics* 5, no. 4.

Turkle, Sherry. 1978. *Psychoanalytic politics: Freud's French revolution.* New York: Basic Books.

van Rossum-Guyon, Françoise. 1977a. Entretien (Cixous). *Revue des sciences humaines* 168:479–93.

_____. 1977b. Questions à Julia Kristeva à partir de *Polylogue. Revue des sciences humaines* 168:495–501.

Variations on common themes. 1980. In Marks and de Courtivron, *New French feminisms*, 212–30. A translation of "Variations sur des thèmes communs." *Questions féministes* 1 (1977):3–19.

Version/feminisms: A stance of one's own. 1981. *Sub-Stance* 32.

Wittig, Monique. 1980a. One is not born a woman. *Feminist Issues* 2. A translation of "On ne naît pas femme." *Questions féministes* 8 (1980):75–84.

_____. 1980b. Paradigm. In *Homosexualities and French literature*, edited by George Stambolian and Élaine Marks, 114–21. Ithaca: Cornell University Press.

_____. 1980c. The straight mind. *Feminist Issues* 1:103–11. A translation of "La pensée straight." *Questions féministes* 7 (1979):45–53.

_____. 1982. The category of sex. *Feminist Issues* 2, no. 2:63–68.

Woman can never be defined. 1980. In Marks and de Courtivron, *New French feminisms*, 137–41. A translation of "La femme, ce n'est jamais ça." *Tel Quel* 59 (1974):19–25.

Women's exile. 1977. *Ideology and Consciousness* 1:57–76.

Writing and sexual difference. 1981. *Critical Inquiry* 8, no. 2.

## Bibliography

Albistur, Maïté, and Daniel Armogathe. *Histoire du féminisme français, du moyen âge à nos jours.* Paris: Ed. des femmes, 1977. An informative survey of French political, social, and literary currents, since the Middle Ages, that centered on the conflicts between women and men and that sought improvement of women's condition.

*L'arc: Jacques Derrida*, no. 54 (1973), and *L'arc: Jacques Lacan*, no. 58 (1974). Special issues that illuminate Derrida's and Lacan's importance for French feminists.

Bovenschen, Silvia. "Uber die Frage: Gibt es eine weibliche Ästhetik?" *Frauen/Kunst/Kulturgeschichte 25 (1976).*

_____. *Die imaginierte Weiblichkeit: Exemplarische Untersuchungen zu kulturgeschichtlichen und literarischen Präsentations-formen des Weiblichen.* Frankfurt: Suhrkamp, 1979. Uses cultural-historical, as well as theoretical perspectives.

Brossard, Nicole. *Mécanique jongleuse, suivi de Masculin grammatical.* Ottawa: L'Hexagone, 1974. Poetic and telegraphic essays that evoke women's relationship to language and try to expand the boundaries of signification.

*Bulletin de Recherches et d'Etudes Féministes Francophones (BREFF)*, Department of French and Italian, University of Wisconsin, Madison. An indispensable newsletter that provides up-to-date information about publications, research, conferences, and events involving French and francophone feminism.

Chawaf, Chantal. *Chair chaude*. Paris: Mercure de France, 1976. Contains a densely metaphorical essay, "L'écriture," that evokes writing in the feminine as a reunion of physical and spriritual forces.

Culler, Jonathan. *On Deconstruction*. Ithaca: Cornell University Press, 1982. An extremely helpful overview of poststructuralist perspectives and their problematic relation to and distinction from structuralist thought.

Derrida, Jacques. *Of Grammatology*. Baltimore: John Hopkins University Press, 1974. A translation of *De la grammatologie*. Paris: Minuit, 1967; *Writing and difference*. Chicago: University of Chicago Press, 1978. A translation of *L'écriture et la différence*. Paris: Seuil, 1967; *Dissemination*. Chicago: University of Chicago Press, 1982. A translation of *La dissémination*. Paris: Seuil, 1972. The works of this philosopher of linguistic and sexual difference that have most influenced French feminists. Dense and specialized, but crucial.

Duras, Marguerite, and Xavière Gauthier. *Les parleuses*. Paris: Minuit, 1974. A series of conversations about Duras's work, which is widely viewed as an important instance of "feminine" writing.

Frabotta, Biancamaria. *Letteratura al femminile*. Bari: De Donato, 1980. A study of Italian women's writings. Contains a section on feminist theory.

Guiducci, Armanda. *La donna non è gente*. Milan: Rizzoli, 1977. An analysis of cultural myths of femininity.

Horer, Suzanne, and Jeanne Socquet. *La création étouffée*. Paris: Pierre Horay, 1973. A somewhat outdated but persuasive critique of the cultural exclusion of women from creativity and creation.

Lacan, Jacques. *Ecrits*. Paris: Seuil, 1966. Some essays translated in *Ecrits: A Selection*. New York: Norton, 1977. Nearly impenetrable but essential pieces by this psychoanalyst-master whose theories of language and sexual difference marked most French and many American and English feminists.

Lemoine-Luccioni, Eugénie. *Partage des femmes*. Paris: Seuil, 1976. A highly specialized Lacanian analysis of women's relation to masculine systems of representation. Argues for a strengthening of what it considers irremediable sexual difference.

Loriga, Mariella. *L'identità e la differenza*. Milan: Bompiani, 1980.

Macciocchi, Maria-Antonietta. *La donna "hera": "Consenso" femminile e fascismo*. Milan: Feltrinelli, n.d. A political critique by an important theorist. Uses little-known documentation and the ideas of Gramschi and Reich.

Mitchell, Juliet. *Psychoanalysis and Feminism*. New York: Pantheon, 1974. An attempt by this British author to reconcile feminism with psychoanalysis. Critiques American readings of Freud, favoring Continental (Lacanian) interpretations.

Mitchell, Juliet and Jacqueline Rose. *Jacques Lacan and the Ecole Freudienne*. New York: Macmillan, 1983.

Montrelay, Michèle. *L'ombre et le nom: Sur la féminité*. Paris: Minuit, 1977. A collection of suggestive but difficult essays that examine femininity through a Lacanian focus on language and the unconscious.

Pusch, Luise. *Das Deutsche als Männersprache.* Frankfurt: Suhrkamp, 1984.

Pusch, Luise, ed. *Feminismus: Inspektion der Herrenkultur.* Frankfurt: Suhrkamp, n.d. Linguistically oriented.

Resnick, Margery, and Isabelle de Courtivron, eds. *Women Writers in Translation, 1945–1982.* New York: Garland Publishing, 1984. An important compilation of those works by nonanglophone women writers that have been translated into English. Provides a useful summary of each work.

Trömel-Plötz, Senta, "Linguistik und Frauensprache." *Linguistische Berichte* 57 (1978):49–68.

――――. *Frauensprache in unserer Welt der Männer.* Konstanz, 1979.

――――. "Sprache, Geschlecht und Macht." *Linguistische Berichte* 69 (1980):1–14.

――――. *Frauensprache—Sprache der Veränderung.* Frankfurt: Fischer Taschenbuch, 1982. Linguistically oriented.

Wartmann, Brigitte, ed. *Weiblich-Männlich: Kulturgeschictliche Spuren einer verdrängten Weiblichkeit.* Berlin: Asthetik Kommunikation, 1980.

Weitz, Margaret Collins. *Femmes: Recent Writings on French Women.* Boston: G. K. Hall, 1985. A useful annotated bibliography of French works published since 1970 in which historical, political, economic and social aspects of women's experience are addressed. Chapter introductions situate authors and issues well. Exhaustively researched.

Yaguello, Marina. *Les mots et les femmes: Essai d'approche socio-linguistique de la condition féminine.* Paris: Payot, 1979. A sociolinguistic and, therefore, unusual study of women's linguistic comportment.

# Politics

*Peggy Simpson*

"By choosing an American woman to run for our nation's second highest office, you send a powerful signal to all Americans. There are no doors we cannot unlock. We will place no limits on achievement. If we can do this, we can do anything."

The speaker was Geraldine Ferraro.

The place was the Democratic National Convention in San Francisco on 19 July 1984, where television cameras recorded one scene after another of women—and men—with tears streaming down their faces at the historic moment. Millions more watching on television felt the same emotion, the same elation.

The Democratic presidential nominee, Walter Mondale, had thrown the dice. He had chosen a woman—some said reluctantly, some said desperately to save his flagging campaign against an overwhelmingly popular President Reagan. Especially in the first weeks of their ground-breaking campaign, the crowds were monumental, the enthusiasm contagious, the press attention overwhelming.

Every incident was a precedent: should the two nominees touch? Should they wave opposite arms so their arms would not lock overhead in the traditional candidates' crowd salute? Would the hairdressers turn half the women of America into Ferraro look-alikes? Could her Queens accent be comprehended in Dixie? Would the First Woman overshadow the presidential nominee?

There were splendid moments, humorous ones, and some that were poignant. One came on the first and only joint trip by Mondale and Ferraro—from her home turf of Queens into the Deep South of Mississippi. The crowds were large in Jackson and respectful, curious. They included famed southern novelist Eudora Welty, who wanted to see the First Woman. There was an encounter with the ultimate southern Good Ole Boy—the Mississippi commissioner of agriculture, who at seventy-nine was courtly and almost awkward in wanting to behave "right" toward the new female nominee.

The telling incident came on a farm, where Mondale and Ferraro joined the commissioner at a makeshift picnic table—news conference table to talk about the declining state of agriculture under Reagan. The commissioner mentioned many of his state's products—such as catfish. He leaned over to ask Ferraro if she'd ever eaten any fried catfish. She allowed as how she hadn't—and he said she'd have to try some soon. A little bit further down his laundry list of Mississippi-grown products, he came to blueberries. She interrupted to say she grew those—at her Fire Island compound. He was delighted—and wanted to know if she could bake blueberry muffins. Ferraro looked nonplussed and then answered she could. And, after another instant, shot him a fast one with a smile: "Can you?" she asked. That did it for the commissioner's composure. He said something about how, in his part of the country, the menfolks don't cook. As Mondale roared, the commissioner stumbled into talk about how Ferraro looked real pretty, however.

It wasn't just a funny moment. It was a challenge for the fledgling Ferraro troops. They couldn't let the traveling national press portray the elderly agriculture commissioner as a chauvinist or as a fool—and they couldn't risk Ferraro coming off as an uppity women, either. At her next stop, in downtown Jackson, she baffled the local folks by talking about how much she looked forward to coming back to Mississippi to eat catfish—and that she'd be bringing some home-cooked blueberry muffins with her.

It solved that immediate political problem. The others weren't so easy.

Ferraro's nomination culminated what many feminists had dubbed "the year of the woman." Some noted feminist activists, such as former representative Bella Abzug of New York and former National Organization for Women (NOW) president Eleanor Smeal wrote books predicting that women would elect the next president. Smeal, in her book and in consulting done for the Democratic National Committee, contended that a woman on a ticket would prove to be a drawing card, not a negative as many skeptics insisted. A coalition of nearly one hundred bipartisan and multiracial women's groups also were actively trying to harness the gender gap with a voter registration drive whose slogan was punchy: "It's a Man's World . . . Unless Women Vote!"

Republicans scoffed at the Democratic activity. Top aides to President Reagan said the Democrats were just leading the women's constituency on with talk of a woman vice president. They portrayed front-runner Democrat Walter Mondale as a "captive" of the women's movement when he was heavily lobbied for a woman veep in speeches to NOW and the National Women's Political Caucus (NWPC).

Even as three-term congresswoman Ferraro commanded growing party and media attention as a strong-gavel chair of the party's Platform Committee, few feminists or party insiders thought that Mondale would choose her—or any woman—as his "heartbeat away" running mate. Ultimately, Mondale gambled on a First Woman—and on the feisty, ambitious, and presumably politically unblemished Ferraro—to revitalize his campaign in his overwhelmingly uphill race against a personally popular president in a bouyant economic climate.

Whether the gamble failed, entirely, with the resounding defeat of the Mondale-Ferraro ticket will be debated for years to come, as the public and

politicians measure the impact of the Ferraro candicacy in toppling or rein-
forcing barriers for all other women. Preliminary results in the months immediately after the election showed that, although few analysts except the
religious Right spokespersons blamed Ferraro alone for the defeat, there
was widespread criticism by conservative and moderate Democrats of the
"special interest" stigma of excessive closeness to feminist issues such as
abortion and pay equity—and battle lines were drawn within the Democratic party on the "legitimacy" of feminists sitting at the power broker tables with the white males. Similar questions were asked of blacks and organized labor.

At the convention, Republicans as well as Democrats predicted after
Ferraro's nomination that 1984 would be the last year with an all-male
ticket by either party. After November, those views were amended. Few
analysts, male or female, would say with as much conviction as in July that
women would be on the 1988 presidential or vice-presidential tickets. The
next woman nominee will have to earn a place in the same way men traditionally have—by running in the presidential primaries. Ironically, Republican women said Ferraro helped them immensely gain credibility within
their own party, whereas Democratic women were far more on the defensive amidst their colleagues, as they tried to prove that she had not been a
major disaster.

Even more ironically, it was clear in retrospect that the Republicans
took the gender gap far more seriously than did the Democrats. The Republicans learned from their losses in the 1982 mid-term elections where at
least three gubernatorial races were decided in favor of the Democrats because of a sizable women's vote. The president's pollster Richard Wirthlin
and the Republican electoral strategists immediately went to work analyzing the gender gap—and instituting damage-control tactics. They conducted more than forty thousand interviews with women and used that
data to divide them into sixty-four subgroups. They found that, although
there was substantial support for feminist issues, women were no different
than men in putting economic and pocketbook issues at the forefront. With
sophisticated polling data that showed how women felt according to their
ages, marital status, income, and interests, the Republicans were able to
shape fine-tuned messages for the 1984 campaign that helped reduce Reagan's negatives among women voters. They made sure that women—old
women and young ones as well—were prominent in Republican television
ads. They played up economic good news such as the sharp drop in infla-
tion, which polls had shown them women had not realized.

In contrast, Democrats never devoted any comparable polling attention to deciphering the women's vote. Nor did they take steps to ensure
that women were visibly a part of the Democratic message—or that a message was tailored to the interests of women. In short, their efforts to nail
down the women's vote did not go much further than the nomination of
Ferraro.

Because of the extensive damage done to her candidacy by continuing
revelations about her husband's financial affairs, it is difficult to measure
Ferraro's impact—good or bad. Those evaluations will be tested against
realities of time and distance in the 1986 and 1988 elections and those
beyond.

Although 1984 had been proclaimed as the "year of the woman," there were few breakthroughs beyond the Ferraro candidacy. Only the incumbent senator, Kansas Republican Nancy Kassebaum, won election out of the ten women nominated for the Senate. The others were badly outspent and outmaneuvered by incumbents. The number of women in Congress remained twenty-two, with the only black woman, Rep. Katie Hall (D-Ind.), defeated in the primary, with Ferraro leaving her seat, and with two new women elected. By the narrowest of margins—sixty-two votes more than the 50 percent mandated by Vermont law—Madeleine Kunin was elected governor on her second try. Women made some other breakthroughs in state legislative leadership positions, and the first woman, a former nun, was elected attorney general in Rhode Island.

There was a gender gap. On the presidential level, it was measured by two television network polls as remaining at the same point as in 1980—8 percent. The third poll said it was half that. The women's vote was the decisive factor in some key Senate races and in Kunin's gubernatorial race. The 1984 elections dramatized, however, that there is no monolithic "women's vote" that can be rallied behind a woman candidate. Instead, the reality is far more complicated, with women being seen as a diverse collection of voters whose pocketbook self-interest can outweigh equity issues such as abortion choice or the Equal Rights Amendment. The votes also proved, however, that women no longer follow men's voting preferences—they can vote decisively in opposite directions from men.

Finally, the elections revealed the rise of a widespread grass-roots backlash movement against Ferraro and "independent" women, as tens of thousands of Christian Right activists participated in elections for the first time—many of them objecting to the very premise of women's equality. With Catholic church leaders opening a new offensive against abortion, with Ferraro again as the catalyst for action, and with the Mormon church taking a far more active role than four years earlier, opposition to women's rights issues and candidacies intensified at the very time it appeared that sex barriers were being toppled.

Whether women increasingly become the targets of campaign opposition or take the offensive to continue their slow climb toward a significant political presence will be shown in the upcoming elections.

## The Ferraro Candidacy

Ferraro arrived in Congress in 1978 as an ambitious, one-of-the-boys politician who had gambled and won on a fast-track career transition from housewife with three children to federal prosecutor to congresswoman. She set her sights even higher upon reaching Washington. As secretary of the Democratic Caucus, she was the only woman in the House leadership, and as the 1984 elections approached, she took on a high-visibility job as chair of the party's Platform Committee for the San Francisco convention.

In the same year, the National Women's Political Caucus and other activist feminist groups launched a campaign to put a woman on the Democratic ticket—to capitalize on the gender gap that had been noted in 1980 when men voted far more heavily for Ronald Reagan than did women.

Many key 1982 congressional and gubernatorial races showed the same pattern, with women putting over New York governor Mario Cuomo, Texas governor Mark White and Michigan governor James Blanchard, all Democrats. In Texas, a woman—Ann Richards—led the ticket in winning the state treasurer's job.

The feminists argued that a woman on the ticket would tap a vast new source of volunteers and donors, as well as voters. They argued that a woman vice president would be the catalyst for an intensity of interest in her victory by Republican feminists as well as Democrats, especially given Reagan's opposition not just to abortion and the ERA but to enforcement of basic discrimination laws and his administration's opposition to affirmative action and sex equity issues. In short, they argued, selecting a woman running mate was a gamble well worth taking. They knew that only Ferraro could pass muster as a packagable First Woman.

No Democratic women were senators. The only woman governor, Martha Collins of Kentucky, had been in office less than year. There was no one of the cabinet or diplomatic stature of UN Ambassador Jeane Kirkpatrick, a conservative Democrat who was the darling of Republican hawks and who finally switched parties in early 1985 (for a possible GOP presidential or vice-presidential bid in 1988).

Although Ferraro was a relative newcomer to Congress, she had quickly moved up the leadership ladder with House Speaker Thomas P. O'Neill as her patron. She was a late-blooming feminist, unlike some of her more experienced colleagues who were judged to be "too" feminist for the outside body politic. Unlike many others among the small bloc of congresswomen, Ferraro not only had a family, a supportive Italian husband and three nearly grown children, she was a "family first" feminist.

In an era when "family values" had become a code word for Republicans to use against Democrats, many women's groups such as the NWPC and, ultimately, Mondale himself saw Ferraro as a person who epitomized those values and could help Democrats retain the defecting middle-class white ethnic voters, especially the Italian-Americans in the high-vote northeastern states. They calculated that her experience as a federal prosecutor in Queens would be a law-and-order credential that would play well in the South, if not totally overcoming the fact that she had a northern liberal's voting record—and a distinctly New York accent.

The convention response to Ferraro's nomination was euphoria. Only her speech and that of the other 1984 stand-out political newcomer, the Reverend Jesse Jackson, overcame the disastrous party-personnel blunders Mondale had made on the eve of the convention itself.

For the first few weeks, it appeared that the euphoria was justified. The "Ferraro factor" was weighed to assess how much she would mean to the ticket, as she returned to Queens and drew much attention in the supermarket, at church, and at a favorite Italian restaurant with her family.

There was temporary panic in the White House, especially as Mondale succeeded briefly in putting Reagan on the defensive about whether he would raise taxes to reduce the huge budget deficits—but just not tell the voters in advance. Reagan, moreover, made a major flub in a sound-test joke about bombing the Soviets.

As Republicans undertook a major offensive against Ferraro—challenging her lack of experience for the "heartbeat away from the presidency" job and filing legal challenges to her House campaign finance reports from previous races—investigative reporters also looked hard at Ferraro's husband, realtor John Zaccaro, and his properties in the Little Italy section of New York. The core question: was he tied to organized crime? He was, after all, an Italian in real estate whose father had done similar work in an era when these ties were assumed to be almost automatic.

No such ties were proven. His Little Italy rentals, however, included tenants who were pornography distributors and Chinese gamblers. Zaccaro initially balked at fully disclosing his own finances, which added fuel to the firestorm of speculation that he—if not she—was tainted. The financial flap consumed nearly a full month after the convention. Even in the fall there were allegations that her parents had been small-time gamblers or numbers-runners forty years earlier and that an indictment was the cause of her father's death by heart attack when she was eight years old.

Ferraro called the charges about organized crime ties to her family "lies . . . awful lies" and condemned the news media for their probes. "I think the story is how much money some of those newspapers have spent on investigative reporters. . . . Would they have done it if I were male? Would they have done it if I were not Italian-American?"

The financial furor, compounded by the organized crime allegations, took a severe toll, however. After two weeks of the controversy, a relieved Reagan-Bush campaign manager Ed Rollins said, "St. Geraldine is now back to earth. If she can move forward and solve her problems, fine, but she is not quite the factor she was two weeks ago."

It was clear by Labor Day that the Mondale campaign advisers had failed to do an adequate job of scrutinizing the Ferraro-Zaccaro finances. Some time bombs should have been anticipated and defused in advance. More questions should have been asked before her selection. The fact that she survived—and was masterful—at a two-hour news conference revealing the family finances (their net worth was $3.78 million; they paid more than 40 percent in taxes) was a moot point. The damage was irreversible. At least some blame had to be laid to Ferraro—to her inexperience, to politically unwise decisions made earlier on family finances, and to her own ignorance of her husband's affairs when she should have realized these would be scrutinized closely as part of the First Woman phenomenon.

The fact that Ferraro had never run for statewide office and therefore had never been exposed to close probes of her personal and family finances proved a major impediment. She had exacerbated matters by choosing to separate her financial affairs from those of her husband when she entered Congress, thus exempting herself from the full-disclosure mandates about spouses' finances required by House rules. Although the exemption might have been taken in good faith, it fed the paranoia that she had something to hide (and a House Ethics Committee later judged she was in technical violation of the rules).

So did her famous "Italian husband" jibe, when she revealed at a brief Washington news conference as she began her first solo campaign swing that her husband had balked at releasing his tax returns as she had said he

would. Zaccaro felt that "his business interests would be affected by releasing" the returns. She told reporters that her husband said, "Gerry, I'm
not going to tell you how to run the country, and you're not going to tell
me how to run my business." And then came the zinger: "If you've ever
been married to an Italian man, you know what it's like." That crack—
which came after a breakfast fight with her husband over the tax return issue—ensured that the financial flap would eclipse any other news from her
West Coast trip, including the fact that she drew crowds up to fifteen thousand in Seattle, which exceeded even those of John F. Kennedy's campaign
rallies there.

The Mondale-Ferraro ticket never regained its footing. The financial
flap paled, but it became clear that Mondale had no game plan to follow up
on his other convention gamble, the tax issue. He proved unable to con-
vince the voters that the deficit was a looming national disaster, let alone
that raising their taxes was the way to avert it. Nor could he rouse people
about the danger of Reagan naming up to five new Supreme Court justices,
who could then overturn not only the 1973 *Roe* v. *Wade* abortion rights ruling but many other significant decisions as well.

Ultimately, the election was one of the most one-sided ones in history,
with Mondale-Ferraro winning only the state of Minnesota and the District
of Columbia. She did carry her home borough of Queens but made little
impact on the state of New York as a whole.

The results, however, did not eclipse the significance of the Ferraro
candidacy or of her own special talents. Despite never having given a major
national speech before nor having dealt with huge crowds and telepromp-
ters and hecklers, she proved to be a charismatic candidate. She was a political natural, even though a novice. She was equally at ease in delivering
a stump speech and in confiding intimacies to a television interviewer.

After only six years in Congress, she was able to master a learning
curve that encompassed foreign policy and arms control—and performed
credibly in a national debate with the vastly more experienced vice president, George Bush. She held her own, despite noticeable softness on foreign policy questions, and got off a few licks of her own. Ferraro's debate
demeanor was so subdued, however, so professional, in contrast to her on-
the-stump fervor, that many onlookers thought she lost valuable points.
She seemed too hesitant, too cool. Her strategists said that being cool—
and, especially, competent with the foreign affairs questions—was part of
the goal. She took the offensive against a reporter who asked if she was
competent to be the person with a finger on the nuclear button—the core
"heartbeat away" question again—by saying just because she hadn't been in
the military didn't mean she wasn't tough. At another point, after Bush offered to "help" her with the facts of a foreign issue, she accused him of
patronizing her.

Bush's trauma at being pitted against the First Woman had been evident even before the debate. After her net worth was revealed, he mocked
as a fraud her political stance as an "Edith Bunker housewife from
Queens." His wife, Barbara, expressed outrage at her in a thinly disguised
comment that she was a "rich bitch." And Bush's press secretary, too, accused Ferraro of being "bitchy." The day after their historic debate, an up-

beat Bush told longshoremen, in a "just one of the boys" crack, that he had had "to kick a little ass" the night before.

Ferraro continued to draw crowds in huge numbers even as the Democrats slid into oblivion. People brought their children to see history in the making, and fans young and old cheered her on in far more than symbolic perfunctory ways. She was also a magnet for protestors, however, especially the religious Right and the Catholic church hierarchy. The Protestant fundamentalists opposed her as a symbol of everything that has gone awry with "family values," and many pastors talked openly about the God-given Biblical agenda, which holds that women are subordinate to men, wives to husbands—and that a woman as vice president would violate that imperative.

The issue was different for Catholic leaders, most notably New York Archbishop John O'Connor, a point man for Pope John Paul II on abortion and morality issues. Although as a resident of Queens rather than Manhattan Ferraro was not in O'Connor's parish, he began to challenge her abortion views directly, especially her support, starting in 1982, of the abortion position of Catholics for a Free Choice. That year, she wrote a foreword to the group's publication on abortion and politics that said "Catholic lawmakers deal each day, both personally and politically, with the wrenching abortion issue. . . . We confront special problems in communicating with Catholic clergy and our Catholic and non-Catholic constituents. Some of us have taken strong pro-choice positions. Others are uncertain. But all of us have experienced moral and political doubt and concern. That is what the briefing, and this monograph, are all about. They show us that the Catholic position on abortion is not monolithic and that there can be a range of personal and political responses to the issue."

That statement ran counter to the pope's views and to O'Connor's, who told a news conference on 24 June that "I don't see how a Catholic in good conscience can vote for a candidate who explicitly supports abortion." These sentiments were later criticized by another Italian-American Catholic, Governor Cuomo, who said the archbishop in essence had said "that no Catholic can vote for Ed Koch, no Catholic can vote for Jay Goldin, for Carol Bellamy nor for Pat Moynihan or Mario Cuomo."

O'Connor later said that wasn't what he had meant—that he would not attempt to dictate anyone's vote. Ferraro, however, continued to face protests and pickets, including some calling for her excommunication from the Catholic church because of her views on abortion. She noted wryly that in trying to "separate my religious views from my standing on the issues" she was only emulating the precedent set by the first Catholic to be elected president, John F. Kennedy. He had had to prove convincingly that he would not be dictated to by the Vatican—but now the pope was calling on her to accept just such dictation.

As the abortion controversy intensified amid a rising tide of bombings of family-planning clinics, a full-page advertisement was placed in the *New York Times* by ninety-six Catholic theologians, including twenty-four nuns and four priests, reiterating that there were divergent views on abortion within the Catholic church. This move was seen as an affront to authority, and soon after the election, the pope ordered the priests and nuns to renounce their views or face expulsion from their orders. The priests complied, but by spring 1985 none of the nuns had budged, with a confrontation with the pope increasingly likely.

Reagan, meanwhile, strengthened his antiabortion rhetoric with publicaton of a book that condemned abortion as murder (1984). With the Republican platform calling for a total ban on abortion and appointment of Supreme Court justices with antiabortion views, Reagan denied that Moral Majority founder Jerry Falwell would have a hand in selecting the justices if vacancies occurred—but he did not back away from Falwell's contention that antiabortion justices would be sought to overturn the 1973 *Roe* v. *Wade* abortion decision.

In the end, the amplification of abortion controversies by the Ferraro-O'Connor collision was seen as costing the Democrats some of the blue-collar, white-ethnic votes it had hoped Ferraro could attract.

Another controversy occurred over whether she should be appealing more overtly to women—whether her campaign should spell out more specifically the ways in which a Mondale-Ferraro presidency could make a difference on equity and other issues. The Mondale campaign made the strategic decision that she should run as a traditional vice-presidential nominee—that her very presence on the ticket was signal enough of the changes that would occur if they, not the Republicans, were elected.

Some election analysts called this a major mistake. GOP pollster Richard Wirthlin said Ferraro was a unique resource who wasn't wisely used—especially to highlight the vulnerability of the Republicans on issues relating to rich-poor inequities and the "fairness" of their budget and tax programs. Ferraro made her only speech on women's issues the final weekend of the campaign, and Mondale made his single bow in her direction—noting the significance of her selection—the day before the election when polls showed Republican moderates might be moving in their direction.

Republicans were taking no chances that Ferraro might tip the balance toward the Democrats. Wirthlin's polls, begun after the 1982 election losses, had broken down the women's vote into sixty-four sub groups, with eight major categories ultimately isolated for special attention. These included young married nonworking women and both married and single older women. Saturation advertising about economic gains was beamed at these groups, using daytime television as one vehicle and making sure that women of these age and occupation groups were used in the ads.

Republican businesswomen who had never been active in politics were recruited for a top-level policy council, with the pitch again being the economic boom rather than single-issue "women's" concerns. Republican women in Congress took the lead in pushing through legislation on expanded child-care and pension rights—with Reagan's blessing. The president's daughter Maureen joined the GOP campaign to ride herd on sex-related issues—and to dismiss, for instance, criticism of pay-equity proposals by conservative presidential assistant Faith Whittlesey. Republican state legislators, who had been critical of Reagan budget cuts and who had complained of being ignored by the White House, were courted for a full year before the election.

The Democrats, meanwhile, never did see fit to go beyond Ferraro's candidacy to court the women's vote and never developed the data base necessary to identify weak links among its targeted voters or to fine-tune messages to them.

## The Results—and What They Meant

The election was a near shut-out for Democrats on the national ticket. Reagan's electoral vote margin of 525 to 13 was exceeded only by the 1936 crushing of Alf Landon by Franklin D. Roosevelt. Reagan won a far larger share of the popular vote than had been expected in a year when dozens of groups had registered low-income voters as well as blacks, Hispanics and women. The Mondale-Ferraro showing, then, raised questions about whether a long-debated ideological and party preference realignment was underway.

Doubts about whether any woman should be next in line for the presidency, as well as about Ferraro herself, cost the Democratic ticket support, pollsters said, but their numbers showed that, among people who based their vote on the vice-presidential nominee, she drew more votes to Mondale than she cost him.

She did not keep the Italians hitched to the Democratic ticket, however, although Italian women voted for her more than did Italian men in a reversal of previous trends; the women voted Democratic 52–47 in eastern states, whereas Italian men voted for Reagan 58–41, according to CBS exit polls. ABC exit polls found that white Prostestants voted Republican by more than a 2–1 margin, and Catholics went narrowly with Mondale-Ferraro. Overall, the networks found a gender gap of between 4 and 9 percent with men favoring Reagan by a margin that much larger than did women.

Reagan's huge personal mandate carried no coattails, however. Only in Texas and North Carolina did Republicans make major inroads; in other areas voters kept the status quo or gave Democrats a slight advantage, enabling them to pick up two additional Senate seats to shave the GOP margin of control to three seats and to cut their House losses to 14. In many state races, a discernible gender gap was noted that favored the Democrats. Kunin eked out her narrow win in Vermont with the votes of 53 percent of the women but only 42 percent of male voters. The women's vote also was a major factor in the upset victories of Democrats Paul Simon of Illinois and Tom Harkin of Iowa over the incumbent Republicans, in reelecting Democratic Senator Carl Levin of Michigan, and in delivering a huge victory margin for Democrat John Kerry in an open seat in Massachusetts.

Census Bureau figures showed in January 1985 that, contrary to initial projections, the overall vote did increase slightly—and the votes of women rose significantly while the men's voting rate stayed even. Women cast 53.5 percent of all votes compared to 46.5 percent for men. Overall, there was a one percentage point rise in voter turnout, the first increase in a presidential election since 1964, and this was nearly all a result of the increased turnout among women: 61 percent of all voting-age women said they had voted, 2 percentage points higher than in 1980. Turnout for men remained at 59 percent, the same since 1976. This meant that 71 million more women than men voted in 1984. There were notable increases in voting by black and Hispanic women, whose participation is now higher than that of black or Hispanic men.

The Women's Vote Project exceeded by 300,000 its goal of registering 1.5 million women. Among the seventy-five groups participating in the pioneering effort, six registered more than 150,000 each: a black sorority, Alpha Kappa Alpha; the American Association of University Women; the National Organization for Women; the League of Women Voters; the National Women's Political Caucus; and the YWCA. Harvard political scientist Dr. Ethel Klein (1985) said the 1984 elections show clearly that "the women's vote can deliver neither a resounding defeat nor victory by itself. But in competitive races waged between candidates sharply divided on the issues, the women's vote can, and will, make the difference."

If women had voted like men, the Republicans would have won four Senate races for a net pickup of two seats; instead, they lost two seats. The GOP gain of only fourteen House seats is typical of a "highly competitive—not a historically lopsided—presidential contest. Without a substantial gender gap in these races, the results would have shifted dramatically in the president's favor," she said. In short, "the gender gap helped keep Reagan's coattails shorttails. The women's vote is part of a complicated process forestalling realignment in this country."

The women's vote is unlike the group-conscious bloc voting by blacks, Jews, and, to a lesser extent, Hispanics and labor. Instead, Klein said, the women's vote "arrived in 1980 and persists through 1984 because of the growing independence of women and the significant differences on the issues between the two political parties." The issues driving the women's vote, she said, "can be loosely clustered into three often interlocking categories: economic equity, violence/war/foreign policy issues, and women's rights. Women as a group tend to be more liberal on these policy areas than men but different subgroups of women have their own issue priorities."

The gender gap was no larger in 1984 because Republicans worked actively to defuse its impact on Reagan and because Democrats backed away from emphasizing issues of concern to women after nominating Ferraro, which Klein called "an approach/avoidance strategy toward the women's vote." The Republicans, in contrast, targeted messages to specific groups of women by age and economic and marital status, attempting to "sell the Republican economic plan as a success. The Republicans appealed to women on the basis of their economic interests divorced from their identity as women."

Democratic pollster Dotty Lynch, who had worked for primary contender Gary Hart and subsequently advised the Mondale-Ferraro campaign, said that the Mondale message focused on deficits and a strong defense in an attempt to regain support of white male ethnics. She said differences in money was not the cause of the problem, although Republicans had far more private donor sources than the Democrats. The difference was the targeting of resources—and, in the Democrats' case, the decision to let the nomination of Ferraro stand alone without supporting paid media messages on issues. Ultimately, Republicans increased their share of the women's vote to 57 percent, a full 10 percent higher than in 1980.

A Republican feminist who runs a campaign consulting firm in New York, Tanya Melich (1984, 19), said that the perceived damage by the Ferraro defeat after the initial inflated expectations will be short-lived. "Women have become politically activated. Nothing in 1984 points to a slowing down of this desire for equity. . . . Changing the political status quo is never easy. A superficial assessment of 1984 may try to claim that women are not a political force because Ferraro lost. Such a judgment is wrong," she said.

"The supposition that one pioneering woman's vice presidential candidacy could overcome the unpopularity of her male running mate and her husband's questionable business relationships is based upon a fairy tale understanding of just how deep are the roots of male dominance in politics," Melich said. "It is a tribute to Walter Mondale's faith in the American system of opportunity that he hoped hundreds of years of sexism could be wiped out by one appointment."

## *Other Elections*

Beyond Ferraro, women made few political breakthroughs. Two women who had run convincing races in 1982 found victory in 1984. Missouri State Senator Harriett Woods, who had come close to upsetting an incumbent GOP senator two years earlier, was the only Democratic victor in 1984 to be elected lieutenant governor. Madeleine Kunin, who had served four years as lieutenant governor of Vermont but was defeated in her effort to move up to the top job in 1982, won the governorship on her second try in 1984.

Of the ten major-party nominees for the U.S. Senate, only incumbent GOP Senator Nancy Kassebaum of Kansas won—and she scored a landslide with more than 70 percent of the vote. None of the others came close. All were challenging incumbents, and all were outspent badly. Minnesota's Secretary of State Joan Crowe, for example, raised $1.2 million compared to $5.4 million for her Republican opponent, Senator Rudy Boschwitz and, like Harriett Woods in 1982, had to fight off male primary challengers well into the election season with damaging effect.

The women contenders in 1984 were, as a group, more credible than predecessors from recent campaigns. They raised record amounts of money, and they won endorsements more easily from mainstream political action committees. But they remained uncompetitive with few exceptions. Of the sixty-five women nominated for the U.S. House, only the twenty incumbents and two newcomers won in the general election. Representative Katie Hall (D-Ind.), the only black woman in Congress, was defeated in a primary battle, and Ferraro gave up her seat. The other incumbents won, along with Republican representatives Jan Meyers of Kansas, a feminist and former state senator, and Helen Delich Bentley of Maryland, an outspoken veteran of work with longshoremen and dockers as a reporter and a Nixon adminstration regulator. An antiabortionist who does favor the Equal Rights Amendment, she defeated a veteran Democrat on her third try.

A notable winner was Arlene Violet, the first woman ever elected attorney general. She first ran two years ago and is a Rhode Island law-and-order Republican. A nun for twenty-three years with the Sisters of Mercy, she was ordered by Catholic church superiors to give up her religious life if she ran a second time for public office.

Ten women now serve as state treasurers and eighteen as secretaries of state. In addition to Woods, four other women now serve as lieutenant governor, including Ruth Meiers (D-N.D.) whose election in 1984 was tied to that of the governor.

Women marginally increased their seats in state legislatures, picking up 99 seats for a new total of 1,096 as of 1985 compared to 610 a decade earlier, or 14.7 percent of the total. Democrats hold a partisan edge of 55–45. The National Women's Education Fund said 73 black women serve in legislatures in twenty-nine states, along with eight Hispanic women in six states and two American Indian women legislators. The only woman speaker of a state House of Representatives is Vera Katz, a fifty-one-year-old Portland Democrat who was elected after 101 ballots to the Oregon speakership in November of 1984. Like Kunin, she is a Jewish refugee who fled Nazi Germany as a young girl to make a new life with her parents in the United States.

## What Next

Many women braced for adversity after the Reagan landslide and the humiliation of the defeat of the First Woman ticket. They noted that, while Ferraro was rarely singled out for scapegoating, women's issues such as abortion and comparable worth were targeted for criticism.

In addition to the resurgence of the religious Right with the Biblical agenda dictating the subordination of women, the new level of confrontation with the Catholic church on abortion issues, and the dilution of bipartisan support for civil rights enforcement and new pay-equity proposals there was a subtle questioning by many mainstream analysts about the core issues: women's place in society and the penalties of success.

Queens College political scientist Andrew Hacker, for instance, noted in a *New York Times Magazine* article (9 December 1984) highlighting the competition faced by men as women enter more nontraditonal jobs that "with fairer job competition, we are discovering that men cannot depend on their gender for preferment." He talked of the link between high-achievement women and the breakup of their marriages. Men may have to settle for less in wages, Hacker said ominously, but "women will also have to face the prospect of living with men they have outpaced."

Throughout 1984, the drumbeat against pay equity and comparable-worth proposals was steady. Reagan's chairman of the U.S. Commission on Civil Rights, Clarence Pendleton, compared them to "Looney Tunes." The U.S. Chamber of Commerce and antifeminist Phyllis Schlafly led the business opposition to the very premise of evaluating workplace wages to see if critics are correct and the domination of jobs by women in itself results in lower pay than for jobs of equivalent education or experience dominated by men.

Despite the criticism, however, more states launched studies of wage disparities and provided funds in some cases to remedy inequities sure to be found. Their action was speeded, in part, by a federal court ruling against the state of Washington that could cost up to $1 billion in back pay and penalties for pay inequities that the state originally tracked a decade earlier but failed to correct.

Pay-equity issues became political organizing tools for at least two large unions: the American Federation of State, County and Municipal Workers, which brought the Washington state case, and the Service Employees International Union, whose membership is predominantly women.

Proof that pay equity may be a political hot potato came in mid-1984 when the Reagan White House put off until after the election a decision on whether to join the state of Washington in its appeal against the women workers.

Civil rights groups were unsure whether the 1984 election—and the pending 1986 one—strengthened or further weakened their ability to fend off continuing erosion in the enforcement of basic antidiscrimination laws. They lost big only weeks before the election when the Senate tabled the Civil Rights Act of 1984, which would have reversed a Supreme Court ruling requested by the Reagan administration to construct laws banning bias based on sex, race, age, and handicap. With the Justice Department proclaiming the end of affirmative action and case-shopping for a way to reinforce their views with a Supreme Court ruling, the civil rights groups were hard put to hold onto what they had—let alone expand efforts against sex or race discrimination.

Serious erosions were feared not just in civil rights enforcements but in the entire arena of a woman's control over her reproductive capacity. Only a dozen states still provided funds for low-income women to have abortions under the state-run but federally funded Medicaid health system. The Catholic church was initiating lawsuits in New York and other states against expansion of Planned Parenthood family planning and abortion facilities, and on the larger front, the State Department reversed its historic stance, to move toward prohibiting any U.S. funds for family planning in impoverished Third World nations, although that has been the main source of aid for contraceptives and child-spacing help. And, of course, the Supreme Court itself could be substantially changed in a second Reagan term since five of the nine justices are over the age of seventy-five and are in varying stages of ill health.

New coalitions of women of all incomes and colors were being shaped to attempt to meet the new realities. Some of these could come about as a result of first-time cooperative efforts between traditionally strong black sororities and grass-roots Hispanic and black community groups and white-dominated groups that have both grass-roots and national bases. In the past, there has been little more than lip service paid toward unity, let alone any common ground being established for nuts-and-bolts operations. Schisms widened on some levels in 1984 between black and white women, especially, in the aftermath of the Jesse Jackson campaign and the nomination of Ferraro as vice president. Resentment ran high that Mondale did not interview any minority women when screening vice-presidential candidates and, partly because of this, former representative Shirley Chisholm of New York took the lead in forming the Black Women's Political Caucus.

Even as 1984 ended, speculation had begun about whether a woman would be on either major party ticket in 1988. The odds appeared against it. On the other hand, women in both parties were talking about potential nominees who could be drafted to run in the primaries and legitimize themselves for selection in the second slot.

Top contenders included former UN ambassador Jeane Kirkpatrick, Transportation Secretary Elizabeth Dole, and Senator Kassebaum in the Republican party. Democratic contenders were harder to settle on. Ferraro appeared too damaged by her husband's finances to make a credible run, there were no Democrats serving in the Senate, and the only woman governor eligible, Kentucky Democrat Martha Layne Collins, was a newcomer to national politics. Kunin, as a foreign-born naturalized citizen, would be ineligible.

The Year of the Woman ended far differently than anyone could have predicted at the start of 1984. There were roller-coaster rides of exhilaration and exhaustion and disappointment. There was also a greater participation than ever before by women on all levels of politics—from voting to organizing—and that provides a firm foundation for future gains.

As former Democratic National Committee political director Ann Lewis put it (Simpson 1985), "Moving from euphoria to reality isn't always pleasant. But in politics there is no magic button. It is hard work and constant people-to-people contact. How could we even have thought it would be easy when we pride ourselves on knowing our history—when we know how long it took us to get the vote and how to use it in our best interest?"

"I think the learning curve is getting shorter all the time but it is not instantaneous," said Lewis, who after the election took over leadership of the Americans for Democratic Action. "In politics there is no such thing as a self-sustaining victory. Every time you win one, you'd better be prepared to go in and win it again and again and again. And that's no different for women than for men. It's always tough."

## Final Roundup 1984: Women's Consistent Gains as State and Federal Officeholders

### State Legislatures

A total of 1096 women will be serving in state legislatures in 1985. Of those, 195 will serve in state senates, (including 8 in Nebraska's nonpartisan, unicameral legislature) and 901 in lower houses. The partisan breakdown is 55 percent or 594 Democratic and 45 percent or 494 Republican. Of these 1096, 970 women were elected to state legislatures in 1984, the most ever elected at one time. In 1985, 14.7 percent of all state legislators will be women.

A total of 73 black women will serve in legislatures in 29 states. Of these, 45 are reelected incumbents, 9 are newly elected, and 19 are holdovers, not up in 1984. Eight Hispanic women will serve in the state legislatures of 6 states. Of these, 4 are incumbents, 3 newly elected, and 1 a holdover. Two American Indian women have also been elected to serve in state legislatures.

| | Holding Office 1975 | Holding Office 1984 | Holding Office 1985 | Democrats/ Republicans 1985 | Elected 1982 | Elected 1984 |
|---|---|---|---|---|---|---|
| Alabama | 1 | 9 | 9 | 8/1 | 6 | NA |
| Alaska | 9 | 8 | 11 | 5/6 | 8 | 9 |
| Arizona | 18 | 19 | 18 | 6/12 | 19 | 18 |
| Arkansas | 3 | 7 | 10 | 9/1 | 7 | 10 |
| California | 2 | 14 | 15 | 9/6 | 12 | 14 |
| Colorado | 16 | 25 | 24 | 8/16 | 22 | 22 |
| Connecticut | 26 | 43 | 41 | 14/27 | 44 | 41 |
| Delaware | 10 | 10 | 10 | 5/5 | 10 | 8 |
| Florida | 13 | 28 | 30 | 18/12 | 28 | 25 |
| Georgia | 9 | 19 | 23 | 19/4 | 19 | 23 |
| Hawaii | 10 | 17 | 14 | 8/5 | 14 | 12 |
| Idaho | 10 | 16 | 24 | 9/15 | 15 | 24 |
| Illinois | 15 | 28 | 30 | 12/18 | 28 | 25 |
| Indiana | 9 | 18 | 19 | 10/9 | 14 | 18 |
| Iowa | 14 | 17 | 22 | 14/8 | 17 | 21 |
| Kansas | 9 | 23 | 30 | 13/17 | 21 | 29 |
| Kentucky | 5 | 10 | 9 | 7/2 | NA | 7 |
| Louisiana | 2 | 5 | 5 | 5/0 | NA | NA |
| Maine | 24 | 41 | 44 | 23/21 | 41 | 44 |
| Maryland | 19 | 36 | 36 | 32/4 | 36 | NA |
| Massachusetts | 16 | 26 | 33 | 24/9 | 26 | 33 |
| Michigan | 9 | 16 | 16 | 10/6 | 16 | 14 |
| Minnesota | 8 | 28 | 28 | 16/21 | 27 | 19 |
| Mississippi | 6 | 5 | 3 | 3/0 | NA | NA |
| Missouri | 12 | 25 | 26 | 18/8 | 23 | 25 |

Number of Women Holding State Legislative Office 1975–85

Source: National Women's Education Fund, 31 January 1985.

## Statewide Offices

Two women are governors: Martha Layne Collins (D-Ky.), elected in 1983, and Madeleine Kunin (D-Vt), elected in 1984.

### References

Klein, Ethel. 1985. The women's vote. Paper read at conference, The Women's Vote, held by the Women's Vote Project, February.

Melich, Tanya. 1984. The painful climb to women's political equality—circa 1984. *Ripon Forum*, December.

Reagan, Ronald. 1984. *Abortion and the conscience of a nation*. Nashville: Thomas Nelson.

Simpson, Peggy. 1985. What happened in '84: Did women make a difference? *Working Woman*, February, 52–58.

## Bibliography

*The Abortion Issue in the Political Process: A Briefing for Catholic Legislators.* Washington, D.C.: Catholics for a Free Choice, 1982. Contains introduction by the then representative Geraldine Ferraro, and articles by Marquette theologian Daniel C. Maguire, "Catholic Options in the Abortion Debate"; Gannett News Service columnist Jim Castelli, "Abortion and the Catholic Church: Shifting Priorities"; pollster Greg Martire, "Polling the Catholic Public in Abortion"; and political strategist Ken Swope, "Successful Political Responses to the Abortion Issue."

"Abortion, 12 Years Later." CBS News/*New York Times* Poll, 22 January 1985.

Abzug, Bella, with Mim Kelber. *Gender Gap: Bella Abzug's Guide to Political Power for American Women.* Boston: Houghton Mifflin Co., 1984.

Baron, Alan. "Religious Retreat." *Baron Report,* 10, September 1984.

Barone, Michael. "Democrats and Comparable Worth." *Washington Post,* 3 December 1984.

Boone, Carroll. "The Washington State Comparable Worth Trial: A Major Victory for Working Women." *Comparable Worth Project Newsletter,* Fall 1983–Winter 1984.

Cohen, Richard E. "After a Halting Start, the GOP Is Now Taking Aim at Ferraro." *National Journal* [special Convention daily issue], 20 August 1984.

Cohodas, Nadine. "Senate Wrongs Civil Rights Act." *Congressional Quarterly,* October 1984.

"Comparable Worth: Battle of the Sexes." Televised debate sponsored by the U.S. Chamber of Commerce between Chamber President Richard Lesher; Linda Chavez, staff director of the U.S. Commission on Civil Rights; Nancy Reder, chair of the National Committee on Pay Equity, and Winn Newman, attorney, broadcast in October and November 1984.

*Comparable Worth: Women's Issue or Wage Controls?* Washington, D.C.: American Legislative Exchange Council, 1984. Summary of laws, theories and studies underway for the American Legislative Exchange Council.

*Congressional Report Proposes Republican Agenda for Women.* Washington, D.C.: House Wednesday Group, 21 June 1984.

Cooper & Secrest Associates, Inc. "Women as Candidates in the 1984 Congressional Elections. A Postelection Survey of Five Congressional Districts." Opinion survey commissioned by the National Women's Political Caucus, November 1984.

Cowley, Geoffrey. "Comparable Worth: Another Terrible Idea." *Washington Monthly,* January 1984.

Dade, Julie B. "A Black Woman's Place." *Focus* (Joint Center for Political Studies); September 1984.

Dean, Virginia, Joy Ann Grune, Margaret Klaw, and Denise Mitchell. *Who's Working for Working Women? A Survey of State and Local Government Pay Equity Initiatives.* Washington, D.C.: Comparable Worth Project, National Committee on Pay Equity; National Women's Political Caucus, 1984.

"Democratic Presidential Candidates Forum in Issues of Concern to Women." Seminar sponsored by Women in Politics '84 and Emmanuel College, Boston, WBZ-TV, 3 February 1984.

Edmunds, Lavinia. "Women Who Won: New Faces of 1985." Ms, December 1984.

Farney, Dennis. "Kassebaum Passes Political Muster." *Wall Street Journal*, 26 September 1984.

Flick, Rachel. "What do Women Want? The Three Reasons for Ronald Reagan's Gender Gap." *Policy Review* (Heritage Foundation), Winter 1984.

Godwin, Ronald S. "Registering Christian Voters." *Religious Broadcasting*, July-August 1984.

Goldman, Ari L. "New York's Controversial Archbishop." *New York Times Magazine*, 14 October 1984, 38.

Greider, William. "The Ballot Box Revolution." *Rolling Stone*, 13 September 1984.

Griffith, Elisabeth. "My Turn: Why I'm Not Going to Dallas." *Newsweek*, 20 August 1984.

Hacker, Andrew. "Women Vs. Men in the Work Force." *New York Times Magazine*, 9 December 1984.

"How Conservatives Can Appeal to Blacks, Hispanics, Women." *Conservative Digest*, March 1984.

Hurst, Jane. *Abortion in Good Faith: The History of Abortion in the Catholic Church*. Washington, D.C.: Catholics for a Free Choice, 1984.

Hyde, Henry J. "ERA and Abortion." *Human Life Review*, Summer 1983.

"Justice Delayed Is Justice Denied: Removing Sex Bias from the Wage Scale." Pay equity brochure published in January 1985 by the American Federation of State, County and Municipal Employees, AFL-CIO.

Klein, Joe. "Abortion and the Archbishop." *New York*, 1 October 1984.

Krauthammer, Charles. "From Bad to Worth." *New Republic*, 30 July 1984.

LaMaye, Tim. "The Election of Our Lifetime." *Religious Broadcasting*, July-August 1984.

Ledewitz, Bruce S. "Who Did in the Democrats?" *New York Times*, 8 November 1984, A-31.

Maguire, Daniel C. "Abortion: A Question of Catholic Honesty." *Christian Century*, 14–21 September 1983.

Mann, Judy. "Assessing the Women's Vote." *Washington Post*, 9 November 1984.

_____. "The Gender Gap from the Reagan Camp: Elizabeth Dole." *Ms.*, March 1984.

Marks, Marilyn. "State Legislators, Judges and Now Congress Examining 'Comparable Worth.' " *National Journal*, 8 July 1984.

Marttila and Kiley. "A Study of Attitudes toward Pay Equity." Polling data commissioned of Boston firm by the National Committee on Pay Equity, December 1984.

Michaels, Marguerite. "Myth of the Gender Gap." *Parade*, 4 March 1984.

"Moral Majority Mobilizes Huge Voter-Registration Drive." *Moral Majority Report*, April 1984.

Newman, Winn, and Christine Owens. "Race and Sex-Based Wage Discrimination Is Illegal." Testimony before Consultation of the U.S. Commission on Civil Rights, *Comparable Worth: Issue for the 80s*, 6–7 June 1984.

Norwood, Janet L. "Working Women and Public Policy." Speech by the Commissioner of Labor Statistics, U.S. Department of Labor, to National Conference on Women, the Economy, and Public Policy, 20 June 1984.

Osborne, David. "Registration Boomerang: The Democrats Delivered the Republican Vote." *New Republic*, 25 February 1985.

Perlez, Jane. "Ferraro the Campaigner." *New York Times Magazine*, 30 September 1984, 22.

_____. "Women, Power and Politics." *New York Times Magazine*, 24 June 1984.

Quinn, Jane Bryant. "Is the Heat Off? Keep Their Feet to the Fire." *Common Cause*, March-April 1983, 28–34.

Raines, Howell. "GOP Seizes 'Genderless Issue' of Tax Returns to Attack Ferraro." *New York Times*, 14 August 1984.

Schlafly, Phyllis, ed. *Equal Pay for Unequal Work: A Conference on Comparable Worth.* Alton, Ill.: Eagle Forum Education and Legal Defense Fund, 1984.

Schneider, William. "Reagan Lead Not Secure or Commanding." *National Journal* [special Convention daily issue], 20 August 1984.

Simpson, Peggy. "A 'Sophie's Choice' for Republican Women." *Working Woman*, September 1984.

_____. "Turning Point for the Women's Vote: Can Women Swing the Election in '84? Our Clout for Years to Come Is Riding on the Results." *Working Woman*, June 1984, 70–72.

_____. Woman in the News: Nancy Landon Kassebaum." *Working Woman*, March 1984, 106–9.

"Singles Show Less Support for Reagan." CBS/*New York Times* Poll, December 1984.

Smeal, Eleanor. "The Ferraro Euphoria." *Eleanor Smeal Report*, 25 July 1984.

_____. "Momentum Increasing for Woman on Presidential Ticket." *Eleanor Smeal Report*, 22 May 1984.

_____. *Why and How Women Will Elect the Next President of the United States.* New York: Harper & Row, 1984.

Smith, James P., and Michael P. Ward. *Women's Wages and Work in the Twentieth Century.* Washington, D.C.: Rand Corporation, October 1984.

Steinem, Gloria. "What No One Else Would Tell You about the Ferraro Campaign." *Ms.*, December 1984, 53.

Stokes, Bruce. "GOP Women Say They're Left Out in Cold." *National Journal*, [special Convention daily issue], 20 August 1984.

*Voting and Registration in the Election of November 1984.* Washington, D.C.: U.S. Department of Commerce, Bureau of the Census, January 1985.

*The Wage Gap: Myths and Facts.* Washington, D.C.: National Committee on Pay Equity. Graphs and tables on sex-based wage differences when adjusted for education and experience.

Wall, James E. "Lazy Churches and Voter Registration." *Christian Century*, 20–27 June 1984.

"Why the Defeat? A Talk With Chief Civil Rights Lobbyist, Ralph Neas." *Women's*

*Political Times*, October 1984. Questions and answers about the October 1984 defeat of the Civil Rights Act in the U.S. Senate.

*Women 1984: A Year in Review.* Hudson, N.Y.: Education Fund; National Organization for Women Legal Defense, 1984.

Woodward, Kenneth L., and Eleanor Clift. "Playing Politics at Church." *Newsweek*, 9 July 1984.

Yankelovich, Skelly, and White, Inc. " Sex Stereotypes and Candidacy for High-Level Political Office." Polling data commissioned by the National Women's Political Caucus, February 1984.

# Popular Culture

*Katherine H. St. Clair*

In 1984, for the first time, a woman was nominated by a major party to run on a national ticket. Geraldine Ferraro stated in her concession speech that this fact alone changes the course of American history. Political campaigns have become media events and, as such, are part of a national dialogue in much the same way that an episode of "Dallas" or Shirley MacLaine's part in *Terms of Endearment* are active ingredients in conversations at the beauty parlor or the dinner table. Millions of television viewers across America witnessed Ferraro's speech and her televised image takes its place next to that of Joan Collins and Jane Curtin. Will her part in the campaign accelerate the changes we are already seeing in representations of women in television and other arenas of popular culture? Or was her appointment somehow a result of these changes?

Popular culture includes the most accessible of the arts—our major source of entertainment and information—television; the dominant cinema—movies playing at the mall; and romantic fiction—best-sellers in airports and bus stations. Popular culture is collective: every story is, finally, a mix of many people's craft and history. The original point of view envisioned by the writer is often molded, softened, or redirected to suit the expectations of a corporate group. Popular culture is sensational: the viewer/reader must cry, laugh, scream—participate. She must respond emotionally in some way or the effort is not a success, and the show is canceled. This feeling of connectedness is what makes popular culture so much a part of our daily lives and so powerful. Endlessly repeated images and formulas seep into a collective picture of what life should be like. We often speak of portrayed characters in the same way we might of our family or close friends. Our family simply becomes larger.

These representations or images, then, are highly influential. It makes a difference how certain groups appear. Since the first angry editorials against nickelodeon theaters in Chicago in 1907, the "effects" of the media have been examined and reexamined. How do these visual and other popular media create or reflect an image of women in our culture? Is what we see a reflection of a perceived reality or the creation of some sort of myth? A future historian or cultural anthropologist looking at artifacts of television, movies, and popular literature to achieve a deeper understanding of the relative status of men and women in the 1980's might come to some startling conclusions. All women over forty-five seem to have disappeared. Asian-American or lesbian women won't be seen at all.

Roles for women on television and film have changed many times and in many directions over the years and not always in a positive direction. We move from the moms of the fifties to the machisma women of the eighties. Any change is slow in coming in both the entertainment and publishing businesses. Since each new venture requires enormous sums of money, significant risks in content are unlikely. Those of us who are divorced, single, mothers, political, or ambitious are only beginning to see serious and careful representations of ourselves in the media.

## Television

Hawkeye:    Clamp, sponge. Margaret, will you please hand me these things on the beat?

Hotlips:    You are the one that's off.

Hawkeye:    Well, let's get together. Clamp, 2, 3, 4; sponge, 2, 3, 4.

Hotlips:    Why can't women lead?

—M*A*S*H, 1977

Prime time succeeds where Hollywood fails in creating stories that express the daily realities of women's lives. The content of several new evening shows deals directly with single parenting, working women, and personal relationships. The scripts convey a surprising understanding of the depth of these problems, not just a nod in their direction. What a difference from Lucy's attempts to manipulate Ricky into buying her a fur coat!

This is not to say that the networks have cured themselves of male chauvinism or that sexism has disappeared from television. There are still plenty of the "Charlie's Angel's" variety of leg-showing crime fighters. And sexism, after all, is alive and well in America. In order to deliver a large audience to the advertiser, producers take as few risks as possible in the creation of new programming. Television constantly imitates itself in the hope that what worked before will work again. It is the land of the commonplace. In *Demographic Vistas*, David Marc (1984) says that the goal of television is to be normal. The regular viewing of a favorite program is as much a ritual as a morning cup of coffee or a weekly bowling night. But there is a virtue in this ordinariness. It allows for incremental changes within the formula that gradually lead to significant changes in the depiction of women's lives. The standard familiar set remains; only the staircase has moved. While woman still appears in the age-old roles of housewife and mother, waitress and secretary, she can also be seen as lawyer, hard-working detective, or single mother.

"Kate and Allie" (CBS), starring Jane Curtin and Susan St. James, is a situation comedy set where situation comedies began—in the home. The key change in the formula is that there is no male head of household presiding over the escapades of his spacey wife and family; instead two divorced women share a home and raise their kids. Weekly episodes are concerned with the everyday problems of interfering ex-husbands and the enormous adjustment to being single and making a new life. The beauty of the show is largely in the familiarity of these situations. A new audience of women sees aspects of themselves represented on the screen. Finally we have an alternative to cop and doctor shows with the token wise woman. Kate and Allie are supportive of each other. They are honestly and openly caring. They are not working for men, scheming against men, or in competition for men. The comedy lies in the differences between the two women. Kate is livelier, more outspoken, and sexually more free. Allie liked living in Connecticut and wearing beige. She tends to resort to cooking fancy dinners when depressed.

In an effort to get on with her life, Allie decides to go back to school. She is filled with fears that she is too old, that her brain will no longer function. As expected she runs into a professor who confirms all her fears, telling her she is stupid, she doesn't need this education, she already has too many advantages. This is a straightforward depiction of the obstacles newly single women face everyday. Fortunately for Allie the dean of the college is also a divorced mother who understands her dilemma. Returning to school is threatening in many ways, not the least of which have to do with practice and time. Younger students are used to memorization. They can devote hours to studying, but mothers of sick children cannot. Many women could write scripts for this show—the women up there are us, maybe not in every way, but certainly in more ways than prime time has offered in the past.

A working relationship and friendship is the basis of "Cagney and Lacey" (CBS), another breakthrough prime-time series. Sharon Gless and Tyne Daley play two detectives who work as a very close team. Personal as well as work-related problems are the focus of each episode. Chris Cagney, independent and living on a trust fund, is unmarried and likes it that way. Occasionally, she has dinner with her alcoholic father, her only family. She is aggressive in her police work and ambitious. Marybeth Lacey, on the other hand, is married and has two sons. Hers is a working-class family with traditional attitudes and goals. Lacey, very professional and a good detective, is less vocal about her desires for advancement. The precinct office is the main location of the show. It contains all the expected ethnic mix of characters, wisecracks, and some of the visual "messiness" brought to us by "Hill Street Blues" (NBC). Most television strives to be not only "normal" but neat, with uncluttered stage sets and clear lines of vision. Stories are also neat, with tidy resolutions at the end of each episode. Problems must be resolved within the length of a show; endings cannot be ambivalent. Perhaps messiness is becoming normal as the nuclear family breaks down and old rules become irrelevant. Perhaps television is moving away from showing us life as it should be and toward showing us life as it is.

Cagney and Lacey are given assignments or take on emergencies as in most cop shows. The solving of the crime is, however, only one element in the evening's program: a parallel focus may be a personal problem of one of the pair, a difference of opinion on how to handle the case, or a problem with the department itself. This kind of emotional analysis is peculiar to women and to this show. The script gives as much weight to these more personal issues as to the crime at hand.

In a recent episode Chris Cagney is assigned to work with a detective who wants sexual favors from her. His power as a superior officer threatens her future advancement in the force if she refuses. She decides to risk pressing charges against the implicit advice of other male officers, who say it is the officer's word against hers. In the final scene the incidents are explained to her as personal misunderstandings and she is offered the guarantee of a good report if she lets it drop, but she continues in the suit. We know that this has as much to do with her own personal esteem as it does with the principle that other women have or will have to confront this particular officer or situation in the future. We know this partly from the script but as weekly viewers we also know it because we know her character. This is as close to a feminist consciousness as you'll see on the tube.

Chris and Marybeth deal with the virtues of marriage in an episode in which Chris decides to break her engagement. "Sex isn't even fun anymore," she says. In a wonderful scene, Dorey, the prospective fiancé, speaking from his male prerogative, suggests that he and Chris combine their incomes. She is resistant; she has been independent for too many years. Lacey, who has a good marriage and understands the value of a lifetime commitment to another person, is frustrated by Chris's ambivalence. But, according to Chris, it was the idea of marriage that changed the feelings in an otherwise positive relationship. In deciding to remain unmarried, Chris again feels strong. The two women struggle to understand each other's point of view on this important question. Two unusual things are happening here: an independent woman is deciding against marriage, but it is a difficult decision to make; two close friends are struggling with deeply felt differences and agree to disagree. These subtle ideas have not been popular prime-time themes.

One of the most noticeable qualities that the actresses involved in these two shows bring to their performances is that of understatedness. The extremes of sex-kitten cops or dithery housewives are gone. Instead, out of the sit-com and cop show format have grown scripts that acknowledge that women want to be taken seriously.

There are other working-woman roles in prime time. Joyce Davenport (Veronica Hamel) on "Hill Street Blues" is a serious public defender who has just gotten a job as assistant district attorney. Although her concerns seem to be related too often to her personal needs and/or her sex life, her role as a career women is generally a serious one. The people who work with her unquestionably respect her and look upon her as a hard worker. The same is true of Lucy Bates, the show's woman dectective. Both are strong characters, tough yet uncertain. But we are much less likely to see a full interchange and working out of a problem between women on this show because these two characters do not work together. The dynamic of the show sets the women in the context of what is basically a male environment. The question then is, do they remain true to themselves or to any feminist vision?

"Magruder and Loud" (ABC) is a more typical police show. Advertisements in *TV Guide* tell us that these detectives are "lovers by night and cops by day." Successfully mixing a romantic/sexual relationship with a daily working partnership has got to be one of the more difficult propositions of the twentieth century, but Magruder and Loud make it seem easy. The show is full of car chases and gun fights. Any real emotional quality brought to the relationship is due to Kathryn Harrold, who plays Jennie Loud. Her acting is very strong and subtle for a show in this genre.

"Remington Steele" (NBC) and "Scarecrow and Mrs. King" (CBS) also feature man/woman detective teams. The woman is usually the intuitive character, while the man takes care of the muscle. In "Remington Steele," a slick detective show, Laura Holt (Stefanie Zimbalist) looks beautiful, and wears fabulous clothes, and is very serious about her work. Steele, her debonair partner, is always trying to romance her away from the case at hand. "Scarecrow and Mrs. King" presents yet another variety of television fantasy. Mrs. King is a widow who lives with her mother and son; she has a secret life working with Scarecrow solving international crimes. On the surface, she is television's typical heroine. She has a nice house and family, above-average income, and attractive clothing. As can happen only on television, she periodically disappears from all this to parts unknown. The viewer is swept from the normal to the exotic in the space of a commercial. The women in these shows have a prefeminist identity. They are strong individuals, anxious to work, but the scripts leave them trapped in a male/female duality in which neither character can be anything but fantasy. Is this life as it should be?

In the evening soaps, such as "Dallas" (CBS) and "Dynasty" (ABC), the leading women are rich and powerful. They are the stuff of dreams and fantasy: they are beautiful, no matter how old they are, their wardrobes are outrageous and extensive; and they are scheming and use their power to selfish ends. They may represent a conservative woman's picture of women's liberation taken to its logical extreme. Excessive ambition leads to the evil embodied in Alexis Carrington (Joan Collins). Through these women we can explore fantasies of power, but deep inside we know that it is not right or good for women to lust for power, so these characters must be villainesses. All soap operas are labyrinthine fantasies of emotional relationships. The time span is endless and the locations are boundless; a recent episode of "General Hospital" (ABC) took place in the Peruvian Andes.

Traditionally, soaps have been the only shows that explored emotional relationships, but the angle has been more romantic than real. Series such as "Cagney and Lacey" and "Kate and Allie" allow for serious discussion of everyday emotional questions, the kinds of issues that recognize the viewer. Women are beginning to be released from patriarchal snares in these shows, and we can only hope that they represent new directions in television scriptwriting, at least in shows dealing with women. Their success will not allow them to be seen only as necessary tokens, but we cannot assume that all new shows will be as fresh. In "Sara" (NBC), a situation comedy that began in February 1985, the lead character is a woman lawyer, and the location is the office, but any hopes of another Cagney or Lacey died after the rest of the cast was revealed. In the San Francisco law firm, we have besides Sara, one black woman, one straight male, and one gay male. The jokes were terrible and self-serving from the start.

Women in top positions in moviemaking for television are beginning to make a creative difference in the final product. Barbara Corday, one of the creators of the television movie "Cagney and Lacey" from which the series was derived, is now president of Columbia Pictures Television; richer roles for women are now possible there. Jane Deknatal of HBO stressed, in an interview for *Working Woman* (Olson, 1984), that her company is interested in producing films that deal with very personal rather than broad social issues, the ordinary stories that have been ignored. Smaller budgets and shorter shooting schedules in all films for television tend to force out science fiction and adventure extravaganzas. These producers, then, appear to be in a good position to produce films that speak to women's lives. Roles for women have, however, only begun to change in films made for television. The change is most readily seen in films dealing with broad social issues.

The most startling of these was *The Burning Bed* (NBC) in which Farrah Fawcett portrayed a battered wife and mother of three. Both her performance and the stark reality of the script were surprising. The script was adapted from Faith McNulty's book detailing the true story of a woman who, after all other resources had failed her, finally burns her ex-husband in his bed. Shelters for battered women across the country reported offers of both help and donations after this film was aired. Battering, one of the most hidden crimes in our society, was brought into the open in this film. Other social-issue films have dealt with incest (*Something about Amelia*, ABC), teenage suicide (*Silence of the Heart*, CBS), and aging (*Heartsounds*, ABC). Several outstanding performances by women have included Glenda Jackson in *Sakharov* (HBO), Jane Fonda in *The Dollmaker* (ABC), and Cybil Shepard in *Secrets of a Married Man* (NBC). The results, however, support the argument that the best work is happening in regular network programming. Films made for television usually focus on exotic or surprising aspects of women's lives, but prime-time programming remains the only place where there seems to be some consistent change and growth.

## Movies

Typically, American film is a male medium even in style. Hollywood has always been a tough guys' town, and the films have reflected this in arrogant attitudes, high-speed chases, and sock-to-the-jaw conclusions. Women can be only adjuncts in this arena. The dream factory creates fantastic and exotic lives and adventures; women must be beautiful and mysterious. Because movie audiences, including women, are conditioned to fast action and moviemakers are tuned into the bottom line, they will continue to make films that meet these expectations. This style contrasts with a realistic presentation of women's lives and relationships. In the thirties and forties, many films dealt with women working. They were doctors (Kay Francis, *Doctor Monica*, 1934), restaurant owners (Joan Crawford, *Mildred Pierce*,

1945), and newspaper women (Rosalind Russell, *His Girl Friday*, 1940). More often than not they sacrificed family for their work. Although they remained unfulfilled or a man rescued them in the end, nevertheless, women as competent workers were central to the film. Women working and relationships between women are only beginning to return to the screen.

Jessica Lange's film, *Country*, is a politically motivated movie revealing the plight of America's small farmers. The film has been cited in many a talk show as instrumental in alerting urban dwellers to the problems of foreclosure facing these farmers. It went a lot further in this direction than did the evening news on inauguration day, when coverage of a farmer's demonstration in Minneapolis occupied about three minutes compared to the fifteen spent on the empty bleachers of the frozen-out festivities in Washington. But Lange's film gives us only a superficial treatment of the problem. It does not seem to take these farmers seriously. When the foreclosures were actually happening in 1982, the farmers were not submissive and suicidal as pictured here. Remember the tractor cavalcade in the streets of our nation's capitol? These people fought and demonstrated publicly to gain their ends. Producer Lange has given herself as the lead a mythical role—she is superwoman. She singlehandedly organizes the community of farmers, all the while cooking dinner and carrying a baby on her hip. Her husband (Sam Shepard) is a drunk and of no help at all. She is beautiful Jessica Lange—no makeup, eyes bright and direct, a symbol of strong, virtuous American womanhood who will hold the family and the country together. None of the other women comes close to her—not in looks (her one concession to some misguided vision of middle America is wearing curlers in her hair once at dinner), not in strength (she beats up her husband, the others sit in pickup trucks and cry), and certainly not in smarts. It is Lange who manages to grasp the figures involved in the foreclosure, not her husband or her father. She plays her own version of strong country virtues to the detriment of everyone else, particularly Sam Shepard. He gives up so quickly you wonder how he ever had the guts to run the farm in the first place.

*Swing Shift*, produced by and starring Goldie Hawn, neither displays its creator's talents nor tells us anything very important about women working during World War II. The film comes off as a bit of period fluff with lots of forties' ambience but none of the political realities. Women needed but were unable to find jobs both before the war began and after it was over. What we see here is a romp through the excitement of "exotic" factory work, a little sexual fling, and a glimpse of a growing friendship between Kay (Goldie Hawn) and Hazel (Christine Lahti). The potential of the film is the most staggering loss. Connie Field's excellent documentary film, *The Life and Times of Rosie the Riveter* (1980), revealed the realities of the period. Hawn, or perhaps Jonathan Demme, the director, had an opportunity to do the same with a narrative approach, but chose instead to give us a film that softens the real economic issues, avoids dealing with the potentially interesting relationship between Kay and Hazel, and gives us instead a nostalgia piece with a great part for Kurt Russell, who plays Kay's lover. Once again we are given, instead of a real bit of our history, more Hollywood pastiche.

Sally Field, whose popularity and reputation have grown since her days as the Flying Nun, has not based her image on glamor. The characters she has played in *Norma Rae, Absence of Malice,* and *Places in the Heart* seem to need star quality less than real acting or storytelling. She does not function on her own, nor is she the perfect problem solver. In both *Absence of Malice* and *Norma Rae,* Field plays a woman whose realization of her place in the system of a particular institution is the main focus of the film. Although there are feminist/political problems in both scripts, the films nevertheless present some important contradictions in the daily lives of working women.

*Norma Rae* takes place in a southern factory during an effort to unionize the workers. Field's character is at the heart of the organizing effort, and she is closely involved with the northern Jew, Ron Leibman, who is the union representative. Her house, children, and husband, Jeff Bridges, becomes less interesting to her as she becomes engrossed in the fulfilling work of organizing. She spends late hours working, to the point where her husband wants to know if she has slept with the union representative. Her answer is no but "he's in my head." This is possibly more dangerous.

The film unfolds slowly so that we can see the laundry building up, the poor meals the kids are getting. Field and Bridges do not rearrange household responsiblities to avoid this breakdown. When the situation becomes unbearable, she is forced to move out. Clearly, she is caught between her old traditional values and the new ones brought about by her organizing efforts. The beauty of the film is that it concentrates here on this conflict; it does not diffuse its energy by having her fall into bed with Ron Leibman or run away from home and family.

In *Absence of Malice,* Field, as an ambitious young woman reporter on a mid-sized city newspaper, is forced to play by a certain set of rules. As the film opens, she discovers that she has been left out of an important informational meeting concerning a new story. She reacts with anger and goes after the story herself. In her zeal, however, she makes some stupid mistakes and finds herself up against the U.S. Department of Justice. The film is important from a woman's point of view in that it addresses the issues of men's and women's working styles and the barriers that militate against success for working women. Since she is not allowed access to certain information, she must make inquiries on her own. She is dealing in an area deemed inappropriate for women. But if she wants to be taken seriously, she cannot avoid the traps. This approach may reap rewards in her professional life, but it gets her nowhere in her romantic life. She makes the first move in her relationship with Paul Newman and he resents it.

These are dilemmas that young professional women are facing today. Unfortunately, the script also calls for her to act extremely insensitively to other women and to enjoy a rough-and-tumble with Newman during which he angrily tears her clothing.

*Places in the Heart,* the second in what seems to be a trilogy of back-to-the-land movies for 1984, takes place in the small Texas town of Waxahatchee during the depression. Field plays the widow of a local sheriff who must try to hold onto her farm. She accomplishes this against the odds of surprisingly unscrupulous bankers and merchants and with the help of Moze (Danny Glover), a black farmhand who happens to be passing through at just the right time. Through hard work and a lot of free labor, Edna manages to get her cotton crop in on time. But, again, the film is historically misleading. Banks did foreclose on most farmers, resulting in the triumph of agribusiness. The film, ultimately optimistic, is simplistic and loaded with American/Christian cliches. Edna stands for church, family, and the land; it is a very personal view of the depression.

The tendency in Hollywood films is to deal with exotic stories and situations. These films about working women qualify because factory or farm or other repetitive physical work is exotic to the upscale audience for which the films are intended. Meryl Streep's *Silkwood* is another example. Within the major focus of the film, a discussion of the events leading to Karen Silkwood's death, we are given an almost documentary treatment of her daily life and the lives of her lover and roommate. The grueling conditions of the nuclear plant and the fear of the workers are achingly clear. Cher plays Streep's lesbian roommate with incredible sensitivity.

Lesbianism is seldom dealt with directly in the movies. Two exceptions, John Sayles's *Lianna* and Robert Towne's *Personal Best*, are worlds apart in treatment. Sayles's film explores several relationships, those of Lianna and her tense untenured professor husband, Lianna and her lover Ruth, and Lianna and her close friend. The problem with the movie is that Lianna arrives at her lesbianism almost too easily; Ruth is depicted stereotypically; and the lesbian love scenes seem to lack energy. We are really seeing a film about the difficulties of a bad middle-class marriage. But the film is far more realistic and honest than *Personal Best*, where the point of view of the camera*man* is all too clear. The women are objects in this film as they never are in Sayles's work. The love and competition between the two women is seen in a great variety of body shots. The lesbianism is seen as a rite of passage, with a male "rescue" as the conclusion.

Winner of three Academy awards in 1984, *Terms of Endearment* describes in detail the relationship between a mother and daughter, a relationship that hasn't been explored in a film since *Stella Dallas* in 1932. Emma (Debra Winger) and Aurora (Shirley MacLaine) are clearly each other's lifeline. The telephone connects them constantly whether they are living thousands of miles apart or in the same town. The connection between mothers and daughters is one of the most abiding and universal of relationships and therefore one of the most problematic. MacLaine and Winger show us in detail the painful process they go through to try to find each other. Working through this just may have been beyond the director's skill, however; so he avoids the need for a true resolution by having Emma die of cancer.

Neither Emma nor Aurora work outside the home, and the women who do are narcissistic and shallow. While visiting her friend Patsy (Lisa Hart Carroll) in New York City, Emma meets some career women who haven't the time for children. They talk of yeast infections, lousy lovers, and shrinks. Emma suddenly becomes Mother Earth, the standardbearer of all that is secure, Patsy's "anchor." Women and families are what's right in the world; women and careers are not. Isn't there some middle ground missing here? Most of us have built lives somewhere between complete sacrifice to our families and complete devotion to careers. It is interesting to speculate on the outcome of the story had Emma divorced her wandering husband instead of dying. Presumably she would have had to find some balance between family and career.

MacLaine's performance as a vivacious woman of fifty-five or so is extraordinary. Beyond an occasional made-for-television film about older people and Tillie Olsen's *Tell Me a Riddle*, there is, sadly, not much to compare it to. Aurora is conflicted; she is dependent; she is trying to make a life for herself outside of her children and grandchildren. The struggle is so real it often makes the viewer squirm.

The opener of the New York Film Festival for 1983, *The Big Chill*, received less than the boiling reception anticipated in the preopening publicity. The reunion of a group of sixties' college activists at the funeral of their friend Alex gives Laurence Kasden, the director, an opportunity to discuss what they've done with themselves since graduation. There are no stars. The film is a beautiful piece of ensemble acting, but that seems to be all that's left of a sixties sensibility. Meg (Mary Kay Place) has become a real estate lawyer. She gave up legal aid because she found her clients were not always the victims of societal injustices. She has also abandoned the idea of finding a husband so is looking to the men in this group of trusted friends to help her become a mother. Her performance is a joy, but her part is a caricature of the career woman racing the biological time clock. JoBeth Williams plays a dissatisfied bitchy wife of an advertising executive, out to rekindle the flame of an old college romance. Sarah (Glenn Close), the weekend's hostess, is a doctor. But the characters have nothing very interesting to say. The men go running and talk about business deals, while the women change their clothes or sit in the kitchen and discuss methods of birth control. This is another film of missed possibilities.

The life of Shirley Muldowney, top fuel car driver, as presented in *Heart Like a Wheel*, is an exotic one by most people's standards. Shirley Muldowney was the first woman to go 0 to 250 in sixty seconds. She succeeded in breaking down many of the sexist barriers on the tracks in her determination to race. Few women, however, have followed her lead. Muldowney's relationships with men, as pictured in the film, always came second to her career as a driver. Joe Muldowney, her husband, was instrumental in encouraging her at the beginning of her career but never earnestly believed that it was any more than a temporary infatuation. Connie Kaletta, her lover, another first-class driver, took over after she left Joe but turned out to be a womanizer. If she had women friends, the film does not present them. Bonnie Bedelia plays Muldowney as cool and strong. Her single-minded devotion to driving must have led to emptiness and some sadness in her life, but this we do not see. The film presents her as yet another mythical woman.

## Romance Novels

"To Bill, who said I could. With love, d.s." Dedication of
Danielle Steele's novel, *The Ring* (Dell, 1980).

The writing and reading of romance novels is serious business. Publishers' operating profits range from $10 to $15 million annually and $20 million is spent on advertising the product (Jennings 1984). The competition among publishers for good writers of happy-ending romances has escalated since 1957 when the Harlequin brand name was first introduced. What is the magnet-like draw of these stories? Why are they read and reread by millions of women? Contrary to assumptions, the audiences for these novels are just as likely to have a college education as not. Many are career women. The majority of readers, however, are women who live in rural or suburban areas and do not work outside the home. Many of the novels are set in a historical context and so offer information as well as momentary escape.

The value of these books has been questioned by many groups but especially by librarians. With shrinking budgets, the question of what types of reading to provide becomes more and more crucial. In Westville, Illinois, the public library has devoted an entire room to romances. The romance novel collection, now 4,000 titles, was largely donated by staff and patrons and is only minimally catalogued to save on processing costs. This decision has brought in scores of new library patrons. Other librarians and critics will argue that the poor writing and repressive politics of these novels far outweigh any educational benefit that may be derived. The novels are best left to the individual to purchase at the supermarket, airport, or paperback bookstore.

Like prime-time television, the plots of most romance novels follow a formula. For example, the heroine is virginal (in teen romances), or, hardened against men after the failure of her first romance/marriage through mental or physical battering, she has thrown herself into a career or vowed to remain single. She may be very successful in her chosen work, but aspirations and ambitions disappear as the romance takes hold. The hero appears in the first chapter—on page one if possible—with the woman being simultaneously intrigued and repulsed. He is eight or twelve years older than she, seasoned and somewhat cynical and moody. In the end he conquers her resistance with what are sometimes surprisingly violent sexual encounters, and they discover that they have loved each other all along. There is a strong sense of both sexual release and relief that she can relinquish responsibility for herself to this powerful male.

In *Reading the Romance* (1984), Janice Radway describes the act of reading romances as opposed to but at the same time supportive of male dominance. The time taken to read a novel removes a woman from daily chores and cultural expectations. She is patently not responding to the needs of those around her when immersed in romantic adventures. She is also making a connection between herself and millions of other feminine readers. One has only to pick up a recycled romance at a tag sale and note the list of initials on the inside to see the connections being made. The network creates its own common interest and common dialogue.

But these stories reinforce a strong patriarchal message. The man provides the woman with her key to happiness in the end. The hero's original bad behavior was misunderstood by the heroine and the reader. He has been transformed, presumably by her, into the perfect lover/provider. No other woman could have done this for him. Romances affirm the belief that marriage will satisfy all female needs. Marriage was what the heroine secretly wanted all the while she was protesting any involvement with the hero. There is no place for the woman who finds fulfillment in other ways. The stories reflect and reinforce the culture from which they grow. Issues of feminism, therefore, do not appear. Women are never troubled with unwanted pregnancies or abortions. The forceful taking of a woman by a man who truly loves her is a compliment. Rather than a stark indication of his power over her, it is taken as a testament to her real desirability. This obvious consequence of patriarchy characteristically goes unchallenged.

Contradictions arise when we realize that all romance novels are written by women. Are these writers further enslaving their sisters? Reading itself may be a small act of rebellion in the short run, but does the intent continue? Perhaps there is no need for a major expression if a minor one has been performed.

But the fact is that the women who are writing these stories have become more aware to themselves as a group. The Romance Writers Association was founded by a group in Texas in 1981. This organization has grown to involve romance writers, editors, and some readers on a national level in questions of contract negotiations and story content. Through the work of this and similar groups, writers now compose a strong bargaining unit. A combination of the power of these quasi unions as well as the changing demands of the audience has resulted in changes in some of the story elements as well. Recent stories involve women who are more independent and somewhat ambivalent about marriage. The major changes, however, seem to be in the area of sexuality. Women are now allowed to be, if not the aggressors, at least active participants in the sexual process. Tipsheets for new series include requests for long languorous sex scenes. Perhaps a somewhat liberated sexuality will lead to greater awakenings. Perhaps there will be changes in more important or at least more far-reaching areas as well.

As we have seen in television, film, and romance fiction, change takes place in glacial time so that even incremental adjustments are significant. The representation of women in all arenas of popular culture seems to be growing in a more positive direction. The picture of women in the media moves slowly toward a more serious and realistic one in a course parallel with the vision of society in general. Each area of popular culture discussed here seems to deal with this change in a slightly different way. We can see in "Kate and Allie," for instance, an impulse in television production to imitate reality in some of its more complicated aspects rather than molding it in a tidy pattern. Although women in films and romance novels are still rather exotic, some stories speak directly to the real problems women experience in work and in relationships. Movies such as *Country* and *Norma Rae* also explain aspects of larger societal problems that need to be addressed more often in popular culture. The hope is that these trends will grow stronger and that the women who are in positions of power within these industries will be inclined and able to speed the process.

## References

Jennings, Vivien Lee. 1984. The romance wars. *Publisher's Weekly* 226, no. 8 (24 August): 50–55.

Kael, Pauline. 1984. The current cinema. *New Yorker* 60 (1 October):108–13.

Kopkind, Andrew. 1984. Countrification. *Nation* 239, no. 13 (27 October):425–27.

Marc, David. 1984. *Demographic vistas: Television in American culture.* Philadelphia: University of Pennsylvania Press.

Olson, L. 1984. On the firing line. *Working Woman,* 9 (February):90–93.

Radway, Janice. 1984. *Reading the romance.* Chapel Hill: University of North Carolina Press.

Springer, Greg. 1983. Romance in Westville. *New York Times,* 30 March, sect. 3, p. 12.

## Romance Novels

Dailey, Janet. *Calder Born, Calder Bred.* New York: Pocket Books, 1983.

————. *Night Way.* New York: Pocket Books, 1981.

Kelrich, Victoria. *High Fashion.* New York: Richard Gallen Books, 1981.

Steele, Danielle. *The Ring.* New York: Dell, 1980.

Woodiwiss, Kathleen. *Ashes in the Wind.* New York: Avon Books, 1979.

## Television Shows

"Cagney and Lacey," CBS, with Sharon Gless and Tyne Daley.

"Kate and Allie," CBS, with Jane Curtin and Susan St. James.

"Scarecrow and Mrs. King," CBS, with Kate Jackson and Bruce Boxleitner.

"Remington Steele," CBS, with Stephanie Zimbalist and Pierce Brosnan.

"Dallas," CBS, with Linda Gray and Victoria Principal.

"Hill Street Blues," NBC, with Veronica Hamel and Daniel Travanti.

"Sara," NBC, with Geena Davis.

"Magruder and Loud," ABC, with Kathryn Harrold.

"Dynasty," ABC, with Joan Collins and Linda Evans.

## Films

*Absence of Malice.* 1981. Written by Kurt Luedtke, directed by Sydney Pollack. With Sally Field and Paul Newman.

*The Big Chill.* 1983. Written and directed by Laurence Kasden. With Glenn Close, Mary Kay Place, Jeff Goldblum, JoBeth Williams, and William Hurt.

*Country.* 1984. Written by William Witliff, directed by Richard Pearce. With Jessica Lange and Sam Shepard.

*Heart Like a Wheel.* 1983. Written by Ken Friedman, directed by Jonathan Kaplan. With Bonnie Bedelia and Beau Bridges.

*The Life and Times of Rosie the Riveter*. 1980. Produced and directed by Connie Field.

*Lianna*. 1983. Written and directed by John Sayles. With Linda Griffiths.

*Norma Rae*. 1979. Written by Irving Ravetch, directed by Martin Ritt. With Sally Field and Harriet Frank.

*Personal Best*. 1983. Written and directed by Robert Towne. With Mariel Hemingway and Patrice Donnelly.

*Places in the Heart*. 1984. Written and directed by Robert Benton. With Sally Field.

*Silkwood*. 1982. Written by Nora Ephron, directed by Mike Nichols. With Meryl Streep, Cher, and Kurt Russell.

*Swing Shift*. 1984. Written by Rob Morton, directed by Jonathan Denme. With Goldie Hawn, Kurt Russell, and Christine Lahti.

*Terms of Endearment*. 1984. Written and directed by James Brooks. With Shirley MacLaine, Debra Winger, and Jack Nicholson.

## Additional Films

*Doctor Monica*. 1934. Written by Charles Kenyon, directed by William Keighley. With Kay Francis and Warren William.

*Mildred Pierce*. 1945. Written by Ronald MacDougall, directed by Michael Curtiz. With Joan Crawford and Zachary Scott.

*His Girl Friday*. 1940. Written by Ben Hecht, directed by Howard Hawks. With Rosalind Russell and Cary Grant.

*Stella Dallas*. 1932. Written by Victor Herman, directed by King Vidor. With Barbara Stanwyck and Anne Shirley.

*Tell Me a Riddle*. 1980. Written by Joyce Eliason, directed by Lee Grant. With Lila Kedrova and Melvyn Douglas.

## Bibliography

Cassata, Mary B. *Life on Daytime Television: Tuning-in American Serial Drama*. Norwood, N.J.: Ablex Publishing, 1983.

Dowell, Pat. "Ladies Night." *American Film* 10, no. 4 (January-February 1985):44–49.

Ehrenreich, Barbara, and Jane O'Reilly. "No Jiggles, No Scheming: Just Women as Friends." *TV Guide*, 24–30 November 1984, 6–10.

Gitlin, Tod. *Inside Prime Time*. New York: Pantheon Press, 1983.

Hoberman, Jim. "In Defense of Pop Culture: Life and Death in the American Supermarketplace." *Voice Literary Supplement*, November 1982, 1, 10–22; *Village Voice*, 12 November 1982.

Kaplan, E. Ann. *Woman and Film: Both Sides of the Camera*. New York: Methuen, 1983.

Meehan, Diana. *Ladies of the Evening*. Metuchen, N.J.: Scarecrow, 1983.

Schickel, Richard. "Something Is Missing in Hollywood." *Esquire*, June 1984, 119–24.

# Psychology
## Women, Work, and Stress: Another Look

### Rosalind C. Barnett

The question of women's proper social role continues to draw attention. The voices of politicians have recently been added to those of social scientists, mental health workers, and religious leaders. More specifically, the question usually addresses the consequences of women's assumption of the role of paid employee. We are all familiar with the dire warnings: as a result of adding on the role of paid employee, women, especially married women with children, will turn themselves into nervous wrecks and will drag their children and husbands with them into a state of familial disharmony, disaffection, and mental illness.

This chapter attempts to draw together research findings that bear directly on the actual relationship among women, work, and stress. I will discuss the major theories and related paradigms underlying research on women and work. My intention is to discuss the findings and highlight the biases inherent in these theories and to point out how knowledge about women and work has been shaped by these biases. My focus will be on the paradigm guiding mainstream research on the relationship between paid work and stress, specifically research on the effects of multiple role involvement.

By convention three roles are implied in research on women, namely, wife, mother, and paid worker. Two major and conflicting hypotheses have been put forward concerning the effects of occupying multiple roles. The first, referred to as the *scarcity hypothesis* (Marks 1977), was put forth by the sociologist Goode (1960) and extended by Coser (1974), Slater (1963), and others. This information rests on two premises: (1) that individuals have a

Based on a paper presented to the Project on Women and Social Change, Smith College, Northampton, Mass., June 1984.

limited amount of energy, and (2) that social organizations are greedy, demanding all of an individual's allegiance. Goode concluded that an individual's total role obligations are overly demanding, making role strain normal. According to the scarcity model of human energy, people do not have enough energy to fulfill their role obligations; thus compromises are required. Hence, the more roles one accumulates, the greater the probability of exhausting one's supply of time and energy and of confronting conflicting obligations. The scarcity hypothesis implies that role overload and role conflict are typically associated with psychological distress and symptomatology.

Role overload is defined as having so many demands related to one's role(s) that satisfactory performance is improbable. Role conflict arises when the demands from two or more roles are such that adequate performance of one role jeopardizes adequate performance of the other(s).

The scarcity hypothesis was challenged when Gove and Tudor (1973) suggested that men experience fewer symptoms of psychiatric dysfunction than do women because they are committed simultaneously to work and family roles; that is, multiple role involvement was viewed as *enhancing* well-being. A second formulation thus emerged in the mid-1970s that focused on the net positive gains to be had from multiple roles. The major theorists of this revisionist *expansion hypothesis*, Marks (1977) and Sieber (1974), emphasized the privileges rather than the obligations that accrue to role incumbents.

This revisionist view is supported by the work of researchers from several disciplines (Crosby 1983; Epstein 1983; Thoits 1983; Verbrugge 1982). Thoits reports a positive association between the number of roles a person (woman or man) occupies and psychological well-being. In analyses of within-sex differences in women's physical health, Verbrugge (1983) concluded that occupancy of numerous roles was related positively and monotonically to physical health for men as well as women.

Since the 1970's, the expansion hypothesis has been predominant in the research literature. However, with the massive entry of women into the paid labor force, there has been a resurgence of interest, in both the research literature and in the popular press, in the scarcity theory. The assumption is that, for women, employment is the added-on role, the catalyst for feelings of role overload and role conflict, and hence of psychological distress and decrements in well-being. Studies were published indicating that full-time workers experienced more feelings of time pressure than either part-time workers or homemakers. The implication was that women, especially married women with children, who took on paid employment, would necessarily be stressed. A further implication was that not only they but their families would suffer. Such women, the theory suggests, will be overloaded, conflicted, and anxious. Their irritability will distress their families, and the chances for serious family health problems will increase. If married employed women with children experience symptoms of stress, it must be their jobs that are responsible.

It is important to note that many studies supporting this view were not designed to test the assumption that paid work was the stressful role. For example, studies indicating that full-time female workers experienced more feelings of time pressure were interpreted to mean that those feelings were indicators of stress and therefore negative and were caused by the paid employee role. It was left to later researchers to assess more adequately the degree to which full-time female employees were suffering from the negative effects of stress predicted by this theory. Jumping ahead slightly, the results of more unbiased research indicate that while feeling harried, full-time employees are more satisfied and less stressed, and prefer their life style more than do other women.

Like the scarcity hypothesis, the expansion hypothesis also focuses on number of roles. Unlike the scarcity hypothesis, however, the expansion hypothesis predicts not greater role strain as the individual accumulates roles but less psychological distress. That is, the consequences for well-being are positive. Until recently, few predictions were made from the expansion hypothesis to women. The hold of the scarcity hypothesis was tenacious.

That one has difficulty extending these theories to women should not be too surprising. The basic theoretical work was formulated with men in mind and with traditional organizations as the setting in which the paid worker role was enacted. To illustrate, the senior vice president of a company may have responsibility for many aspects of the organization. However, his power in the organization permits him to delegate onerous tasks and, thereby, derive a net gain in terms of rewards, monetary and psychological.

Women's occupations as paid workers tend to have low social value and an excess of obligations over privileges; hence, they may not fit the model implicit in theories of multiple roles. Moreover, women's traditional social roles of wife and mother do not fit easily into these theories. Many married mothers who enter the labor force find themselves in low-status jobs that do not permit the kinds of tradeoffs that accompany higher prestige occupations. Further, such women often cannot trade off obligations associated with the roles of wife and mother, since in our culture failure to perform these duties is often associated with guilt and role partners are not usually willing to make the required trades.

Another major gap in both approaches is that neither hypothesis specifically differentiates among various social roles. Yet whether occupancy of a role will result in an excess of privileges over obligations and in increased status and self-esteem clearly depends upon the role and role combination in question. Specifically, for women the role of paid worker may differ from that of wife or mother in the patterning of privileges and obligations. Moreover, the combination of paid worker and mother may differ from that of wife and mother in the particular package of possibilities for status, role bargaining, tradeoffs, and negotiating for accumulations of privileges. Research in this area is in its infancy (Long and Porter 1984).

Before discussing the data on women and multiple roles, I would like to highlight the view of workplace roles that derives both from the scarcity hypothesis and from another body of research and theory that is important for understanding the direction that research on women and work is taking. Within the scarcity hypothesis, workplace roles are viewed solely as stressors. Little attention has been paid to work as a source of positive feelings, as an arena in which people can experience challenge, achievement, and heightened self-esteem. Few studies investigate the rewarding aspects of workplace roles; yet recent evidence suggests that for women holding a paid job, almost any paid job, is associated with positive feelings of well-being. Future research on women and work must examine the positive, that is, health-enhancing, effects of work, as well as the negative or distressing effects.

The treatment of work as exclusively stressful is especially strong when it comes to thinking about women. A similar view of the negative effects of workplace roles on women emerges from the enormous body of research on stress and coronary heart disease. Drs. Friedman and Rosenman, two cardiologists whose book, *Type A Behavior and Your Heart* (1974), popularized the serious study of the negative effects of stress on health, predicted that Caucasian women would lose their survival advantage over men as they entered the labor market. According to them, women too would begin to fall victim to coronary heart disease and other stress-related illnesses. They viewed women as less vulnerable to coronary heart disease because at that time comparatively few females were "as completely immersed as males in the contemporary economic and professional milieu that nourishes the development of Type A Behavior Pattern." They went on to say, "Most American women, at least in the immediate past, have remained in their homes, and although they have had many chores to do, relatively few were constrained to work under conditions whose essence consisted of deadlines and competition and hostility. The mother of growing children, of course, does suffer many anxieties, but the effects are clearly less pernicious." Unfortunately, Drs. Friedman and Rosenman were unable to test their own predictions, because the large-scale prospective study they designed included approximately 3,500 men and no women.

In addition to treating the workplace as exclusively stressful, this quotation reflects a second major bias that permeates this literature: namely, that home is a haven, for women and for men. In studies of men and stress, inquiries are never made about home life. Married male employees are considered more desirable than their unmarried counterparts because of the presumed stabilizing effects of marital and parental roles on men. I'll say more about this bias later.

Based on the assumption that the workplace is the setting that nourishes the Type A behavior pattern, which is related to the development of coronary heart disease, a massive endeavor was undertaken and continues today to determine which aspects of workplace roles are the most problematic. Briefly, the initial assumptions of Rosenman and Friedman, that job conditions reflecting time pressure and urgency are the villains and that high-level executives are the primary victims, have been challenged. Although this group may be the most likely to describe their jobs as stressful, men (and perhaps women) in such occupations are not as likely to develop symptoms of stress as are men in much less responsible positions. Recent studies in this country and abroad provide strong evidence that two conditions of work are consistently related to symptoms of diseases associated with stress. These conditions are (1) having many demands, and (2) having little authority. Thus the doctor who is under constant pressure because of heavy demands but who has the authority to make decisions will experience less stress than the nurse who works under similar demands but has little authority. Figure 1 is a graphic presentation of occupations distributed along these two dimensions.

This particular combination of job conditions characterizes many of the jobs that women occupy. It is important to note that these two stressful job conditions also characterize women's nonworkplace roles. Having too many demands is a primary occupational hazard in the job of mother. Simultaneously wives and mothers experience as much stress over negative events that happen to those close to them as they do when negative events occur to them personally. When other's behaviors, which are by definition out of one's control, have a profound effect on someone's well-being, that person, according to this model, has a very stressful job.

The scarcity hypothesis concerning multiple role involvement and the paradigm underlying research on stress and coronary heart disease together constitute the underpinnings of research on women and work. These traditions converge in several key respects; both assume that women are by nature wives and mothers and that when they add on the role of paid worker, they pay with distress and negative well-being. It is important to note that these research traditions also perpetuate a narrow one-dimensional

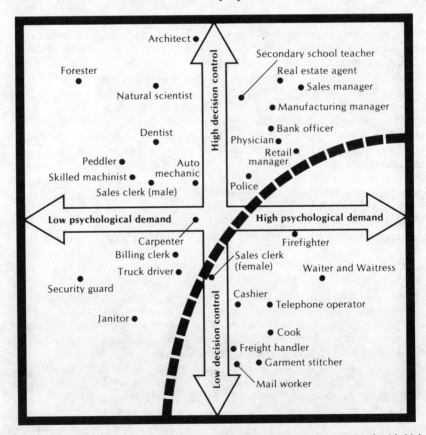

Figure 1. Distribution of male occupations on two job characteristics associated with high risk of coronary heart disease.

*Source:* Columbia University Department of Industrial Engineering and Operations Research.

view of men: men as workers. The mainstream literature on stress focuses on men at work; that they also function as husbands and as fathers is, with few exceptions, ignored. The idea that performance in one role affects performance in others is also ignored, with few exceptions. Clearly, future research paradigms need to include positive aspects of work place roles and both positive and negative aspects of nonworkplace roles.

In the remainder of this chapter, I will review the major findings regarding the effects of multiple role involvement, in general, and of occupancy of the paid worker role, in particular, on women's well-being. Given the negative bias in this literature, my comments will focus on the questions of whether multiple roles are related to distress or to well-being and whether work per se is a source of stress or a source of well-being. I will also review some of the literature that explores the relationship between women's several social roles and their experience of well-being and stress.

Recent findings are in unanimous agreement that, in contrast to the predictions of the scarcity hypothesis, the more roles a person occupies the better her or his mental and physical health. Moreover, this linear, monotonic relationship holds for as many as eight roles, the maximum number so far studied (Thoits 1983; Verbrugge, 1983, 1984). Thus roles on balance seem to add to or enrich a person's feelings of well-being.

What aspects of the paid employee role contribute to well-being for women? A beginning answer to that question comes from a study (funded by the National Science Foundation) I recently completed with my colleague Grace Baruch (Baruch, Barnett, and Rivers 1984). Its aim was to understand psychological well-being among Caucasian women thirty-five to fifty-five years of age. The sample consisted of 238 women who represented four family statuses and two employment statuses. The design allowed us to explore, among other things, the relationship between occupancy in each of three social roles (wife, mother, and paid employee) and the experience of well-being. Moreover, we were able to examine which aspects of particular roles were related to well-being.

To understand well-being, we asked the women in our study about several aspects of their personalities, including their self-esteem, the degree to which they felt they had control over the events that happened to them, the frequency with which they complained of symptoms of anxiety and depression, their overall satisfaction with life, their optimism about the future, and their level of happiness.

When all the interviews were completed, we put the results of these individual measurements together statistically. Our results indicate that there are two major dimensions of well-being, which we call Mastery and Pleasure. Mastery refers to coping well and being free of symptoms. Women who have high scores on Mastery are positive about themselves, they have high self-esteem, and they believe that the actions they take today can change their futures in positive ways. Pleasure refers to the emotional tone of a women's life. Women who are high in Pleasure describe themselves as satisfied, happy, and optimistic about the future.

Our next research question concerned how women who were in different social roles scored on these two dimensions. In other words, did scores on Mastery and Pleasure differ among women who were married or not, employed or not, or mothers or not? Figure 2 shows how the six groups of women in the study scored on Mastery. All four groups of employed women scored higher on Mastery than did the two groups of non-employed women. In fact, paid employment status was the single best predictor of Mastery. This positive effect was for the most part independent of the occupational prestige of the job. In other words, if one wants to know something about a woman's feelings of Mastery and can ask only one question, the question should be: does she hold a paid job?

Although the figure also shows how the six groups scored on the Pleasure dimension, which is related to the emotional side of a woman's life, I will concentrate here on the Mastery dimension, because women's feelings of competence and well-being and their relation to paid employment have been so neglected in research.

In addition to knowing that a woman is employed, one needs to know about the *quality* of her experience at work to gauge her feelings of Mastery. Interestingly, recent work (Verbrugge 1984) suggests that a subjective report of satisfaction with one's roles, particularly the work role, is a main predictor of physical health status. As we defined it, quality of experience at work was the difference between the degree to which a woman felt rewarded at her job and the degree to which she was distressed about aspects of her job. How did we know which aspects of a job women found reward-

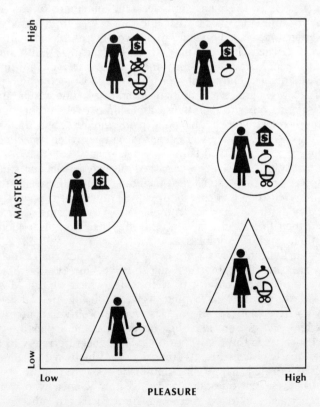

Figure 2.   Distribution of six groups of women on mastery and pleasure.

ing and which they found distressing? Rather than assuming that items used to assess men's work experience were automatically relevant to women, we did a preliminary interview study designed to have women tell us in their own words about the positive and negative aspects of their current jobs. Working from these interviews, we developed scales that reflected the most frequently mentioned rewarding and problematic aspects of women's work. These scales were administered to the women in the main study.

A few of the rewarding items women mentioned that never appear on measures used in studies on men were "the hours fit my needs"; "getting out of the house"; and "helping others / being needed." Items that women mentioned as problematic and that, again, never appear on scales used with male employees included "problems due to your being a women" and "having to do things that shouldn't be part of your job."

A positive quality of experience at work does not require the absence of problems. It merely requires that the rewards outweigh the concerns. It is useful to think of quality of experience much as one would think of balancing a checkbook. The balance is positive as long as deposits outweigh withdrawals.

Each employed woman in the study was asked to tell us how rewarding each of nineteen aspects of work were to her. She also indicated how concerned she was about nineteen problematic aspects of work. For each employed woman, we computed a quality-of-experience, or balance, score; having a positive balance score was related to feelings of Mastery. In other words, women who on balance experienced their jobs as rewarding also experienced heightened levels of Mastery.

We then asked whether the nineteen rewarding and nineteen problematic aspects of work formed any patterns that might be useful to us in understanding specifically what it was about work that had the potential for enhancing women's feelings of well-being.

As can be seen in Figure 3, the rewarding items formed two clusters; that is, a woman who found an item in a cluster to be rewarding was also likely to experience the other items in that cluster as rewarding. The first cluster, called Challenge, concerns opportunities for advancement and learning. Scores on this cluster are strongly related to feelings of Mastery. In other words, among employed women, those who experience a great

## CHALLENGE
The job offers challenge and stimulation
There is a variety of tasks
There is an opportunity for learning
The job fits your skills
You get a chance to make decisions

## SOCIAL RELATIONSHIPS
Liking the people you work with
Liking the boss
Being able to help people and interrelate with them

Figure 3. Work concern clusters.

deal of reward from the challenging aspects of their current jobs also experience heightened well-being.

Women in jobs at all levels of occupational prestige found challenge an important part of their work. I'd like to share with you some comments made by a forty-two-year-old woman, whom we've called Esther. Esther has been a self-employed free-lance typist for thirteen years. While some people might think of her work as tedious, she finds it a great source of self-esteem and an opportunity to grow. She said:

> I love it. It's very interesting. I'm getting an education. I type all kinds of journals; I typed a whole study on economic conditions in India. And then I typed all these other books and doctoral theses and it's very gratifying because, when I looked at the list of graduate student theses at the university, there were thirty-six, and I typed twelve. That's a third. I do résumés and these hard statistical tables with numbers and it's very challenging. Out of everything I do in my whole life—I always say I can do very little—but I know I do one thing very well, and that's type.

The second cluster, Social Relationships, was unrelated to the sense of Mastery. A woman may enjoy her coworkers and her boss, but that enjoyment is not reflected in her sense of well-being. Stated differently, an employed woman who wants to improve her feelings of self-esteem and mastery at work will have greater payoffs if she concentrates on the amount of challenge she has in her job and not on the quality of her relationships with her fellow workers.

Thus, work, and certain aspects of work in particular, can enhance a woman's sense of well-being. It is also true that certain aspects of work can detract from feelings of well-being. Figure 4 shows the clusters of problematic aspects.

## DULL JOB
There is little challenge
The work is dull and monotonous
The job doesn't fit your skills

## DEAD END
Little chance for advancement in the organization
Lack of recognition
Poor opportunities for professional development
Inadequate pay

Figure 4.

Both the dull-job and dead-end clusters were strongly associated with diminished feelings of well-being. Here we can see that a woman's well-being can suffer if she is not challenged enough. In other words, too few demands and too few challenges can be experienced as stressful. Women thrive when they are challenged and suffer when they are not.

Having demonstrated that work often contributes to women's well-being, we are ready to address the second question, namely, how do women's roles interact?

There is amazingly little recognition that conditions outside the workplace may affect a woman's experience in the workplace. This tunnel vision has two sources. First, studies of men and work focus exclusively on the workplace, and there has been a tendency to apply the same focus to studies of women. Second, for women, the roles of wife and mother are assumed to be natural, that is, performed without negative consequences; therefore, those roles have been virtually ignored in research on work and stress. Researchers have tended to treat women as if their lives before nine and after five did not exist, as if the boundaries between their work and nonworkplace roles were made of concrete. Events at home are ignored, treated as if they do not permeate the awareness of women at work. Similarly, events at work are treated as if they are locked securely behind iron doors when a woman leaves work to return home. I doubt that those rigid role boundaries exist for men; I know that they do not exist for women.

Common sense, our own experiences as women, and a small but growing body of research suggest that to understand women's (and perhaps, men's) experience at work it is absolutely necessary to take into account events in their lives outside the workplace. Research aside, the widespread assumption is that for women, in addition to the negative additive effects of multiple roles, there is a negative interactive effect. For example, the negative effects of the paid employee role are assumed to be heightened for women who are simultaneously wives and mothers. There are two glaring omissions in this literature. First, no attention whatsoever is paid to the positive aspects of combining roles. Rarely is the following question considered—what are the positive aspects of combining the roles of mother and paid worker? Second, for men, when there is acknowledgment of the interaction of roles, it is assumed that workplace roles impinge negatively on nonworkplace roles: the harried executive has less time to spend with his wife and children. Never examined is the possible negative or positive effect of men's family roles on their workplace roles. However, when a woman experiences a divorce or has a sick child at home, it is assumed that the experience will have a negative effect on her performance of her workplace role. However, several recent studies (Bersoff and Crosby 1984; Crosby 1983; Gove and Zeiss, forthcoming) suggest that satisfaction with work is closely related to one's home life for both men and women. Clearly the paradigm for future research needs to reflect the fact that men and women function in workplace and nonworkplace roles, and that these two sets of roles impact on each other.

To illustrate some of the interactive effects of workplace and nonworkplace roles for women, let me share with you some of the findings of a major on-going study, conducted in Framingham, Mass., on factors related to the development of coronary heart disease. The sample includes approximately 1,300 adults, 387 of whom are employed women. At the beginning of the study all the subjects were free of symptoms of coronary heart disease. After the first ten years it was possible to tease out the factors that differentiated those subjects who developed health problems from those who did not (Haynes and Feinleib 1982). Among the working women, the group highest in risk for developing coronary heart disease (CHD) was that of clerical workers, but not *all* clerical workers were high in risk. The vulnerable group was clerical workers who were married and had children, as is shown in Figure 5. Further, among married clerical workers with children, those who had blue-collar husbands were three times more likely to develop CHD than were non-clerical worker mothers with white-collar husbands, as is shown graphically in Figure 6. Mothers married to white-collar workers and performing clerical work were at no special risk of developing CHD. And the incidence rates of CHD among non–clerical worker mothers were not affected by the husband's occupation.

How can we understand these results? One interpretation is that a woman who has a demanding clerical job, a job that has little decision-making authority, and who is married to a man who has stereotyped views of women's and men's roles may experience lack of authority and excessive demands at home as well as at work. Having children and a hostile boss may add to the demands she experiences and underscore her lack of authority in dealing with them. One intriguing question raised by this study is the possibility that a woman's roles at home may be the major contributor to her sense of being stressed.

The conclusion that women's experience of stress cannot be understood by looking solely at the workplace is supported by another study that my colleague Grace Baruch and I recently completed on the sample that I described earlier (Barnett and Baruch, 1985). As you may remember there were four groups of employed women. With respect to their nonworkplace roles, some were neither married nor had children, others occupied both roles, that of wife and that of mother, and two groups occupied one non-workplace role. The divorced women were mothers; the married childless women were wives. The nonemployed women were all married; one group had children, and the other was childless.

We inquired into the women's experience of anxiety as well as two forms of role strain. The women in the study indicated the degree to which they felt that the things they had to do added up to being too much—an indication of their sense of being overloaded. They also reported on how often they felt they had to juggle things—an indicator of role conflict. Finally, they completed a form inquiring about the frequency with which they experienced several symptoms of anxiety. Our research question concerned which of the roles that women typically occupy was related to their experience of role strain and stress as measured by their scores on the three indices. Surprisingly, the experience of role strain and stress, as measured by any of the three indicators, was unrelated to whether a woman was employed or not. In other words, employed and nonemployed women were indistinguishable with respect to the level of role strain and stress they reported. However, mothers were higher than nonmothers on both forms of role strain. Mothers, regardless of whether they were married or not, or employed or not, experienced higher levels of role overload and role conflict than did nonmothers. Thus, being responsible for a dependent child appears to be uniquely stressful for women. Symptoms of anxiety were reported more frequently among married than among nonmarried women, regardless of employment or parental status. However, as we'll see later, for married mothers, the experience of anxiety was also related to the quality of their relationship with their children.

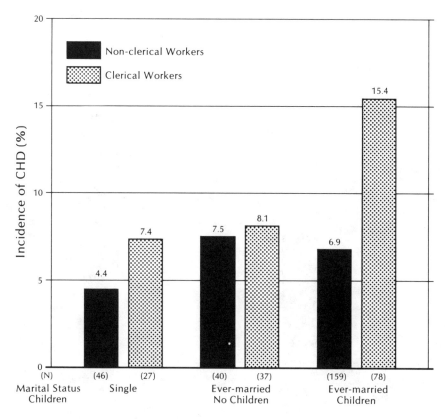

Figure 5.   Relationship between occupation, marital status, parental status, and incidence of coronary heart disease.
*Source:* Haynes and Feinleib, 1982.

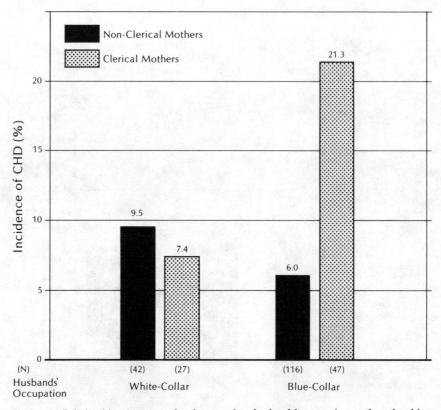

Figure 6. Relationships among mothers' occupation, husbands' occupation, and mothers' incidence of coronary heart disease.

*Source*: Haynes and Feinleib, 1982

A nonemployed mother in our study said this about the pace of her days:

> My day is fairly frantic. There are a couple of hours a day where there are household things to do—folding laundry and such. I spend a tremendous amount of time in children's activities, which is to say, driving them. I think that's the suburban life. I spend a lot of time in a station wagon driving children to activities of all kinds and to Camp Fire girls—when I'm not a troop leader—and violin lessons and swimming, and it's endless. I drop them and do shopping errands, dry cleaning. I'm very involved in activities of the college I attended, and go to numbers of meetings. I'm active in town politics, and we go out socially once or twice a week. It's such a busy life. There are always a million chores. I never do get things finished, there's never a sense of completion about anything.

Other findings from this study suggest that in addition to the strain and stress experienced by having children, the quality of a woman's relationship with her children further affects her experience of role strain and stress. Having a conflicted relationship with her child adds to the stress she experiences, whereas having a rewarding experience reduces the stress associated with being a mother. Thus, it appears that being a mother is the primary source of stress in women's lives. When women feel stressed, then, rather than focusing on the workplace as the source of that stress, it might be well to look at what is happening with their children. It follows that stress reduction should include strategies for managing children, getting assistance with child care, perhaps from husbands, and so forth.

Another interesting finding from the same study suggests that having a rewarding experience at work can actually reduce the stress experienced in the role of mother. One possible interpretation of this finding is that work has a beneficial effect on women at least in part by setting limits around the demands imposed by children.

What have we learned? First, certain work conditions, especially having too many demands and too little authority, are associated with the development of stress-related illnesses. Second, these illness outcomes are more likely to emerge among women who are also experiencing stress at home, especially the stress of rearing children and having a nonsupportive husband. Thus, to understand women's experience of stress at work, one must take into account the whole context of a woman's life. Although it may be possible to reduce a woman's stress by altering certain conditions at work, it might also be possible to reduce her stress by focusing on her nonworkplace roles. Biases in this area of study have caused us to neglect what appears to be women's major source of stress, namely, their supposed natural role, that of mother.

In addition, there is evidence to suggest that women who have a sense of mastery and self-esteem are less likely to experience stress when problems arise in their lives. In other words, women with a sense of mastery are less vulnerable to stress than are women whose sense of mastery is diminished.

Thus, for women, work can be both a source of stress and a source of reward. Certain aspects of work, especially work that is perceived to be challenging, enhance a woman's sense of mastery and can offset some of the stress associated with the role of mother. On the other hand, when the demands of a woman's job are excessive and her control over decision making is negligible, work can be stressful. Further, the absence of challenge and opportunity for growth in one's job is also stressful. How work is experienced depends both on particular aspects of the job and on the other circumstances of a woman's life. If a woman is married, her husband's attitudes and whether she has children affect her vulnerability to stress at the workplace. Thus, women's roles interact in producing stress or well-being, and future research paradigms need to take into account the whole of a woman's life if the role of work is to be adequately understood.

## References

Baruch, G.K., R.C. Barnett, and C. Rivers. 1984. *Lifeprints: New patterns of love and work for today's women*. New York: New American Library.

Barnett, R.C., and G.K. Baruch. 1985. Women's involvement in multiple roles, role strain, and psychological distress. *Journal of Personality and Social Psychology* 49:135–45.

Bersoff, D., and F. Crosby. 1984. Job satisfaction and family status. *Personality and Social Psychology Bulletin* 10:79–83.

Crosby, F. 1983. Work satisfaction and domestic life. In *Managing work and home life*, edited by M.D. Lee and R.N. Kanungo. New York: Praeger.

Coser, L. (with R. Coser). 1974. *Greedy institutions*. New York: Free Press.

Epstein, C. 1983. The new total woman. *Working Woman*, April, 100–103.

Friedman, M., and R.H. Rosenman. 1974. *Type A behavior and your heart*. New York: Knopf.

Goode, W.J. 1960. A theory of strain. *American Sociological Review* 25:483–96.

Gove, W.R., and J. Tudor. 1973. Adult sex roles and mental illness. *American Journal of Sociology* 78:812–35.

Gove, Walter, and Carol Zeiss. Forthcoming. Multiple roles and mental health. In *Modern woman managing the dual role*, edited by F. Crosby. New Haven: Yale University Press.

Haynes. S.G., and M. Feinleib. 1982. Women, work, and coronary heart disease: Results from the Framingham 10–year follow–up study. In *Women: A developmental perspective*, edited by P. Berman and E. Ramey. NIH Publication no. 82–2298. Washington, D.C.: U.S. Government Printing Office.

Long J., and K.L. Porter. 1984. Multiple roles of midlife women: A case for new directions in theory, research, and policy. In *Women in midlife*, edited by G. Baruch and J. Brooks-Gunn. New York: Plenum.

Marks, S.R. 1977. Multiple roles and role strain: Some notes on human energy, time, and commitment. *American Sociological Review* 39:567–78.

Sieber, S.D. 1974. Toward a theory of role accumulation. *American Sociological Review* 39:567–78.

Slater, P. 1963. On social regression. *American Sociological Review* 28:339–64.

Thoits, P.A. 1983. Multiple identities and psychological well-being: A reformulation and test of the social isolation hypothesis. *American Sociological Review* 48:174–87.

Verbrugge, L.M. 1982. Women's social roles and health. In *Women: A developmental perspective*, edited by P. Berman and E. Ramey. NIH Publication no. 82–2298. Washington, D.C.: U.S. Government Printing Office.

Verbrugge, L.M. 1983. Paper presented at the annual meeting of the American Psychological Association, Anaheim, Calif.

Verbrugge, L.M. 1984. Role burdens and physical health of women and men. Paper presented at conference, "Modern Woman: Managing Multiple Roles," May, Yale University, New Haven, Conn.

## Bibliography

Barnett, R.C., and G.K. Baruch. *The Competent Woman: Perspectives on Socialization.* New York: Irvington/Halstead, 1978.

Barnett, R.C., and G.K. Baruch. "Women's Involvement in Multiple Roles, Role Strain and Psychological Distress." *Journal of Personality and Social Psychology,* 49 (1985):135–45.

Baruch, G.K., and R.C. Barnett. "On the Well-Being of Adult Women." In *Competence and Coping During Adulthood*, edited by L.S. Bond and J.C. Rosen. Hanover, N.H.: University Press of New England, 1980.

Baruch, G.K., and R.C. Barnett. "Role Quality, Multiple Role Involvement, and Psychological Well-Being." Forthcoming. In *Modern Woman Managing the Dual Role*, edited by F. Crosby. New Haven: Yale University Press.

Rivers, C., R.C. Barnett, and G.K. Baruch. *Beyond Sugar and Spice.* New York: Ballantine, 1979.

Veroff, J., E. Douvan, and R.A. Kulka. *The Inner American: A Self-Portrait from 1957–1976.* New York: Basic Books, 1981.

# Science
## Women in Science and Engineering

### *Betty M. Vetter*

During the middle decades of the twentieth century, only a relative handful of women worked as scientists, and comparatively, half a thimble full were employed as engineers in the United States. After World War II, the number of men earning bachelor's degrees in engineering or doctorates in science doubled in less than a decade, while the number of women earning these degrees remained almost static. Not until the early 1970s did large numbers of women enter and remain in these fields.

### *Education*

Between 1972 and 1982, women's share of all earned degrees increased from 41.9 percent to 50.3 percent at the bachelor's level and from 40.6 percent to 50.7 percent at the master's level (National Center for Education Statistics 1972–82). In science and engineering, the proportion rose from 28 percent to 36 percent of bachelor's degrees and from 18 percent to 28 percent of master's degrees during that decade (National Science Foundation 1982). The largest increases, both numerically and in percentage of total degrees, occurred in the life sciences and the social sciences including psychology. The largest percentage increases were in engineering and in the physical sciences, where the proportion of women earning degrees in 1970 was small (see Figure 1).

Between 1965 and 1983, women earned more than 49,400 doctorates in science and an additional 900 in engineering, with 36,700 being awarded between 1973 and 1983 (National Science Foundation 1982; National Research Council 1971–84). Women's share of science doctorates increased from 8.8 percent of the total in 1965 to 15.5 percent in 1973 and 29.4 percent in 1983. Although the proportion is increasing in every field of science and engineering, the relative proportions of women in each broad field of

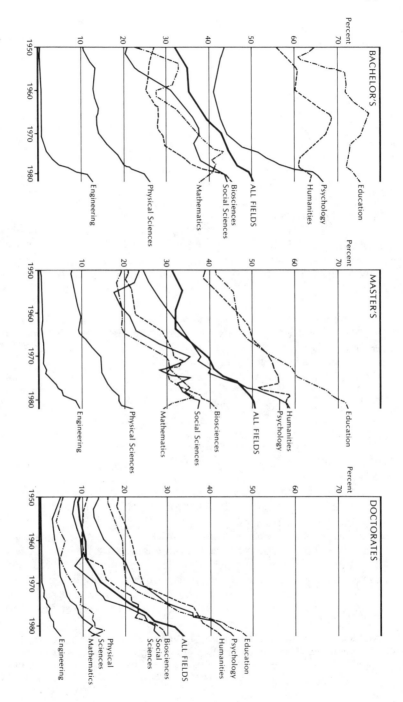

Figure 1.  Percent of degrees awarded to women, 1950–82.

*(Source:* Betty Vetter and Eleanor Babco, *Professional Women and Minorities: A Manpower Data Resource Service,* 5th ed. [Washington, D.C.: Scientific Manpower Commission, 1984]. Used with permission.)

science remain about what they were two decades ago, with almost half (49 percent) of women who earned science doctorates in 1983 earning them in the social and behavioral sciences and 35.5 percent earning them in the life sciences. These are also the broad science areas of first choice for men, where about one-third chose each of these fields in 1983. Physical sciences and engineering continue to have the lowest representation of women.

This phenomenal proportionate increase of women in the doctorate population has occurred both because the number of women earning science and engineering doctorates has risen so fast since 1965, increasing 540 percent in those eighteen years, and because the number of men earning these degrees increased only 47 percent during the same years. Between 1973 and 1983, the number of science doctorate degrees awarded to men actually dropped 14 percent, while the number awarded to women increased 177 percent.

Almost half (49 percent) of all science and engineering doctorates awarded since 1950 were earned between 1971 and 1983. Male as well as female scientists in today's doctoral work force are somewhat more likely to have earned the doctorate in the past twelve years than in the preceding twenty-two years, with 45 percent of men and 76 percent of women in this category.

Judging from current enrollment trends, the increasing number and proportion of science and engineering degrees granted to women can be expected to continue upward, at least over the next several years. The proportion of freshmen women planning majors in science and engineering (including premed) has risen from 24 percent in fall 1973 to 27 percent in fall 1984 (Astin et al. 1974–84). The number of undergraduate women enrolled in science and engineering fields is rising steadily (National Center for Education Statistics 1982, unpublished), as is the proportion of baccalaureate graduates entering graduate study.

In doctorate-granting departments, women were 28 percent of full-time graduate students in science and 4 percent of those in engineering in 1974, rising to more than 40 percent in science and 9 percent in engineering in 1982–83 (National Science Foundation 1984a). Annual increases in full-time science enrollment in Ph.D. departments over these eight years averaged 4.1 percent per year in science and 15.2 percent in engineering for men, while the increase in women students averaged 19.2 percent per year in science and 67.7 percent per year in engineering.

Master's degree attainment rates for men with science and engineering bachelor's degrees have dropped slightly over the decade, from 22.5 percent of 1970 bachelor's graduates to 21.5 percent of 1980 bachelor's graduates, while the rate for women has increased from 13.9 percent to 14.9 percent during the same period. Rates of attainment of Ph.D.s for male science and engineering bachelor's graduates of 1965 were 13.1 percent, dropping to 6.7 percent for the graduates of 1975. For women, the rates also dropped, but neither so far nor so steadily—from 5.8 percent to 4.4 percent. These rates assume a seven-year time span from bachelor's to doctoral degree (Vetter and Babco 1984).

In those undergraduate fields (principally engineering and computer science) where a bachelor's degree is the first professional entry level, all available information indicates a continuing increase in the proportion of women enrolled and graduating, although the rate of increase is slowing. The number of undergraduate women enrolled full time in engineering has grown from 6,064 in 1973–74 to almost 65,000 in 1983–84, an increase of 966 percent in ten years. The increase for men over that period was 89 percent. In 1983–84, women are 15.9 percent of total full-time undergraduate enrollment compared with 3.2 percent a decade earlier. The 358 women who earned bachelor's degrees in engineering in 1970 represented 0.8 percent of the graduating class, while the 10,693 women who earned this degree in 1984 made up 13.9 percent of the graduates, and the 1987 class should be about 17 percent women, based on first-year engineering enrollments in fall 1983 (Engineering Manpower Commission 1969–85).

## Employment

Once prepared with the necessary education credentials, women have been moving into the science and engineering labor force in record numbers, but it takes a long time for their proportionate share of the total group to be affected. They were 8 percent of the science and engineering labor force in 1974 and climbed to 12.2 percent in 1982. The numerical increase is 224,100 in eight years, representing an increase of 122.3 percent from 1974, compared with an increase of 815,100 or 38.7 percent for men during that time (National Science Foundation 1982, 1984). Still, women increased their share of the science and engineering labor force by only four percentage points, or half a percentage point per year. If we assume continuation of this trend—a rise of only one-half of a percent each year—it will take seventy-six years for women to make up half of the science and engineering labor force.

The gains made by women over the past decade have occurred in a positive policy climate of legalized opportunities for educational access, supportive changes in society's view of the role of women, and a favorable political backing. A change to a hostile or even a neutral climate might be expected to slow proportionate growth in the participation of women in science, so that even seventy-six years may be an optimistic assessment. Nonetheless, continued progress at some rate appears probable.

A major component of the science and engineering labor force is composed of those members of the group who have attained doctorates. The 1973 labor force of doctoral scientists and engineers was estimated by the National Research Council to total 229,400 persons, including about 18,050 women (7.9 percent). The 1983 Ph.D. labor force of about 365,400 doctoral scientists and engineers includes about 48,400 women (13.2 percent) (1974, 1984).

With women now constituting at least 12 percent of the science and engineering labor force, they form a large enough group that their progress, relative to men, may be measured by examining some of the factors that govern career advancement and satisfaction. Although individual case studies would show both many similarities and wide disparities between men and women, comparison of average statistics indicates that equality of opportunity has not yet been achieved.

## Unemployment Rates

In each of six biennial surveys of the doctoral population since 1973, the National Research Council has found unemployment rates for women to be two to five times higher than for men, with some variation by field (1974, 1976, 1978, 1980, 1982, 1984). Generally, the higher the unemployment rate for men, the wider the gap in unemployment rates between men and women, which would seem to indicate that women are more likely to have difficulty finding jobs in a tight job market than are men. Unemployment rates for doctoral men and women scientists and engineers were 0.9 percent and 3.9 percent, respectively, in 1973. In 1983, the rates were 0.8 percent and 2.6 percent.

Unemployment rates among all scientists and engineers also continue to be higher for women than for men. In 1974, the National Science Foundation reported unemployment rates of 1.6 percent for men and 4.1 percent for women. In 1976, these rates were 2.8 percent and 7.4 percent, respectively, and in 1980, 1.4 percent and 2.7 percent (1982). By 1982, unemployment rates had climbed again to 1.9 percent for men and 4.5 percent for women (1984c).

More illuminating than these overall rates, however, are the unemployment rates for recent science and engineering graduates at the bachelor's and master's levels. Among 1980 and 1981 bachelor's graduates surveyed in 1982, 7.7 percent of women and 5.1 percent of men were unemployed and seeking work. At the master's level, however, the sex gap widened as the rates rose to 7.3 percent for women, while dropping to 2.3 percent for men (National Science Foundation 1984b). Although the unemployment rates for doctoral scientists and engineers are lower than for these recent graduates at lower degree levels, the gap in unemployment rates between men and women carries across all degree levels, all experience levels, and almost all fields.

Even among those who are employed, men trained in science or engineering are considerably more likely to find jobs in science or engineering than are women with such training. The National Science Foundation developed the concept of "underemployment" to describe the combined effect of involuntary employment outside of science and engineering and of involuntary part-time employment when full-time employment was sought. The underemployment rate for scientists and engineers in 1982 was 5 percent for women and 1 percent for men (1984c). Part of this difference is explained by the greater concentration of men in engineering, but when only scientists are compared, women are still twice as likely as men to be underemployed—6 percent versus 3 percent. Underemployment rates for women were higher than for men in every field of science except among computer specialists, where the rates were essentially equal. This is true also at the doctoral level, where underemployment rates for women are above those for men in all major fields of science and engineering.

*Underutilization* is the National Science Foundation term for an even more comprehensive indicator of relative opportunity for men and women in these fields. This category includes those who are unemployed but seeking employment plus those who are underemployed, expressed as a percentage of the labor force. By this measure, the underutilization rate for women scientists and engineers in 1982 was 9 percent and for men, 3 percent (1984c). Again, the rates are very low and essentially equal for men and women in computer specialties, but they are higher for women than for men in every other field (see Figure 2).

Among recent graduates, women again show higher unemployment rates, higher underemployment rates, and higher underutilization rates than do men (National Science Foundation 1984b). Among recent bachelor's graduates, the underutilization rates were 11.2 percent for men and 20.4 percent for women. At the master's level, they were 5.7 percent and 13.6 percent, respectively.

Much of this difference lies in field of degree, since men were more likely to major in engineering, where the bachelor's degree is a professional entry level, and women were more likely to major in the social and behavioral sciences, where graduate degrees are generally required for professional employment. The differences resulting from field of degree disparities, however, cannot account for the gap between the sexes.

Thus, for whatever reasons, women with science degrees are more likely to be unemployed and less likely to find employment in science and engineering than men, whether they are recent or more experienced graduates, and whatever their degree level and their field.

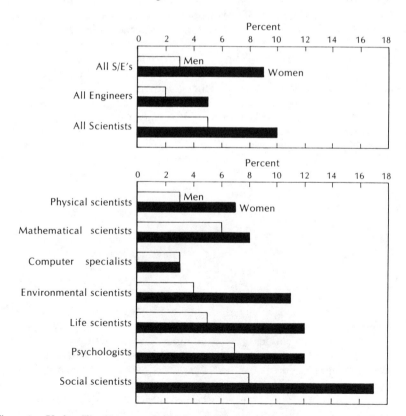

Figure 2. Underutilization rates of scientists and engineers by field and sex, 1982
(*Source:* National Science Foundation, *Women and Minorities in Science and Engineering*, January 1984. Used with permission.)

## Employment Sector

Women scientists, particularly at the doctoral level, are more likely than men to work in academic institutions, hospitals and clinics, nonprofit organizations, and state and local governments. They are less likely than men to be employed in industry or in the federal government. This is true regardless of field or degree level (Vetter and Babco 1984). But women continue to fare less well than men in terms of status or rank, tenure or other job security, salary and promotion, regardless of employment sector. Although some lessening of the differences between men and women in all these factors can be seen among younger scientists and engineers, the differences still persist, and because these differences widen with age and years of experience, it cannot yet be said that today's younger women will not find that same widening as they grow older.

Women were 19.4 percent of all academically employed scientists and engineers at colleges and universities in 1983, but their proportion of faculty positions, tenured positions, and tenure track positions is far below this figure.

Among all academically employed doctoral scientists and engineers in 1983, 65.6 percent of men but only 39.2 percent of women were tenured. An additional 14 percent of men and 21 percent of women were on the tenure track, while 8.4 percent of men and 19.9 percent of women were neither tenured nor in tenure track positions. More than a fourth (26.2 percent) of academically employed doctoral women in the life sciences are neither tenured nor on a tenure track, compared with 10 percent of men. This is not just a function of age, since even among those age thirty-six and older, one in four women (24.3 percent) compared to one in thirteen men (7.5 percent) is neither tenured nor on a tenure track (National Research Council 1984). Although this differential is widest in the life sciences, it occurs in every field. Thus, the possibility that within the coming decade women might substantially increase their proportion of tenured positions and top academic ranks does not appear very bright.

## Salaries

The only clear measure of comparison between women and men in industry and government is their salaries. Except for a few beginning salaries, women earn less than men in every field of science, in every employment sector, and at every level of experience. The salary gap grows wider with age and is wider at each succeedingly higher degree level.

Beginning salaries of men and women graduates at the end of the bachelor's degree are more nearly in balance than at any later career stage. In 1984, salary offers to women graduates ranged from slightly over 100 percent of salary offers to men in engineering to 84.7 percent in the biological sciences (College Placement Council 1984) (see Table 1). For several years, the gap in starting salaries generally was higher in the humanities than in most of the sciences. However, in 1984, in addition to the wide disparity in biology, women's offers in the social sciences other than economics were only 86.4 percent of men's, compared with 90.7 percent in the humanities.

Table 1

Beginning salary offers to women bachelor's graduates as a percentage of men's offers

| Year | Mathematics | Computer sciences | Chemistry | Biological sciences | Economics | ENGINEERING | | | | |
| --- | --- | --- | --- | --- | --- | --- | --- | --- | --- | --- |
| | | | | | | Chemical | Electrical | Civil | Mechanical | All |
| 1974 | 99.2 | 97.3 | 97.3 | 88.4 | | 99.1 | 101.5 | 100.4 | 100.3 | 100.3 |
| 1975 | 98.1 | 99.4 | 98.1 | 92.0 | | 100.1 | 103.3 | 103.2 | 100.5 | 101.5 |
| 1976 | 98.9 | 100.9 | 104.0 | 96.9 | | 100.4 | 101.8 | 104.4 | 102.6 | 102.3 |
| 1977 | 98.6 | 98.8 | 99.8 | 96.7 | | 101.1 | 101.4 | 105.8 | 102.7 | 102.7 |
| 1978 | 98.7 | 98.9 | 98.1 | 88.0 | 97.2 | 100.3 | 101.1 | 104.3 | 101.6 | 101.8 |
| 1979 | 97.3 | 97.8 | 98.4 | 93.0 | 96.8 | 100.5 | 101.8 | 102.7 | 101.0 | 101.5 |
| 1980 | 97.6 | 98.5 | 97.1 | 89.6 | 97.4 | 100.2 | 99.8 | 102.3 | 101.5 | 100.9 |
| 1981 | 97.9 | 98.4 | 97.5 | 92.9 | 96.2 | 99.8 | 100.2 | 101.4 | 100.2 | 100.1 |
| 1982 | 97.9 | 100.1 | 100.6 | 94.1 | 93.8 | 100.4 | 100.8 | 100.3 | 100.8 | 101.3 |
| 1983 | 97.2 | 97.5 | 96.6 | 91.7 | 100.3 | 100.7 | 100.2 | 100.9 | 100.5 | 100.7 |
| 1984 | 96.8 | 96.9 | 97.9 | 84.7 | 97.8 | 101.1 | 100.2 | 98.8 | 100.8 | 100.7 |

*Source:* College Placement Council, Annual *Salary Survey*, July 1974–July 1984.

The 1984 dollar differences range from $-\$2,784$ per year in the biological sciences to $+\$312$ per year in chemical engineering. There has been little or no change in these differentials over the past decade.

A significant change may be occurring, however, in the first year or two of employment. Earlier studies show a widening of about five to eight percentage points within two years. But in 1982, women one and two years after the bachelor's degree had generally improved their salary status relative to men, or at least had held on without further widening of the salary gap. In the biological sciences, women's salaries in this group of recent bachelor's graduates were 94 percent of men's; in engineering, 101 percent; in chemistry, 93 percent; and in mathematics, 89.2 percent (National Science Foundation 1984b).

At the master's level, however, recent women graduates in 1982 earned only 89.4 percent as much as men in the physical sciences and 90.3 percent in the math sciences, but 98.4 percent in engineering, 102 percent in the biosciences, 96.1 percent in psychology, and 84.1 percent in the social sciences (National Science Foundation 1984b). Thus, no sure change in trend is yet detectable.

Salary differences between men and women also increase with additional years of experience. For example, in 1983, women master's-level chemists employed full time in industry who had earned their bachelor's degrees fifteen to nineteen years earlier earned only 86 percent of salaries earned by comparable men, and among those who were twenty-five to twenty-nine years past the bachelor's degree, women's salaries were only 69.4 percent of men's (American Chemical Society 1983).

At the doctorate level, there appears to be improvement in the ratio of women's to men's salaries over the decade from 1973 to 1983 only in the fields of computer sciences, environmental sciences, and life sciences (see Table 2). The dollar amounts represented by the ratios in 1983 range from a difference of $9,500 per year in engineering and $8,700 in chemistry to $1,200 per year in computer sciences, $4,900 in math, and $5,700 in the social sciences. Because of the greater concentration of women in the lower paid fields, the average difference across all science and engineering fields is $9,100 per year, up from $8,600 in 1981 (National Research Council 1982, 1984a).

Table 2

Women's salaries as a precentage of men's for doctoral scientists and engineers

| Field | 1973 | 1975 | 1977 | 1979 | 1981 | 1983 |
|---|---|---|---|---|---|---|
| All fields | 82.3 | 80.8 | 79.6 | 77.3 | 75.9 | 77.8 |
| Physical scientists | 81.4 | 79.3 | 70.1 | 80.0 | 78.8 | 80.1 |
| Math scientists | 87.8 | 85.5 | 84.3 | 81.3 | 83.6 | 87.2 |
| Computer scientists | 79.4 | 76.3 | 79.7 | 79.2 | 87.3 | 97.2 |
| Environmental scientists | 81.6 | 80.9 | 75.8 | 79.3 | 83.3 | 87.3 |
| Engineers | 87.0 | 82.5 | 79.8 | 80.1 | 81.6 | 85.0 |
| Life scientists | 76.6 | 83.6 | 83.7 | 79.6 | 78.9 | 80.6 |
| Psychologists | 87.6 | 86.3 | 82.7 | 82.9 | 79.6 | 82.6 |
| Social scientists | 84.4 | 83.1 | 81.8 | 84.3 | 81.2 | 84.5 |

*Source:* National Research Council biennial profiles of U.S. doctoral scientists and engineers.

Further, the salary gap, which exists in every field at the start of a Ph.D. career in science, widens with age. Examined by years since Ph.D., the ratio of women's to men's salaries continues to decrease with time. For example, among biological scientists in 1983, the ratio of women's salaries to men's salaries widens from 93 percent at five or fewer years since the Ph.D. to 88.4 percent at sixteen to twenty years, and 82.6 percent at twenty-six to thirty years (National Research Council 1984). Other fields show similar changes over time.

No available data allow us to ascertain what proportion of scientists and engineers of either sex may have interrupted their careers for military service, family responsibilities, illness, or other reasons, so we cannot tell how much the increasing salary erosion over time for women compared to men may be attributed to such career breaks. We do know that the labor force participation rates of men are slightly higher than for women.

Among all scientists and engineers in 1982, 95.2 percent of men and 92.2 percent of women were in the labor force. Among recent graduates in 1982, 97 percent of men and 92.3 percent of women bachelor's graduates, and 97.7 percent of men and 95.2 percent of women master's graduates were in the labor force (National Science Foundation 1984b). At the doctoral level in 1983, 94.7 percent of men and 91.8 percent of women scientists and engineers were in the labor force (National Research Council 1984). Thus, although either men or women may have been out of the labor force for some period in the past, the participation rates show only relatively small sex differences and can account for only a fraction of women's salary disadvantage relative to men. Despite women's increased participation in the labor force over the past decade, the wage gap over time is not significantly different in 1983 than it was in 1973.

Another factor that may contribute to the salary gap is differences between the sexes in the amount of voluntary part-time employment that may have occurred in the past. Although salary comparisons never match part-time with full-time workers, advancement in a career may be slower if significant periods of voluntary part-time employment have occurred previously. We cannot measure this effect, if any, with presently available data bases.

## Social and Philosophical Barriers

Several areas of science and engineering still include less than 10 percent women, and this in itself constitutes a social barrier to increased participation. Only when a critical mass of some undetermined size has been attained will all women with an interest in these fields feel comfortable in planning a career in them. The social barriers to participation in these and other areas that are still predominantly male include sex discrimination in the workplace—not so blatant as in earlier years, but still present. Even in work situations where employers pride themselves on their lack of discrimination, old mythologies about the place of women and their competencies still persist. Said one women chemist: "My growth and career development have been hampered most by the prevailing attitude of my supervisors and peers. They are less willing to trust, support and assume risks with a woman than a man" (Vetter 1980). A woman engineer pointed out that "women are required to prove their worth, while men only have to prove their lack of worth" (Vetter 1980).

Barriers from the past continue to have adverse effects on women. For example, the GI bill following World War II, which opened up higher education to 2.2 million veterans, mostly men, nearly doubled the prewar enrollment, taxing existing facilities to the point that there was little room for women. Quotas on female enrollment were commonplace, as were higher standards for admission. Many women were pushed into less desirable institutions, where a lower quality undergraduate education decreased their chances for successful graduate work and employment (Hornig 1984).

Long after the World War II veterans were out of college, admissions policies continued to discriminate against women. Since such discrimination was not a federal offense before the Civil Rights Act of 1964, most major universities continued to require higher credentials from women than from men applicants, and quotas were not an embarrassment but a fact of life. Even as late as 1969, financial aid for male undergraduates exceeded that awarded to women by 30 percent (Hornig 1984). The results of these policies continue to be felt in many ways.

Although differences in opportunity are more subtle today than in earlier years, they continue to exist. For example, among persons who earned their doctorate in 1983, approximately equal proportions of men and women had university fellowships, but women were much less likely than men to have had research assistantships in any of the science fields. It is not surprising to find that higher proportions of new women doctorates than men were still seeking employment at the time the degree was awarded—16.5 percent of women and 12.3 percent of men in the physical sciences, 11.1 percent and 9.9 percent in the biosciences, and 28.0 percent and 23.1 percent in the social sciences.

Inequities in the early career stages continue to affect women scientists as they move forward. Men are still more likely than women to be hired for academic tenure track positions, to be promoted to tenure, and to achieve full professorships. Women hold assistant professorships and non-faculty positions more than twice as often as men, and there has been little change in these distributions since 1977.

The Women Chemists' Committee of the American Chemical Society found that in 1983, women held only 188 of 4,400 faculty positions in chemistry departments that grant doctorates (4.1 percent), although women have earned 9.5 percent of all doctorates in chemistry awarded by these universities in the past twenty years and 11.5 percent of those awarded over the past decade (Vetter 1984). In industry, doctorate women chemists remain underrepresented by about 50 percent (National Research Council 1980).

Would science policy and scientific research be different if more women were involved in all aspects of the scientific enterprise? Many feminist scholars, historians, and critics believe that there would be radical differences both in the perception of science as a rigorous, quantitative, and therefore "masculine" activity and in the subjects chosen for research. At the June 1984 annual meeting of the National Women's Studies Association at Douglass College, Harvard biologist Ruth Hubbard pointed out that "there is nothing intrinsically male about science." It is "male because men have been doing it." There is, and ought to be, a lot of subjectivity in science, but white males who have dominated the discipline have perpetuated the myth that science is an exercise in objectivity and, therefore, tailor-made for the male temperament (Coughlin 1984).

These scholars agreed that feminist science would not be a discipline in which control over the subjects to be studied would be left to a chosen few, but would relate closely to the social context in which it operated. Women would make value judgments about the desirability of acquiring certain knowledge of scientific techniques. For example, women would abandon or curtail certain areas of genetic engineering and reproductive biology, questions about the biological bases of human behavior, and cloning.

Engineer and computer consultant Evelynn Hammonds pointed out that in the "computer revolution," for example, both the hardware and the software involved have been designed almost entirely by white men. "Women are in the react mode," she said. They need to become involved in the creation and production of computer technology, not just in its consumption (Coughlin 1984).

There is a whole body of research on the different ways in which women and men solve problems—men use quantitative tools and women use qualitative tools. Associate Professor Sherry Turkle of the Massachusetts Institute of Technology (1984) says her research suggests that some of the problems girls experience in introductory courses in computer programming have to do with the "social construction" of programming as male. She believes that important decisions that will affect women's relationships with the growing computer culture are being based on a fallacy: "that programming is a thing of one kind," attacked through a structured approach to goal setting, breaking down into subgoals, and plotting strategy through a carefully defined sequence of moves. She found that when allowed to program according to their own styles, boys and girls may do it differently. She compares the "hard mastery" of the boys as the mastery of the engineer and the "soft mastery" of the girls as the mastery of the artist, which tries something, waits for a response, tries something else, and lets the overall shape emerge from an interaction with the medium. "We must recognize that what may be characterized as 'male mastery' is not the only type of mastery," she says.

There are signs of progress in overcoming some of the remaining barriers. Beginning in 1982, the National Science Foundation (NSF) set up a program of visiting professorships for women to increase the visibility of female scientists and engineers, give them better opportunities for research of their own choosing, and encourage more women to enter those fields. In its first year, this program awarded grants totaling $1 million to seventeen women; the second year, twenty-eight women were awarded $2 million in grants. The number of research proposals submitted increased from 118 in the first year to 150 in the second. Although the ultimate effect of this program in increasing the numbers of women seeking careers in science or in encouraging the research of a small number of grant recipients cannot yet be assessed, the program itself is an encouraging statement for women.

## Conclusions

Women have not yet moved into science and engineering in proportions equivalent to their representation in the population. Except in the behavioral and social sciences, their proportions in the labor force remain below 25 percent. Because of the strong predominance of males in the professional community in science, many years will pass before men and women are represented equally.

Despite the evidence of continuing inequality for those women who have entered the science community as shown by unemployment rates, academic rank, and salary levels, women have made real strides in increasing their participation in science and engineering over the past decade at every degree level and in every field and employment sector. Continuing increases in participation through the 1980s are indicated by both undergraduate and graduate enrollment patterns, and there is evidence that an increasing proportion of precollege women are taking the essential high school courses in mathematics and science that will open up the option of choosing to pursue a science career.

Although women still face more difficulty than men in finding employment (and especially employment in science or engineering), achieving promotions, increasing their salaries, and thus advancing their influence and prestige, real progress is occurring, particularly in their increasing numbers and proportion in the science community.

This does not mean, however, that all past gains have been consolidated and will remain, nor that future gains are assured. Continued monitoring through data collection and analysis will be essential in order to assess further progress as well as to identify any loss of gains apparently already achieved. So long as the proportion of women in the U.S. scientific community remains below 20 to 25 percent, their influence within that community is not likely to result in policy changes.

### References

American Chemical Society. 1983. *Salaries, 1983*. Washington, D.C.: American Chemical Society.

Astin, Alexander, et al. 1974–84. *The American freshman: National norms for fall 1973 through fall 1984*. Los Angeles: American Council on Education/Cooperative Educational Research Program, University of California, Los Angeles, Graduate School of Education.

College Placement Council. 1974–84. *A study of beginning offers, final report, July 1974 through July 1984*. Bethlehem, Pa.: College Placement Council.

Coughlin, Ellen K. 1984. Confronting social and philosophical barriers to the participation of women in science. *Chronicle of Higher Education*, 5 July.

Engineering Manpower Commission. 1969–85. *Engineering and technology enrollments fall 1969* through *fall 1983*, and *Engineering and technology degrees 1969* through *1984*. New York: Engineers Joint Council (through 1979) and American Association of Engineering Societies (1980 through 1985).

Hornig, Lilli S. 1984. Women in science and engineering: Why so few? *Technology Review* 87, no. 8:29–41.

National Center for Education Statistics. 1972–82. *Earned degrees conferred by institutions of higher education, United States, 1969–70* through *1979–80*. Washington D.C.: Government Printing Office, 1972 through 1982. *1980–81*, and *1981–82*. unpublished.

———. 1982. *Fall enrollment in higher education, 1980*. NCES 82–323. Washington D.C.: U.S. Government Printing Office, 1982; and *1982*, unpublished.

National Research Council. 1974, 1976, 1978, 1980, 1982, 1984. *Science and engineering doctorates in the United States, 1973 profile* and *1975 profile; Science, engineering and humanities doctorates in the United States, 1977 Profile, 1979 Profile, 1981 Profile*, and *1983 Profile*. Washington D.C.: National Academy of Sciences.

———. 1971–84. *Summary report, 1970* through *1983 Doctorate recipients from United States universities*. Washington D.C.: National Academy of Sciences.

———. 1980. *Women scientists in industry and government—how much progress in the 1970's?* Washington D.C.: National Academy of Sciences.

National Science Foundation. 1982. *Science and engineering degrees: 1950–80*. NSF 82–307. Washington D.C.: U.S. Government Printing Office.

———. 1982 and 1984. *U.S. scientists and engineers, 1980* (NSF 82–314) and *1982* (NSF 84–321). Washington D.C.: U.S. Government Printing Office.

———. 1984a. *Academic science/engineering graduate enrollment and support Fall 1982* (NSF 84–306). *Detailed statistical tables*. Washington D.C.: U.S. Government Printing Office.

———. 1984b. *Characteristics of recent science/engineering graduates 1982*. NSF 84–318. Washington D.C.: U.S. Government Printing Office.

———. 1984c. *Women and minorities in science and engineering*. Washington D.C.: U.S. Government Printing Office, January.

Turkle, Sherry. 1984. Women in computer programming: A different approach. *Technology Review* 87, no. 8:48–50.

Vetter, Betty. 1980. Working women scientists and engineers. *Science* 207 (4 January): 28–34.

———. 1984. Women and minorities in chemistry. *Professional Relations Bulletin* (American Chemical Society) 33 (June): 8–9.

Vetter, Betty, and Eleanor L. Babco. 1984. *Professional women and minorities: A manpower data resource service*, 5th ed. Washington D.C.: Scientific Manpower Commission.

## Bibliography

Berryman, Sue E. *Who Will Do Science?* New York: Rockefeller Foundation, 1983. The trends and their causes in minority and female representation among holders of advanced degrees in science and mathematics.

Briscoe, Anne B. "Phenomenon of the Seventies: The Women's Caucuses." *Signs* 4. no. 1 (1978): 152–58. Describes the growth and effectiveness of women's caucuses in scientific societies.

Cole, Jonathan R. *Fair Science: Women in the Scientific Community.* New York: Free Press of Macmillan Publishing Co., 1979. Examines studies of men and women scientists, and concludes that science is more fair to women than many other professions.

Fennema, Elizabeth. "Increasing Women's Participation in Mathematics: An Intervention Study." *Journal for Research in Mathematics Education* 12, no. 1 (1981): 3–14.

Haas, Violet B., and Carolyn C. Perrucci, eds. *Women in Scientific and Engineering Professions.* Ann Arbor: University of Michigan Press, 1984. Papers from the Conference on Women in the Professions: Science, Social Science, Engineering, held at Purdue University in 1981.

Malcom, Shirley M., Paula Quick Hall, and Janet Welsh Brown. *The Double Bind: The Price of Being a Minority Woman in Science.* Washington, D.C.: American Association for the Advancement of Science, 1976. Minority women suffer from both sex and racial discrimination, with sex discrimination being the stronger of the two.

National Research Council Commission on Human Resources. *Climbing the Academic Ladder: Doctoral Women Scientists in Academe.* Washington, D.C.: National Academy of Sciences, 1979, and *Climbing the Ladder: An Update on the Status of Doctoral Women Scientists and Engineers,* 1983. The relative status of men and women in academic institutions is examined, with the conclusion that women do not advance at the same rate as comparable men. The updated study shows little change from 1979 to 1983.

————. *Career Outcomes in a Matched Sample of Men and Women Ph.Ds.* Washington, D.C.: National Academy of Sciences, 1981. Triads (two men and one woman) were matched for field and year of Ph.D. and prestige of Ph.D. university. Salaries and other indicators of progress were then compared, with the finding that sex is a consistently negative factor for women in the recognition of achievement.

Rossiter, Margaret W. *Women Scientists in America, Strategies and Struggles to 1940.* Baltimore: Johns Hopkins University Press, 1983. This first volume in a study of U.S. women scientists describes in rich detail the contributions of women to U.S. science up to 1940, the barriers erected to exclude them, and the strategies women used to surmount some of the barriers.

Vetter, Betty. "Women Scientists and Engineers: Trends in Participation." *Science.* 214 (18 December 1981): 1313–21. Describes and documents changes in educational attainment and labor force experience of women, and compares their salaries and opportunities with those of men.

"Women in Technology." *Technology Review* 87, no. 8 (1984): 31–41. A special section including several articles, of which two (Hornig and Turkle) are referred to in this chapter.

# Work
## Challengers to Occupational Segregation

*Carroll Wetzel Wilkinson*

Sara Garrigan Burr (1981) raised one of the most intriguing issues about women and work in her 1980 essay in the *Women's Annual:* the matter of nontraditional work for women. This chapter will take up that subject, focusing both on the latest published information and on critical issues for women who have chosen to pioneer on male occupational frontiers.

The variety of nontraditional jobs that women have moved into during the last ten years is startling and impressive (although their numbers are still small); this suggests a picture of significant social change in America, not just in the professions and management, which has been so well documented, but in all parts of the American work force.

Barbara Haber, the originator and first editor of the *Women's Annual*, has pointed out that by studying work we clarify the allocation of sex roles in our society (1981). By studying women in nontraditional occupations, we see who has refused to accept the idea of "men's work" and "women's work" and how many female challengers to occupational segregation in the United States there are now. The women who move beyond gender boundaries and into territory presumed exclusively male are harbingers of a new age; their accomplishments bring an additional dimension to the study of women and work, which in turn demands further study and a deeper understanding (Hacker 1984).

## Trends and Issues for All Female Pioneers

A literature review reveals similarities among female occupational pioneers, no matter what the job area. This is not surprising, since all women share the characteristic of being outsiders in a culture in which another group is dominant. In some nontraditional areas, there is evidence that a postpioneer era with a whole new set of concerns has developed (Harlan and O'Farrell 1982; Crocker 1984). Conferences, support groups, awards programs, new periodicals, regional meetings are evidence of the networking among women working in nontraditional fields and indicate women workers' recognition of mutual need for support and encouragement.

The novelty factor is a pervasive nuisance for women in nontraditional fields. The curiosity of the media and their readers and viewers is seemingly endless; yet once the public congratulations are over, probing insights rarely follow. Moreover, the women frequently suffer a painful loss of privacy. Only from serious studies of groups of pioneers in similar occupational categories can we begin to learn what is changing on the American employment frontier.

A review of the writing and research about women in nontraditional fields uncovers some interlocking and vital issues. They include the pervasive and persistent occupational segregation in American society; the barriers to women entering a nontraditional field in the first place; and the barriers they encounter once they are actually working. In high school or earlier, a woman often meets vocational counselors, teachers, parents, and peers who unconsciously or consciously steer her away from certain occupations. If she goes on to higher education, she may encounter professors and/or university officials as well as friends who discourage her along with her parents. Once working, she has the prejudice of coworkers and supervisors to deal with as well as deeply rooted sexism within the organization. No matter what her original intention, sexism often tracks a woman into a traditional role within the field (in medicine, for example, toward pediatrics or psychiatry and away from surgery).

Finally, for some women there is the crushing recognition that the first stage of pioneering may not be the last if no career ladder exists for women in their field. This may add up to as many as twenty years of hurdles lasting from young adulthood through the early years of midlife. Nevertheless, some women, for psychological reasons, will deny they have had any trouble along the way as they establish and develop their careers (Crosby 1984).

## First Women

The subject of women in nontraditional jobs makes its way into the national consciousness each time another barrier is broken by an extraordinary woman who achieves a "first." The year 1984 will be remembered for the historic moment Geraldine Ferraro stood before the delegates at the Democratic National Convention in San Francisco and said to them and the American viewing public, "My heart is filled with pride. I proudly accept your nomination for vice president of the United States" (Ferraro 1984). She was the first female in U.S. history to receive the nomination of a major party, and many hoped her candidacy would strengthen Walter Mondale's chances for winning the presidential election.

Other recent firsts that have captured national attention are Sandra Day O'Connor's appointment to the Supreme Court in 1981 by President Ronald Reagan and the appointment on 16 January 1978 by the National

Aeronautics and Space Administration of six women astronauts, two of whom, Anna L. Fisher and Sally Ride, completed successful space flights in 1983–84. On another front, in late December 1984, Georgeann Wells of West Virginia University became the first woman to score a slam dunk in a basketball game (*Washington Post* 1985). A fascinating summary of some other firsts by women is found in Joseph Nathan Kane's *Famous First Facts* (1981), which reveals that women have been breaking gender barriers in the United States since 1696, when Dinah Nuthead of Annapolis, Maryland, received a license to carry on the printing business of her deceased husband. There may have been other pioneers before her whose achievements have not yet been documented.

Less publicized but no less significant than these achievements are the women who have ignored sex segregation to become coal miners (1973), railroad conductors (1979), carpenters, Coast Guard airplane pilots (1977), electricians, rabbis (1972), jockeys (1969), bodybuilders (1984), and surgeons, or have entered numerous other occupations previously closed to women. On 6 June 1979 the first railroad train operated exclusively by women was placed in service by the Long Island Railroad (Kane 1981). In December 1983, sixteen women attended the National Conference of the United Mine Workers of America in Pittsburgh, Pennsylvania, as elected delegates representing locals from all over the country. This was the first time women delegates had attended the national UMWA conference and illustrates their genuine participation in the union (Wilkinson 1985).

All kinds of firsts will continue for women as individuals and in groups until sex segregation in the workforce no longer exists. But while women move toward the goal of equal representation in all occupations, gains previously established will be lost because of changes in the economy, political shifts, and countless other factors. At its peak, for example, the female work force in the American coal fields rose to 3,773 employees. But the recession and the government's failure to endorse coal as an important energy alternative has caused high unemployment in this industry, particularly in the eastern United States. No one knows exactly how many women have been laid off during this quiet crisis, but it is estimated that 40 percent of the women originally employed by American coal companies in the 1970s are now unemployed (Wilkinson 1985). Similar setbacks have occurred for women in other trades, such as steelmaking, and there is evidence that it is difficult for women engineers even to be hired once their training is completed (Finn 1983).

## Nontraditional Work Defined and Described

Brigid O'Farrell and Sharon L. Harlan (1982) provide a working definition: "Non-traditional jobs are those predominantly held by men and considered atypical for women, such as managers, machinists, and craftworkers." The Women's Bureau of the U.S. Department of Labor (1983) defines nontraditional occupations as those where women constitute less than 25 percent of the total number of workers. Although no one agrees on a precise definition for research purposes, this chapter will pay particular attention to jobs where women now occupy up to 5 percent of the work force but ten years ago there were no women at all. Though actual numbers are tiny, the variety of new positions women occupy nationwide indicates a trend that may grow even more significant by the 1990 national census.

What are the positions women have entered during the last ten years? They include not just extraordinary jobs that receive national media attention, such as astronaut, Supreme Court justice, and 6' 7" basketball star, but also skilled trades including carpenter, mechanic, repair worker, supervisory blue-collar worker, and electrician. Women have made inroads into engineering, medicine, and dentistry, and so many advances have been made in such professions as pharmacy, computer science, and operations research that they are no longer considered nontraditional for women (U.S. Department of Labor, Women's Bureau 1983). In traditionally male sales occupations such as insurance agent, broker, and underwriter, women's participation has increased to 24 percent, and 20 percent of all manufacturing industries' sales representatives are now women. In management there have been major changes in sex distribution. By 1981 38 percent of bank officers and financial managers were female.

Substantial increases in female employment have occurred too in the protective service occupations, such as guard, police officer, and detective; women now hold 6 percent of these jobs (U.S. Department of Labor, Women's Bureau 1983). And the number of women in public office has more than doubled over the last decade to almost eighteen thousand. For example, there were over nine hundred women serving in state legislatures in 1982 (Wright 1984). There has also been a tremendous rise (43 percent) in the number of self-employed women in the United States during the last decade. The Bureau of Labor Statistics found that there were 1.9 million women working from their homes as artists, lawyers, physicians, importers, detectives, media consultants, horticulturalists, party planners, and clothing manufacturers, among other job titles (Wright 1984). Female entrepreneurs starting, for example, balloon and custom-made-cookie delivery services, are also becoming more common.

## Basic Statistics

There are now 2,000 women firefighters, over 1,000 female pilots and navigators, 2,700 female crane and tower operators, 12,600 female professional athletes, 45,500 policewomen and detectives, 3,600 female fishers, 12,000 auto mechanics, 20,200 female carpenters, 12,000 female electricians, 6,200 female plumbers, over 3,500 female coal miners, and 44,000 female heavy truck drivers (Dion 1984).

Perhaps the most interesting data of all regarding women in nontraditional fields has come to light through the "1980 Census/EEO Special File" (U.S. Department of Commerce, Bureau of Census 1984). Originally produced to help meet the needs of both government and private-sector employers in planning equal employment opportunity and affirmative action programs, it is based on a sample of approximately 120,000 persons in the civilian labor force in 1970 and 1980. Officials point out that readers must take into account the potential for error when dealing with a sample so small. They especially warn that zeros in the 1970 data mean that there were no cases in the adjusted sample, not that there were no cases at all.

Still, it is instructive to look at the occupations registering no females in 1970 and compare them to the percentages of women discovered in 1980. Keeping all the warnings firmly in mind, the data of the sample reveal the following: there were no female nuclear engineers in 1970 and 343 (3.7 percent) in 1980; no female agricultural engineers in 1970 and 390 (8.7 percent) in 1980; no female mapping scientists or surveyors in 1970 and 1,321 (4.2 percent) in 1980; no female medical science teachers in 1970 and 2,123 (23.6 percent) in 1980; no female fire inspection or fire prevention specialists in 1970 and 2,145 (9.5 percent) in 1980; no female pest control specialists in 1970 and 2,173 (5.8 percent) in 1980; no female managers of horticultural specialty farms in 1970 and 2,573 (16.4 percent) in 1980; no female inspectors of agricultural products in 1970 and 196 (17.1 percent) in 1980; no female hunters or trappers in 1970 and 250 (11.4 percent) in 1980; no female electricians or power transmission installers in 1970 and 459 (1.2 percent) in 1980; no female paving, surfacing, and tamping equipment operators in 1970 and 235 (3.1 percent) in 1980; no female water and sewage treatment plant operators in 1970 and 1,062 (3.2 percent) in 1980; no female roasting or baking machine operators in 1970 and 1,044 (14.5 percent) in 1980; no female longshore equipment operators in 1970 and 128 (3.0 percent) in 1980; and finally, no female bridge, lock, and lighthouse tenders in 1970 and 435 (8.4 percent) in 1980. Surely we can at least deduce that, as Grace Forster (a black woman who graduated in 1984 from a Santa Claus training school) said to her three sons, "The times are changing, boys" (About New York . . . 1984).

Looking critically at new occupations for women, one finds that they fall into six basic areas: high technology, the arts, the trades, public life, the professions, and the remaining fields including sports, management, and the clergy. Table 1 lists some specific job titles in each classification to show the variety and breadth of employment of women in nontraditional fields in 1984.

## Background Research Trends For Blue-Collar Women

Although much of the research has centered on women in higher education, law, medicine, and management, larger numbers of female pioneers in the nation are found in the semiskilled and skilled trades (U.S. Department of Labor, Women's Bureau 1983). It is interesting to consider what is known about women in blue-collar occupations and what questions have been raised regarding the meaning of their accomplishments (O'Farrell 1982).

Full understanding of women's participation in nontraditional blue-collar jobs requires an acknowledgment of the mixture of pressures, strains, and motivations they experience. Being first, they are always examined for their motives. They face the real problem of being an outsider in a foreign culture. They risk sexual harassment and unemployment. They must combat stereotypes and assumptions, usually incorrect, about why they have made their career choice. But they have assumed a lifelong commitment to

Table 1.
Job titles for women in nontraditional jobs, 1984–85

| High Technology | Public Life |
|---|---|
| astronaut | judge |
| electronics technician | mayor |
| pilot | state trooper |
| | FBI agent |
| | probation/parole officer |
| | prison official |

| Arts | Trades |
|---|---|
| composer | ironworker |
| dramatist/playwright | printer |
| rock musician | construction worker |
| movie director | longshore person |
| photographer | coal miner |
| stage technician | trucker |
| stage manager | telephone worker |
| conductor | machinist |
| artistic director | firefighter |
| special effects technician | craftworker |
| sound technician | carpenter |
| studio recording engineer | welder |
| sculptor | electrician |
| landscaper | plumber |
| | sprinkler fitter |
| | forklift operator |
| | elevator mechanic |
| | chain inspector |
| | cable splicer |

| Professions | Other |
|---|---|
| engineer | administrator |
| trial lawyer | manager |
| surgeon | investigator |
| architect | jockey |
| business executive | umpire |
| chemist | rabbi/minister |
| astronomer | adventurer |
| mapping scientist/surveyor | stuntwoman |
| | bodybuilder |
| | policewoman |
| | military officer |
| | mail carrier |
| | woodstripper |
| | soldier |
| | farmer |

an unconventional job and find it to be a central part of their lives from which great meaning is derived.

In 1976, the sociologist Mary Lindenstein Walshok, who had been involved with a women's storefront project to train handywomen, began field research on invisible female participants in the labor force. She studied 117 blue-collar women—welders, carpenters, forklift operators, cable splicers, mechanics, and machinists among others—in three metropolitan areas in California over a three-year period. Eighty-one of the women in the sample were white, fifteen black, four Asian, fourteen Latina, and three represented other racial groups. Her book, *Blue Collar Women: Pioneers on the Male Frontier* (1981) is one of the best comprehensive resources available on women in nontraditional blue-collar jobs.

She introduces these women as the "Risk Takers" and studies their family and young adulthood experiences in order to probe the roots of their motivations. She finds a "dazzling array" of women representing a spectrum of ages, races, educational attainments, and previous work experiences. After exploring their on-the-job experiences, she discusses the meaning of nontraditional employment in their lives and presents an agenda for future research and social policy implications.

Carol Tropp Schrieber has studied both men and women in nontraditional jobs. Her book *Changing Places: Men and Women in Transitional Occupations* (1979) sheds welcome light on men and women who have moved into technical, clerical, and craft jobs previously occupied by members of the other sex.

Schrieber points out that "little or no attention has been directed to the study of women in the lower status skilled or semi-skilled trades and occupations traditionally occupied by men." She finds that women experience far more stress upon entry into a new job than men, but says that both groups have experienced assessment as "tokens" as well as self-consciousness and performance pressure. Schrieber's sample for this research was a hundred employees in a single organization.

Finally, Carroll Wetzel Wilkinson has explored the women who have chosen to become coal miners in the United States. This field was virtually closed until November 1973 when the first woman signed on in West Virginia. Their experiences during the last decade tell us much about what happens to women who choose nontraditional employment.

Wilkinson's study of the literature regarding women miners during this period uncovers and clarifies a number of pressing issues that affect the lives of this unique group of women (1985). For example, there is a need for more research into special safety and health requirements of women miners, including investigating the risks of working during pregnancy and the results of wearing ill-fitting work clothing designed for men. A demographic profile of the women who choose mining would be helpful for future research on women in all nontraditional occupations. There is a need, too, to answer the questions: After the pioneer stage of development is over for women miners, what then? Are avenues for further career frontiers opening up or are they caught in a deadend situation? Finally, she found, like Walshok and Schrieber, that serious researchers have taken little interest in blue-collar women. Instead, the popular press has capitalized merely on the curiosity factor of their employment.

## Why the Research Gap for Blue-Collar Women?

Many women who have chosen to pioneer in the trades do not openly acknowledge a debt to the women's movement; nor do they see their efforts as being feminist in spirit. Their styles of living can be different from the familiar ways of professional life, their numbers are small, and they can seem inaccessible. For all these reasons, blue-collar women may not seem to be fruitful subjects for study and attention. There are factors, however, that some researchers may not have taken into account.

All female pioneers, whether they choose blue-collar or professional work, have to prove themselves and their competency in the work world before doing anything else. In a male-dominated environment, earning respect is a fundamental first goal that is basic to success in their careers. Female physicians, miners, scientists, and electricians share a desire to pass the early tests that earn their acceptance by coworkers. Thus, although their actions are affirmative for all women, gender consciousness is not central to their everyday life in the workplace. Some have found, in fact, that to be openly feminist may be counterproductive to their basic goal of recognition.

Often a first stage of career development takes place, which is characterized by an unconscious feminism. There is preliminary evidence that this stage changes after a decade or so. The pioneers find they recognize the potential benefit of contact with women in similar occupations with whom they share perspectives. At this point, there may be a postpioneer readiness for the feminism that earlier achievement drives and time constraints pushed aside, although it could have provided extremely useful support all along.

The female pioneer's lack of overt feminism can create unfortunate barriers with some feminist researchers and discourage some research exploration. It is no secret that women do not all agree on strategies for liberation and that there are numerous opinions on the role of gender consciousness in the workplace.

If larger numbers of scholars and researchers understood the real pressures and changes going on within the ranks of female pioneers, attitudes might change. The future should include inquiries into the similarities among all pioneers in a variety of occupations and social classes. Research to explore the validity of these observations may relieve the misconceptions. Those open to these ideas may take another look at blue-collar women and their accomplishments and find that the spectrum of unexplored subjects they represent is rich indeed.

## Conclusions

While preparing to write this essay, each newly discovered article or book on women in nontraditional careers led to further sources. Each trip to a library or a bookstore revealed more documents and studies worth citing. Personal contacts with female pioneers, whether in medicine, mining, entomology, carpentry, or law, yielded observations on experiences as well as suggested materials from their literatures. And finally, each contact with a support group for female pioneers (particularly on the West Coast) turned up resources that had not received broad distribution but were of potential use to many others.

This exploration has had a quality of urgency and newness about it that has been captivating. Just as a dazzling array of women have entered nontraditional fields, and a rich selection of print and nonprint material has appeared, so a network has developed around the country of people interested in supporting the entrance of more women into nontraditional careers. Supporters include parents, teachers, counselors, administrators, support group founders, demographers, government researchers, women's studies researchers, sociologists, and public school officials. So far, this network is not joined in a cohesive national whole, but there is no doubt that interest is growing, and there may be an effort to bring people together into a national forum of significance in the near future (U.S. Department of Labor, Women's Bureau, forthcoming). As the appended list of organizations will show, the strength of individual regional efforts is impressive, and the genuine support of and interest in the research for this essay has been heartwarming. In spite of the serious employment problems, the excitement of the potential for future development of women in nontraditional careers is contagious.

There are reasons for this optimism. Counselors are beginning to see the challenge open to them in working with high school girls (Haring and Beyard-Tucker 1984). Curriculum and activity guides have become available (particularly on the West Coast) that address prevailing sex-role stereotypes in the classroom that are transferred to assumptions about jobs (Calabrese 1984; WINC . . . 1984; Moore 1984).

There is evidence of accelerated research activity in, for example, the fields of vocational education, psychology, and sociology (Andrews 1984; Steinberg 1984; Auster 1984). A new seriousness of purpose on the part of researchers studying women in blue-collar occupations (O'Farrell 1982) may offset the paucity of research to date. Much more, however, must be done.

Certainly all the research, the print and nonprint resources, the exploration in the popular press, the support groups documented in the appended bibliography, the potential for more support groups, and, most important, the women themselves in nontraditional occupations are an affirmation that what is happening is not merely a temporary novelty. Instead, a process of permanent social and psychological change is underway in the United States.

## References

About New York: The holiday season: A look beneath the surface. *New York Times*, 21 November 1984, B1.

Andrews, Cecile. 1984. Women in nontraditional vocational training: A case study of the problems. Ed. D. diss., Stanford University.

Auster, Carol Jean. 1984. Non-traditional occupational choice: A comparative study of women and men in engineering. Ph.D. diss., Princeton University.

Burr, Sara Garrigan. 1981. Women and work. In *Women's annual, 1980: The year in review*, edited by Barbara Haber. Boston: G.K. Hall & Co.

Calabrese, Anthony. 1984. *Rainbow shave ice, crackseed, and other ono stuff. Sex equity goodies for the classroom.* Equal Goals in Occupations. San Francisco, Calif.: Far West Laboratory for Educational Research and Development; Honolulu: Hawaii State Department of Education, Office of the Director for Vocational Education. (Eric Doc. #244133).

Crocker, Jennifer, ed. 1984. After affirmative action: Barriers to occupational advancement for women and minorities. *American Behavioral Scientist* 27, no. 3 (January-February), whole issue.

Crosby, Faye. 1984. The denial of personal discrimination. *American Behavioral Scientist* 27, no. 3 (January-February): 371–86.

Dion, Mavis Jackson. 1984. *We, the American women.* Washington, D.C.: U.S. Department of Commerce, Bureau of the Census Public Information Office. For sale by the Superintendent of Documents, U.S. Government Printing Office.

Ferraro, Geraldine. 1984. Acceptance speech. *Vital Speeches of the Day* 50: 644.

Finn, M.G. 1983. Understanding higher unemployment of women engineers. *American Economic Review* 73 (December): 1137–40.

Haber, Barbara. 1981. *Women in America: A guide to books, 1963–1975.* Urbana: University of Illinois Press. (An appendix covers 1976–79.)

Hacker, Andrew. 1984. Women vs. men in the workforce. *New York Times Magazine,* 9 December, 124–29.

Haring, Marilyn J., and Karen C. Beyard-Tucker. 1984. Counseling with women: The challenge of nontraditional careeers. *School Counselor,* March, 301–9.

Harlan, Sharon L., and Brigid O'Farrell. 1982. After the pioneeers: Prospects for women in non-traditional blue collar jobs. *Work and Occupations* 9, no. 3 (August): 363–86.

Kane, Joseph Nathan. 1981. *Famous first facts: A record of first happenings, discoveries and inventions in American history.* New York: H.W. Wilson Co.

Moore, Madeline. 1984. *Expanding the options: Working toward sex equity.* Portland, Oreg.: Career/Vocational Education Department, Portland Public Schools.

O'Farrell, B. 1982. Women and non-traditional blue collar jobs in the 1980's: An overview. In *Women in the workplace: Management of human resources,* edited by P.A. Wallace. Boston: Auburn House.

O'Farrell, Brigid, and Sharon L. Harlan. 1982. Craftworkers and clerks: The effect of male co-worker hostility on women's satisfaction with non-traditional jobs. *Social Problems* 29, no. 3: 252–65.

Schreiber, C.T. 1979. *Changing places: Men and women in transitional occupations.* Cambridge, Mass.: MIT Press.

Steinberg, Jill A. 1984. *Climbing the ladder of success in high heels: Backgrounds of professional women.* Ann Arbor, Mich.: Research in Clinical Psychology Series, no. 9. UMI Research Press.

U.S. Department of Commerce, Bureau of Census. 1984. *Detailed occupations of the experienced civilian labor force by sex for the United States and regions,* 1980 and 1970. Supplementary Report. PC 80–51–15.

U.S. Department of Labor, Women's Bureau. Forthcoming. Conference on the WINC (Women in Non-traditional Careers) program for educational policymakers, 13 February 1985, Washington, D.C. Mary Natani, Co-ordinator.

Not for sale at U.S. Government Printing Office, publication plans not confirmed.

———. 1983. *Time of change: 1983 handbook on women workers*. Bulletin 298. Washington, D.C.: U. S. Government Printing Office, 27–63.

Walshok, Mary Lindenstein. 1981. *Blue collar women: Pioneers on the male frontier*. New York: Anchor Press, Doubleday.

Washington Post. 1985. One small dunk. Editorial, 13 January, B6.

Wilkinson, Carroll Wetzel. 1985. Critical guide to the literature of women coal miners. *Labor Studies Journal*, 10:25–45.

WINC Curriculum Guide. 1984. *Women in non-traditional careers*. Washington, D.C.: U.S. Government Printing Office.

Wright, John W. 1984. *The American almanac of jobs and salaries*. New York: Avon Books.

## Bibliography

*American Bar Association Journal* 69 (October 1983). Issue devoted to women and the law. Includes profiles of Sandra Day O'Connor and Geraldine Ferraro.

Baker, Sally Hillsman. "Women in Blue Collar and Service Occupations." In *Women Working: Theories and Facts in Perspective*, edited by Stromberg and Harkness, 339–71. Palo Alto, Calif.: Mayfield, 1978. Analysis of many low-level blue-collar jobs.

Blaxall, Martha, and Barbara Reagan, eds. *Women in the Workplace: The Implications of Occupational Segregation*. Chicago: University of Chicago Press, 1976. Contains a selection of pertinent papers given at conference on occupational segregation in 1975 sponsored by the Committee on the Status of Women in the Economics Profession, American Economic Association, and the Center for Research on Women in Higher Education and the Professions, Wellesley College.

Briscoe, Anne M. "Roadblocks Remain for Women Scientists: A Review of Vivian Gornick's *Women in Science: Portraits from A World in Transition*." *Chemical and Engineering News*, 5 March 1984. Compares Gornick's book to Rossiter's *Women Scientists in America* (1982). Briscoe likes both books for different reasons and denounces the pattern of discrimination in the sciences which both discuss. Calls on women scientists to keep debate alive by forming "politically enlightened and active coalitions."

Davis, Howard, "Employment Gains of Women by Industry, 1968–78." *Monthly Labor Review*, June 1980, 3–9. Previews trends toward more established nontraditional occupations.

Deaux, Kay. "Blue Collar Barriers." *American Behavioral Scientist* 27, no. 3 (January-February 1984): 287–300. Discusses external barriers to the advancement of blue-collar women, including tracking and enforcement of seniority policies.

Deaux, Kay, and Joseph C. Ullman. *Women of Steel: Female Blue Collar Workers in the Basic Steel Industry*. New York: Praeger, 1983. Thorough look at women workers in the steel industry, including discussion of policy implications.

Doudna, Christine. "Blue Collar Women." *Foundation News*, March-April 1983, 40–49. Summary of work in nontraditional areas the Clark Foundation supported: high-technology repair training, construction, coal mining.

Dukes, Joyce. "Women Underground Come Up Fighting." *New Directions for Women* 13 no. 6 (November-December 1984): 1. Discusses trials and successes of women coal miners.

Enarson, Elaine Pitt. *Woods Working Women: Sexual Integration in the U.S. Forest Service*. Tuscaloosa: University of Alabama Press, 1984. Problems and prospects of women woods workers in Oregon national forests.

"Equal Goals in Occupations: Some Outcomes and Implications of the EGO Project for Secondary Vocational Education in Hawaii (1978–1982)." Honolulu: Hawaii State Department of Education, 1984. Discusses a program of training in sex equity issues and skills for vocational education personnel in Hawaii's public secondary schools.

Ford Foundation. *Women in Blue Collar Jobs: A Ford Foundation Conference Report. 1976.* Reports on the National Conference on Women in Blue Collar Industrial and Service Jobs held in 1974.

Gillis, Phyllis. *Entrepreneurial Mothers*. New York: Rawson Associates, 1984. By women who have gone into business on their own while caring for their children.

Gornick, Vivian. *Women in Science: Portraits from a World in Transition*. New York: Simon & Schuster, 1983. A journalist's perspective on women who work in the sciences.

Gussow, Mel. "Women Playwrights: New Voices in the Theater." *New York Times Magazine*, 1 May 1983, 22. An exploration of women as playwrights and the subjects they discuss.

Harrison, Michelle, M.D. *A Woman in Residence*. New York: Penguin Books, 1982. A feminist physician through her diary challenges the American health care system.

Haas, Violet B., and Carolyn C. Perrucci, eds. *Women in Scientific and Engineering Professions*. Ann Arbor: University of Michigan Press, 1984. Papers presented at a national conference on Women in the Professions: Science, Social Science, and Engineering at Purdue University in 1981. Topics include women in science-based professions, women scientists and engineers in academe, and alternative science careers. Book concludes with a history of similar conferences.

Honey, Maureen. *Creating Rosie the Riveter: Class, Gender, and Propaganda during World War II*. Amherst: University of Massachusetts Press, 1984. Analyzes pop culture; asks why the strong image of Rosie the Riveter was transformed into the childlike image of postwar women.

Koba Associates, Inc. *Women in Non-Traditional Occupations: A Bibliography*. Prepared under contract with the Office of Education, U.S. Department of Health, Education, and Welfare, Bureau of Occupation and Adult Education, Washington, DC 20202. September, 1976. Five sections cover overview materials, skilled vocations, professional occupations, resources for additional information, and sources for materials. Though dated, it is still useful.

Lederer, Muriel. *Blue Collar Jobs for Women: A Complete Guide to Getting Skilled and Getting a High Paying Job in the Trades*. New York: E.P. Dutton, 1979. Includes addresses to write for further information, how to break into training programs, and a list of agencies that may open some doors.

Leon, Carol Boyd. "Occupational Winners and Losers: Who They Were during 1972–1980." *Monthly Labor Review*, June 1982. Outlines trends for women's employment.

Martin, C.A. *Capable Cops: Women Behind the Shield: A Selected Bibliography on Women Police Officers*. Public Adminstration Series. Monticello, Ill.: Vance Bibliographies, 1979.

Moore, Madeline. *Directory of Women Role Models*. Portland, Oreg.: Career/Vocational Education Department, Portland Public Schools, 1984. A directory of female role models in nontraditional fields who have volunteered to serve as resources to Portland-area classrooms.

Morgan, Elizabeth, M.D. *Solo Practice: A Woman Surgeon's True Story*. Boston: Berkeley Books, Little, Brown & Co., 1982.

O'Farrell, Brigid. *Women and Non-Traditional Blue Collar Jobs: A Case Study of Local 1*. Wellesley College, Wellesley, Massachusetts. Center for Research on Women. Final Report of Grant DL-21-25-78-21; report available through National Technical Information Service. May, 1980. Interviews conducted with union officials and women and men workers about women in blue-collar jobs and the barriers they face.

Paramore, K. *Non-traditional Job Training for Women: A Bibliography and Resource Directory for Employment and Training Planners*. CPL Bibliography, no. 45. Chicago: Council of Planning Librarians, 1981.

Patterson, Michelle, and Laurie Engelberg. "Women in Male-Dominated Professions." In *Women Working: Theories and Facts in Perspectives*, edited by Stromberg and Harkness. Palo Alto, Calif.: Mayfield, 1978. Analysis of and statistics on women in medicine, law, and higher education.

Regional Council Board of Trustees. "Women in Medicine: Making a Difference: Third Regional Conference." *Journal of the American Medical Women's Association* 39, no. 3 (May-June 1984): 73. Report on 1983 conference on Women in Medicine: Making a Difference, Rockefeller University.

Sherman, Susan R., and Aaron Rosenblatt. "Researchers in Medical and Surgical Specialties: Kanter versus 'Avis' as Competing Hypotheses." *Sex Roles* 2, nos. 3–4 (August 1984): 203–9. Describes a study on women's performance in non-traditional areas.

Stromberg, Ann H., and Shirley Harkness, eds. *Women Working: Theories and Facts in Perspective*. Palo Alto, Calif.: Mayfield, 1978. Essays.

Streker-Seeborg, Irmtraud, Michael C. Seeborg, and Abera Zegeye. "The Impact of Non-Traditional Training on the Occupational Attainment of Women." *Journal of Human Resources* 19, no. 4 (Fall 1984): 452–71. Points out that the effectiveness of nontraditional vocational training in decreasing occupational segregation has not been addressed in the literature.

Todd, Susan, ed. *Women and Theater: Calling the Shots*. London: Faber & Faber, 1984. Contributions from actresses, artistic directors, playwrights, technical stage managers, costume designers.

Turner, Gurley, and Kathleen Weir. "Working Women." *Sightlines*, Fall-Winter 1982–83, 24–28. Surveys film literature of women and work; gives details for entries in Nonprint Resources section that follows.

U.S. Department of Health and Human Services. Public Health Service. *Minorities and Women in the Health Fields*. Washington, D.C.: U.S. Government Printing

Office, 1984. Statistics on changes for women and minorities in the health fields.

U.S. House. Subcommittee on Manpower and Housing of the Committee on Government Operations. *The Women's Bureau: Is It Meeting the Needs of Women Workers? Hearings.* 98th Cong., 2d sess., 1984. Washington, D.C.: U.S. Government Printing Office. Proceedings of hearings on the controversy surrounding the Cole-Alexander administration at the Women's Bureau.

U.S. Department of Labor. Employment and Training Administration. *Women in Traditionally Male Jobs: The Experiences of Ten Public Utility Companies.* R & D Monograph 65. Washington, D.C.: U.S. Government Printing Office, 1978. (No longer for sale.) Report on study of 164 women in managerial and blue-collar jobs.

U.S. Department of Labor. Women's Bureau. *Job Options for Women in the 80's.* Pamphlet 18. Washington, D.C.: U.S. Government Printing Office, 1980. (No longer for sale.)

———. *Nontraditional Occupations for Women of the Hemisphere: The U.S. Experience.* Report, 9 August 1974. Washington, D.C.: U.S. Government Printing Office.

———. *Problems of Working Women.* 3 April 1984. Washington, D.C.: U.S. Government Printing Office. Hearing on WINC's success, and a conference to inform policymakers about its potential.

———. *Time of Change: 1983 Handbook on Women Workers.* Bulletin no. 298. December 1984, 54–57, "Shifts to Non-Traditional Jobs." Washington, D.C.: U.S. Government Printing Office.

Waite, Linda J., and Sue E. Berryman. "Women in Non-Traditional Occupations: Choice and Turnover." Prepared for the Urban Poverty Program, the Ford Foundation. Rand Corporation, Santa Monica, CA 90406. March, 1984. 91p. Preliminary findings of research on women in nontraditional civilian and military sectors; includes bibliography.

Wallace, Phyllis E., ed. *Women in the Workplace.* Boston: Auburn House, 1982. Essays addressed to management, outlining things they can do to attain equity within their organizations.

Walshok, Mary Lindenstein. "The Paradoxes of Skilled Blue Collar Employment for Women in the United States." Paper presented at the Second International Interdisciplinary Congress on Women, Groningen, The Netherlands, April 1984. Further discussion of ideas in Walshok's 1981 book: *Blue Collar Women: Pioneers on a Male Frontier.*

Wetherby, Terry, ed. *Conversations: Working Women Talk about Doing "Man's Job."* Millbrae, Calif.: Les Femmes Press, 1977. Interviews with women, including a welder, carpenter, butcher, electrical mechanic, and law school dean.

Wider Opportunities for Women, Inc. *All in Her Power.* Washington, D.C.: Wider Opportunities for Women, 1984. WOW 20th anniversary report.

———. *Bridging the Skills Gap: Women and Jobs in the High Tech World.* Washington, D.C.: Wider Opportunities for Women, 1983.

———. *Bridging the Skills Gap Working Paper. Part 1, High Technology Industries. Part 2, High Technology and Related Occupations.* Washington, D.C.: Wider Opportunities for Women, 1984.

———. *Non-Traditional Work Programs: A Guide*. Washington, D.C.: Wider Opportunities for Women, 1980.

———. *Reauthorization of Vocational Education Act*. Washington, D.C.: Wider Opportunities for Women, 1984.

———. *Work Incentive Program 1984*. Washington, D.C.: Wider Opportunities for Women. About the WIN program's history.

Winter, Bill. "Survey: Women Lawyers Work Harder, Are Paid Less, but They're Happy." *American Bar Association Journal* 69 (October 1983): 1384–88.

"Women in Science: Lack of Full Participation." Editorial. *Science* 221, no. 4618 (September 1983): 30. Discusses a symposium on women in science at Stanford University in 1983.

## Nonprint Resources

*Annapurna: A Woman's Place*. 45 min. Color. 1980. Arlene Blum. An all-woman team climbs Annapurna in 1978.

*Breaking Through*. 27 min. 1981. Women's Workshop, 29 Hibiscus Ave., London, Ontario N6# 3P2 Canada. About getting into the trades.

*The Captain Is a Lady*. 13 min. 1983. Joseph Wershba/CBS News. About Capt. Grace Hopper, 76, the oldest officer in the armed forces still on active duty.

*Coal-mining Women*. 59 min. Color. 1983. Appalshop films, Elizabeth Barret. Traces women's involvement in the coal industry before they began mining. Introduces opportunities in the trade.

*Comedienne*. 82 min. Color. 1982. Straightface Films, New York. Profiles two women establishing careers as comediennes in New York.

*Connections: Women at Work*. 20 min. 1981. Boston YWCA. Profiles three women in skilled trades: railroad engineer, maintenance worker, house painter.

*Engineering Skills and Career Planning: A Model Program*. 20 min. 1982. Slides and tape. EDC/WEEA Publishing Center, Newton, Mass. Overview of Purdue University's efforts to attain equity in the engineering program.

*Good Work, Sister! Women Shipyard Workers of World War II: An Oral History*. 20 min. 1982. Slide-tape and videotape. Suppl. study guide. Northwest Women's History Project, P.O. Box 5692, Portland, OR 97228. About women in the Portland-Vancouver area around 1944 who worked as technicians and semiskilled helpers and welders in the shipbuilding crafts.

*It's Her Future*. 17 min. 1978. WEEA, 55 Chapel St., Newton, MA 02160. Talks to parents about their daughters' future in the trades.

*Laila*. 12 min. Color. 1980. National Film Board of Canada; Phoenix Films, New York. The owner of a dry wall and plastering business talks about her work.

*Louise Drouin: Veterinarian*. 21 min. Color. 1981. National Film Board of Canada. About a female vet in rural Canada.

*Make It Happen*. 22 min. Color. 1982. Mobius International, Franklin Lakes, N.J. Achieving careers in finance, engineering, and the skilled trades.

*The Math Science Connection.* 18 min. 1978. WEEA, 55 Chapel St., Newton, MA 02160. About careers in math and science.

*Nothing But Options.* 171/2 min. Color. 1984. Videotape. Produced under a grant from WEAA of the U.S. Department of Education. Winner of the 1984 National Educational Film Festival Award. Distributed by Math/Science Network, c/o Mills College, Oakland, CA 94613. Profiles women in such jobs as environmental scientist and financial investment counselor. Emphasizes need for competence in math, science.

*Overcoming Resentment.* 11 min. Color. 1981. Development Dimensions International, 1225 Washington Pike, P.O. Box 13379, Pittsburgh, PA 15243. About women managers and their male subordinates.

*Sandra, Zelle, Dee and Claire: Four Women in Science.* 17 min. 1978. Education Development Center. Biographies of an astronomer, vet, mechanical engineer, laser physicist.

*Science: Woman's Work.* 27 min. 1981. Distributed by Modern Talking Pictures, 1901 L St. NW, Washington, DC 20056. Career discussion.

*Silver Wings and Santiago Blue.* 59 min. 1980. Adams/King Productions, Washington, D.C. About WAFS and WASPs in World War II.

*Soldier Girls.* 87 min. 1981. Chruchill Films. Young women in basic training.

*We Dig Coal: A Portrait of Three Women.* 58 min. Color. 1981. State of the Art, Washington, DC 20009. Examines the motivations of three women, the reactions of their families, of male co-workers, and of miners' wives. Explores the death of the youngest of the three.

*What You Take for Granted.* 1983. Iris Films, Box 5353, Berkeley, CA 94705. Explores women's experiences in nontraditional occupations.

*Why Not a Woman?* 26 min. Color. 1977. National A-V Center. Addresses male employers about the myths of lost productivity and high rates of turnover and absence.

*With Silk Wings: Asian American Women at Work: Four Women.* 30 min. Color. 1982. Asian American Women United, El Cerrito, CA 94530. An architect, doctor, social worker, and union organizer discuss their careers.

*With Silk Wings: Asian American Women at Work: On New Ground.* 30 min. Color. 1982. Asian American Women United, El Cerrito, CA 94530. A judge, stockbroker, dress designer, welder, police officer, bartender, pharmacist, TV news commentator, and park ranger talk about their work.

*Women under Fire.* 22 min. Color. 1982. WHA Television, Madison, Wisc. About eight women firefighters in Madison.

*Women Working: Blue Collar Pioneers.* 20 min. Color. 1985. 16mm film or video recording. Stephanie Antalocy. Distributed by New Front Programming Services, Minneapolis. Profiles an ironworker, electrician, sprinkler fitter, and welder.

*Working Equal.* 10 min. Color. 1979. National Center for Research in Vocational Education, Columbus, Ohio. Profiles race car driver Janet Guthrie; introduces planning for a nontraditional career.

*Women Business Owners.* 28 min. 1977. Martha Stuart Communications. Entrepreneurs talk about their businesses.

*Women in Business.* 24 min. Color. 1979. LSB Productions. Combining work and family.

*Women in the Corporation: On a Par, Not a Pedestal.* 26 min. Color. 1977. Distributed by Document Associates. Describes an affirmative action program at Connecticut General Life Insurance Company.

## Contact People and Support Organizations

Advocates for Women: A Women's Economic Development Center, 414 Mason St., San Francisco, CA 94102; (415) 391–4870. A nonprofit organization that provides skills training, career counseling, and placement services for women and affirmative action recruitment for San Francisco employers.

ANEW (Apprentice and Nontraditional Employment for Women), 315 Garden North, Reston, WA 98055; Ann Oxrieder (206) 235–2212. Offers basic skills training for blue-collar jobs: math, blueprint reading, use of hand and power tools, strength building, shop projects; offers career planning, job-search training.

Association for Women Geo Scientists, P.O. Box 1005, Menlo Park, CA 94025. Conducts workshops, seminars on job hunting in the sciences; sponsors educational groups at geological society conventions.

Association for Women in Science, 1346 Connecticut Ave., NW, Room 1122, Washington, DC 20036; Pamela Surko (202) 833–1998. Holds annual convention with American Association for the Advancement of Science; for biologists, chemists, physicists, engineers, mathematicians, doctors, veterinarians, psychologists, sociologists, anthropologists.

Association of Women in Architecture, 7440 University Dr., St. Louis, MO 63130; Betty Lou Custer, executive officer (314) 621–3484. For women in architecture or allied arts.

Blue Collar Asian Women's Support Group, San Francisco–Bay Area, California. Contact Cho (415) 775–1651.

Chicago Women in Trades, 4147 North Greenview Ave., Chicago, IL 60613. A support and information-sharing group for women in the trades or seeking blue-collar jobs; an activist organization.

Chinese for Affirmative Action, 121 Waverly Pl., San Francisco, CA 94108, Donna Jung; 586 N. First St., -268, San Jose, CA 95112; (408) 293–3347, Christine Miwa-Pimentel. A civil rights organization for Asian Americans; provides counseling, information, support, workshops, and referrals for women and minority members who want to enter skilled trades.

Coal Employment Project, 16221 Sunny Knoll Lane, Dumfries, VA 22026; (703) 670–3416; Betty Jean Hall, director. A national support group for women coal miners.

Coalition for Labor Union Women, Center for Education and Research, 2000 P St., NW, #615, Washington, DC 20036; (202) 296–3408.

Equals, Nancy Kreinberg, director, Lawrence Hall of Science, University of California, Berkeley, CA 94720. Provides support for entering math and science fields.

Math/Science Network, Math/Science Resource Center, Mills College, Oakland, CA; (415) 430–2230, Jan MacDonald, director. Volunteers working to correct underrepresentation of women in math- and science-based fields.

Metropolitan Women's Center, 22 E. Gay St., Ste. 446, Columbus, OH 43215; (614) 228–0404; Paula Brooks, executive director. Sponsors meetings, workshops, seminars to help women make career choices, fine-tune their skills, enhance their financial and legal knowledge. Classes include basic tool use; electronics and wiring; plumbing and dry walling.

National Association of Female Executives, 120 E. 56th St., Ste. 1440, New York, NY 10022; (212) 371–0740.

National Association of Women Business Owners, 500 N. Michigan Ave., Ste. 1400, Chicago, IL 60611; (312) 661–1700.

Network of Women in Trade and Technical Jobs, 1255 Boylston St., Boston, MA 02215; (617) 868–4476; Sarah Carleton. Publishes a newsletter; holds meetings, social events in the Boston area for women interested in nontraditional jobs.

New Employment for Women, Logan, WV; Sarah Davis (304) 752–3422. Support group.

Non-Traditional Job Opportunities, Lower Columbia College, 1600 Maple, Logview, WA 98632; Julia Armstrong, program coordinator. Offers an overview of women in the work force; practice in goal setting, skills assessment; job search techniques; tours of industry; speakers from the business community; special training programs. Offers tuition assistance, some supportive services.

Northwest Equals, Oregon Museum of Science and Industry, 4015 Southwest Canyon Rd., Portland, OR 97221-2797; (503) 222–2828. A spin-off of Equals. Has similar goals.

Renaissance Center for Educational and Technical Training, 333 Valencia St., Ste. 250, San Francisco, CA 94103; Ana Gonzalcz, administrative assistant (414) 282–9990. Offers technical training in microcomputer repair, office machine repair; includes in-class, hands-on work and on-the-job training.

Roundtable for Women in Foodservice, Inc., 153 E. 57th St., New York, NY 10022; (212) 688–8078; Diane Davis, founding president. Helps women in the food service industry.

SNEWS, Chimney Sweep News, P.O. Box 124, Wilmore KY 40390. Trade journal for chimney sweeps, published ten times a year. Chimney sweeping is a trade with little discrimination, sexual harassment. SNEWS invites sweeping women to contribute.

Society of Women Engineers, 345 E. 47th St., Rm. 305, New York, NY 10017; Julie E. Gibouleau, executive director. Supplies information on achievements of women engineers and opportunities open to them; assists women to return to active engineering work after temporary retirement.

State of Louisiana Department of Health and Human Resources, Women's Advocacy Bureau, P.O. Box 1943, Baton Rouge, LA 70821; (504) 342–2715; Beverly Barrett, director Electromechanical Training Program. Twelve-week programs in Baton Rouge, New Orleans provide hands-on training in basic electronics, mechanics, blueprint reading, mathematics. Includes physical fitness and employment preparation skills. Trains economically disadvantaged women, those who have been laid off; priority given to single parents.

Toledo-Area Affirmative Action Program for the Construction Industry (TAAP),

5515 Southwick Blvd., Toledo, OH 43614; (419) 865–8018; Ruth Montgomery, administrative assistant. Outreach program to help females, ethnic minorities enter the construction skilled trades. Present services include pre-application orientation and information, directive and supportive counseling; hopes to restore testing and tutoring programs in the near future.

Tradeswomen, Inc., P.O. Box 40664, San Francisco, CA; Roberta L. Kierstead, executive director. A grassroots organization of women working in blue-collar jobs and their supporters. Publishes *Tradeswomen Magazine*, the only national publication for women in blue-collar jobs, and a monthly newsletter.

Tradeswomen of Color, c/o Claudia Withers, 2000 P St. NW, #400, Washington, DC 20036; (202) 887–0364. In association with the Women's Legal Defense Fund Employment Rights Project.

Tradeswomen of Philadelphia/Women in Non-Traditional Jobs, P.O. Box 5904, Philadelphia, PA 19137; (215) 643–2175, Sue Mittermaier; (215) 831–9768, Bea Szepesi. Provides referrals, job information, support groups, speakers. A grassroots organization of union and self-employed tradeswomen; newsletter.

Tradeswomen Task Force on Oppression, c/o *Tradeswomen Magazine*, P.O. Box 40664, San Francisco, CA 94140.

Wider Opportunities for Women, 1325 G St., NW, Lower Level, Washington, DC 20005; (202) 638–3143; Cindy Narano, executive director. Operates a program to train and place economically disadvantaged women in entry-level skilled technical jobs in electromechanics and construction trades; involved in advocacy efforts. (See Bibliography for recent publications.)

Women and Employment, Inc., 1217 Lee St., Charleston, WV 25301; (304) 345–1298; Chris Weiss, executive director. Committed to improving the economic position and quality of life of West Virginia women; sponsored a Women in the Trades Conference in March 1985.

Women's Construction Employment Project, Littleton, WV; Carolyn Pearce; (304) 775–2906. Support group for women in construction trades in West Virginia.

Women in Fire Suppression, 18 W. Hudson Ave., Dayton, OH 45405; (513) 277–4145; Terry Floren. A newsletter-based support network for women who are career firefighters, urban or wild land. Works to break down isolation, promote communication, support, and information sharing.

WINC (Women in Non-traditional Careers), Northwest Regional Education Laboratory, 300 Southwest 6th, Portland, OR 97204; Andrea Hunter. Portland schools experimented for several years with a course on women in nontraditional careers at high schools thoughout the city with positive results.

Women in Science Committee, c/o Dr. Linda Butler, 1090 Agricultural Sciences, West Virginia University, Evansdale Campus, Morgantown, WV 26506. Formed to support women students at W.V.U. who select science majors and anticipate careers in nontraditional fields.

Women's Maritime Association, P.O. Box 10534, Bainbridge Island, WA 98110; (206) 842–5472. A network for seafaring women. Gives job and safety information and helps improve conditions for women working at sea; publishes newsletter; holds meetings in several areas. Not a union, membership is open to all seawomen, including students in maritime training programs.

Women's Technical Institute (WTI), 1255 Boylston St., Boston, MA 02116; Sharyn Bahn, executive director. A certified educational institution providing training to women who want to enter technical fields such as computer equipment repair.

# Contributors

*Mary Drake McFeely* is head of the Reference Department and assistant librarian at Smith College. She is the author of *Women's Work in Britain and America from the Nineties to World War I: An Annotated Bibliography* (Boston: G.K. Hall, 1982). She has been a fellow of the Council on Library Resources. A frequent reviewer of books on women and labor for *Library Journal*, she is working on a history of women factory inspectors in Britain.

*Rosalind C. Barnett* is a clinical psychologist specializing in the field of adult development, sex roles, and stress. She received her Ph.D. in clinical psychology from Harvard University and has devoted her professional life to clinical practice and research concerning female development over the life span. Formerly a research associate at the Radcliffe Institute and Brandeis University, Dr. Barnett currently is a research associate at the Wellesley College Center for Research on Women and has a private practice in clinical psychology. She is the author of or coauthor of numerous articles and several books, including *The Competent Woman* (New York: Irvington, 1978) *Beyond Sugar and Spice* (New York: G.P. Putnam, 1979) and *Lifeprints: New Patterns of Love and Work for Today's Women* (New York: New American Library, 1984). Her articles have appeared both in academic journals and in such general publications as the *New York Times Magazine*, *McCall's*, and *Working Woman*.

*Josephine Donovan* is the author of *Feminist Theory: The Intellectual Traditions of American Feminism* (New York: Ungar 1985), *New England Local Color Literature: A Women's Tradition* (New York: Ungar, 1983), *Sarah Orne Jewett* (New York: Ungar, 1980), and the editor of *Feminist Literary Criticism: Explorations in Theory* (Lexington: University Press of Kentucky, 1975). She has taught women's studies/humanities courses for many years and lives in Portsmouth, New Hampshire.

*Elissa Gelfand* is associate professor of French and former chair of the women's studies program at Mount Holyoke College. She has published a study of women's prison literature, *Imagination in Confinement: Women's*

*Writings from French Prisons* (Ithaca, N.Y.: Cornell University Press, 1983), and an annotated bibliography, *French Feminist Criticism: Women, Language, and Literature* (New York: Garland Publishing Co., 1985). She is currently working on Jewish women writers in France.

*Lynn R. Holmes* graduated from Mount Holyoke College and Georgetown Law School. She served as legislative counsel in the office of Sen. Howard Baker, Jr. (R-TN), from 1980 to 1984. She is currently manager of government affairs for Bell South Corporation.

*Katherine H. St. Clair* is director of audio-visual services at Mount Holyoke College. She has taught courses in film history and is currently reviewing films on WFCR, Amherst. In 1984 she produced a video documentary, *Hegira*, describing the shelter for battered women in Westfield, Massachusetts.

*Marilyn Schuster*, associate professor of French and comparative literature and former academic dean at Smith College, has consulted widely on curriculum transformation in colleges and secondary schools. With Susan Van Dyne she is coeditor of *Women's Place in the Academy: Transforming the Liberal Arts Curriculum* (Totowa, N.J.: Rowman & Allanheld, 1985). She received her Ph.D. in French language and literature from Yale University in 1973 and has published articles on such writers as Arthur Rimbaud, Marguerite Duras, Monique Wittig, and Jane Rule.

*Peggy Simpson* is the economics correspondent for the Hearst Newspapers. A Neiman fellow and former president of the Washington Press Club, she is Washington correspondent and contributing editor to *Working Woman* magazine where her column, "Washington," appears monthly.

*Norma Swenson and Paula Doress*, members of the Boston Women's Health Book Collective, are coauthors of *The New Our Bodies, Ourselves* (New York: Simon & Schuster, 1984). *Diana Siegal* and Paula Doress are coauthors of a book on midlife and older women's health and living issues to be published by Simon & Schuster in 1986.

*Susan Van Dyne*, associate professor of English and former academic dean at Smith College, has consulted widely on curriculum transformation in colleges and secondary schools. With Marilyn Schuster she is coeditor of *Women's Place in the Academy: Transforming the Liberal Arts Curriculum* (Totowa, N.J.: Rowman & Allanheld, 1985). She received her Ph.D. in English and American literature and language from Harvard University in 1974 and has published articles on Theodore Roethke, Sylvia Plath, Adrienne Rich, and other American women poets.

*Betty M. Vetter* is the executive director of the Scientific Manpower Commission, a private, nonprofit corporation formed by a group of societies devoted to the various scientific disciplines to serve as a focus for common concerns about manpower. Educated at the University of Colorado, Berkeley, and Stanford, she held academic appointments in California (including the university's Far East Extension Division) and in several universities in the Washington, D.C., area prior to her appointment to the commission in 1963. She is editor of the monthly *Scientific, Engineering, Technical Manpower Comments;* coauthor with Eleanor L. Babco of the annual *Professional Women and Minorities—A Manpower Data Resource Service* (Washington, D.C.: Scientific Manpower Commission); and author of more than a hundred published reports and articles on some phase of scientific manpower production and/or utilization.

*Carroll Wetzel Wilkinson* is the head of the Circulation Department at the Charles C. Wise, Jr., Library of West Virginia University in Morgantown. She holds an M.L.S. degree from Rutgers University and a B.A. from Wells College. She has worked in academic libraries at the University of Illinois and Rutgers University. She is the 1984–87 chairperson of the WVU Council for Women's Concerns; a faculty associate of the WVU Gerontology Center; and the author of two bibliographical studies: *Aging in Rural America: A Comprehensive Annotated Bibliography 1975–1981* (Morgantown, W.V.: West Virginia Gerontology Center, 1982), and "Critical Guide to the Literature of Women Coal Miners," *Labor Studies Journal* 10, no. 1 (Spring 1985). In conjunction with the 1981–82 National Endowment for the Humanities Women in the Community Project, she was local coordinator of a public program in Morgantown, West Virginia, called "Monongalia Women: Living and Working with Coal."

# Index